# AN AMERICAN FAMILY MYTH

Norine G. Johnson

authorHOUSE®

*AuthorHouse™*
*1663 Liberty Drive*
*Bloomington, IN 47403*
*www.authorhouse.com*
*Phone: 1-800-839-8640*

*This book is a work of fiction. References to real people, events, establishments, organization, or locales are intended only to provide a sense of authenticity, and are used fictitiously. All other characters, and all other incidents and dialogue, are drawn from the author's imagination and are not to be construed as real.*

*First published by AuthorHouse 11/2/2010*

*ISBN: 978-1-4520-9273-7 (sc)*
*ISBN: 978-1-4520-9274-4 (hc)*
*ISBN: 978-1-4520-9275-1 (e)*

*Library of Congress Control Number: 2010915926*

*Printed in the United States of America*

*This book is printed on acid-free paper.*

*Certain stock imagery © Thinkstock.*

This book is dedicated to the strong women following in the footprints of Verna Gentry Collins Derby, their husbands and the strong children they're raising together: Cammarie Johnson and Charles Burlile, Kathryn Johnson and Shane Wedge, Margaret Johnson and Matt Fraidin and their children Kate and Evan Burlile, Taylor and Morgan Wedge, and Max and Maya Johnson-Fraidin.

This book happened through the contributions of many individuals and institutions. My husband, Wayne Woodlief, believed in this project from the beginning and kept a steady barrage of support and encouragement. My daughter Kathryn Johnson and my son-in-law, Shane Wedge, actually read the manuscript and helped turn it into a publishable book. A friend, Maynard Poland, encouraged me early and often, including invaluable tips on publishing.

My editor, Peggy Nauf, took the manuscript to its finished form with a steady but firm hand. This project began thanks to Robert Giles, Curator for the Niehman Fellows at Harvard University and Rose Moss, instructor of fictional writing at the Nieman Foundation. Both Rose and Robert are two outstanding individuals who helped me believe in myself as a fictional writer. Also, thanks to Dr. Jan Rabb, a teacher at Lesley College who did an initial editing of the book and was the first to look at the complete work.

This book never would have reached the printers without the continuing support of my network of friends and colleagues. My Women's Group, Dorothy Cantor, Carol Goodheart, Sandy Haber, Alice Rubenstein, Lenore Walker, and Karen Zager, brilliant and creative women all who listened to my stories from a feminist perspective. Another colleague, Ruth Paige read the book in its early stage and helped me stay the course. Boston friends, Lynn Cooper, Ros Moore, and Harvey Waxman each read and commented on the book. Thanks also to John and Caroline Mutz for their enthusiasm about the book and recommending sources for publication.

Grub Street is an invaluable source for writers in the Boston area and in addition to the many forums I attended that helped me develop the craft, I want to thank particularly Mary L. Sullivan and Jenna Blum who reviewed the completed manuscript and gave exceptionally helpful comments and critics.

The personnel at the Masonic Homes of Kentucky and the University of Kentucky were welcoming and are to be commended for their dedication to students of all ages and people in need, now and in the past.

# PART I

## BEREA, KENTUCKY, NOVEMBER 1915

# CHAPTER ONE

## BEFORE DAWN

Verna woke with a sense of dread. Lying on her right side, she inched her left foot out behind her to touch John's space, afraid of cold emptiness. Slowly moving her leg, she felt the damp spot left from their love. Still unwilling to turn over, she whispered a simple prayer. "Please, God." She felt the hair on his leg and stopped moving. "Thank you, God."

"Verna." John's good-natured voice filled the small room. "Verna, you silly goose, I'm here as always." She slipped into his arms and rubbed her cheek against his whiskers.

"John, sleep a little longer. I can get the fire going this morning."

"I'll just do that. It'll be a long day." John rolled over and Verna knew he'd be back asleep before she found her rabbit fur slippers. Verna carefully felt her way in the dark. It would be almost an hour before the sun was up enough to light the back rooms of the house. She didn't want to risk waking her husband by lighting the kerosene lamp. Touching the green cotton flannel robe laid out on the rocker's arm, she inched her small feet into slippers lying scattered on the floor. Picking her ivory comb from the dresser and putting it in her robe pocket, she decided, "This will have to do until I have time later to

3

brush my hair." Except for her long, thick brown hair, Verna allowed herself few vanities, believing that "Pride cometh before a fall."

During the day while she was minding the children, keeping the house, and tending to the garden, cooking, canning, mending and making clothes, Verna forgot her fear of losing those she loved. But on some mornings in the winter when she woke before the sun, the chilled silence of the house reminded her of the cold bed where her grandmother had laid beside her after she died during the night. Verna shivered with the memory. She asked as she did each morning, "Please Lord, don't take another from me. Not yet. Please."

As she reached the bedroom door, Verna had an urge to go back and slip in the bed beside John. She turned, trying to see his form in the dark. Today was different. Didn't matter how much he tried to reassure her, having a Hatfield in the Berea jail was dangerous. Even if he was letting his deputy take that boy to Richmond for trial, until John and Clinton got Clem Hatfield on the noon train anything could happen. Verna started back to the bed and stopped herself. "Verna Gentry Collins, you are just a silly goose."

Verna repeated, "He promised he'd be home by noon. He promised he'd be home by noon." She picked up the cut dried logs John had stacked behind the potbellied stove, opened the door carefully with a double-thick hot pad as the embers still glowed from John's stoking them around midnight. She wanted the kitchen warm for her children.

After seeing the new logs catch fire, Verna got out her Granny's old iron pot to make the porridge, and two smaller pans – one dented tin pan to warm the applesauce and one newer pan to simmer milk the way Darlene liked it. Except when she was laid up with birthing children, Verna loved cooking. People dropped in hoping to be asked to stay for a meal. She smiled whenever John reached across the table and playfully made dimples by squeezing their boy's swollen checks. No one would ever go hungry in her home.

She noticed the vinegar bottle out and put it back in the cupboard. In her haste last night to join John in bed she had forgotten to put it away. She hoped it worked this time. Neither of them felt ready for another child.

Trusting that John had fed the stove on his routine midnight trip to the Outhouse, she quickly but carefully threw branch logs into the belly of the stove. Atop glowing elm embers the dry wood sputtered, and then flamed around the edges. She closed the door, checking it was latched so her inquisitive boy wouldn't get burned, and hummed as she stirred the leftover porridge with a wooden spoon. Seeing bubbles of heat escaping from the porridge, she closed the burner so the oatmeal wouldn't burn but would stay warm.

She went to the kitchen hutch and brought out three clay bowls with blue trim on the lips, a gift from one of the Berea College students made especially for John after he followed the tracks and found her runaway horse. As a prank a student from Appalachia had unfastened the reins and given the horse a spank, sending it speeding to freedom.

Hearing two sets of feet scampering down the stairs, one carefully as if on tiptoes, Verna turned to greet her oldest daughters: "Hey Ellen. Hey to you, Miss Darcine. Don't the two of you look pretty." Eight-year-old Darcine turned, ran to her mother, and gave her a hug, bunching up Verna's apron with a tight squeeze. Her older sister, Ellen, held back, not sure it was proper for a ten-year-old to run to her mother.

"Where's Pa?" Ellen looked around the kitchen, eyes and ears alert like a deer.

Verna wanted to be closer to Ellen but it seemed as if each new child, if she or he survived infancy, took all her attention. She watched Ellen give up her short-lived place in the family as "the baby" in exchange for the lasting power of "big sister." As Ellen got older, some said she looked "the spittin' image" of Verna's mother. Verna would bite her tongue so the words "I wouldn't know" didn't jump out of her mouth.

Verna looked at Ellen as she did each child to make sure they looked as proper as the sheriff's family should. Noticing Ellen's beginning buds of breasts, Verna said kindly, "Child, after school, leave your dress in my basket. I'll let out the seams."

Darcine skipped over and gave her mother a hug, squeezing Verna's thick waist and placing her cheek against her mother's oven-warmed apron. Verna ran her hand over her second-born's hair, feeling the thickness and twisting a curl around her pointing finger. "Did you both get a good sleep? Busy day today. Willa Mae's coming to help me with the canning. And there's a supper at the church tonight in honor of Mrs. Goodfree's newest baby's christening. So you'll be up late."

Verna gave all the news at once because she knew that Son was apt to come bursting through the attic door at any moment. Then there would be no time for anything but watching him and feeding Nanny Marie. She loved the times when her kitchen was bursting with the noise of her children and John was home. For those moments her fears that one of them would vanish were eased.

"Now you two run quick and get me some eggs while I get the young'uns up. The chickens are already slowing their laying and I've yet to fill the water glass with enough to last out the winter. Be sure to watch for snakes." Ellen and Darcine were already out the door before Verna finished her warning.

Just then Verna heard footsteps overhead and went to the attic door, yelling up. "Now Son, wait for me to come and get your sister out of her crib. Don't you help her. You hear now." Verna hurried up the wooden stairs as fast as her short legs would let her. The attic was warming from the kitchen heat and the day's beginning sunlight.

Son greeted her at the top of the stairs with a leg hug. Verna tousled her child's soft brown hair and pulled him close to her still-warm body. "I love you, Son." Looking at his mother with the eyes of a lovesick four-year-old, the boy took her warm chapped hand and put his nose close to smell her morning scent.

"What do you have there?" Verna reached behind her child and rescued Darcine's favorite doll, hanging by one arm from Son's tight grasp. Son, at four years, was into everything. As active as his father, with the face of an angel topped by yellow hair the color of corn, he could be counted on to find mischief anywhere. Verna gently took the doll. "Now hurry down while I change Nanny Marie. Don't wake your father." Verna patted his bottom lovingly, checking if he had wet himself during the night.

Verna heard a buzz and noticed a few flies around the hanging green beans, a reminder to get some chili peppers to keep the bugs away from the drying vegetables. Her eighteen-month toddler reclaimed her mother's attention by chanting, "Ma, Ma, Ma" with increasing vigor.

"Hush, baby." Verna soothed the toddler as she changed Nanny Marie's soaked nappy, wiping and drying before sprinkling powder on the small red bottom. John's voice boomed through the cracks into the attic. Verna cooed, "Oh, baby, your daddy's up. He's goin' to want to see you before he leaves."

As Verna re-entered the kitchen with Nanny Marie in her arms, she saw John buckling his holster on. He never wore his gun in the house. "Do you have to go so soon?"

Feeling impatient, John caught his breath before quietly saying, "Yes, Verna. I do." Then, he turned to his oldest children: "Ellen and Darcine, quick now, I hear the school wagon. Don't make them wait for you." John's stern voice mobilized the two older girls, who quickly jumped up and grabbed their coats with one hand and the strap that held their books together with the other before running out the kitchen door. He finished with "Don't let the door slam."

"Son, come give me a kiss." Verna felt at peace as she watched father and son embrace. She and John didn't kiss in front of the children, but their eyes met briefly before he turned to leave. "See you at noon, Verna. Looking forward to that apple pie."

Verna picked up a jam-stained shoe box and handed it to her young boy child. "Go bring the eggs in, and remember to look out for snakes. You know how they love those eggs. You can wave your father goodbye. But don't get in front of Rex."

Now that John was off to the town jail and Ellen and Darcine to school, Verna poured a cup of coffee, picked up Nanny Marie, and headed for the bedroom to straighten up. Nanny Marie nestled her head against her mother's breast. "Oh, those sisters of yours. I bet they were whispering into the night again. Keeping you awake." She placed the sleeping toddler between two goose-breast-feather pillows in the middle of the bed. The cloudless dawn filtered through the closed curtain.

She heard the door slam and went back into the kitchen. With her finger to her lips, she gently admonished Son. "Shush now. Nanny Marie's gone back to sleep." Verna kissed his smooth forehead. Knowing that like his father, Son needed action, she suggested, "Get your soldiers and put them here on the rug. I'll brush my hair. Let your sister sleep."

Slipping back into the bedroom, she checked on the still-sleeping child, then picked up a fine silver brush from her wood plank dresser next to the silver-plated nail buffer, both out of place in a small, plain bedroom dominated by the four-poster bed John made for them when they were first married fifteen years ago. Anticipating the afternoon harvest celebration, Verna wanted her hair to gleam. Although John called her a flirt, she knew he liked men finding her attractive.

"Ma, can I touch your hair?" With marble-sheen blue eyes agleam, the small boy reached to stroke his mother's thick, brown tresses, left undone to hang to her waist. He imitated his father and brought a hand full of Verna's hair to his lips.

While Son played on the wood plank floor, Verna brushed her long brown hair one hundred strokes and buffed her nails. Humming softly, she stopped only to lean down and kiss the top of her toddler's head.

His tin gray and blue uniformed soldiers held miniature rifles as Son enacted the continuing division within Kentucky, unhealed since the Civil War. But Verna's thoughts were far from killing and war.

"Son, your pa and I were married fourteen and a half years today."

"Mrs. Collins, you there?" A strong melodic voice filtered through the kitchen door.

"Oh, Willa Mae, you can come right in." Son went over and threw his arms around Willa Mae's knees. She tousled his hair.

Nanny Marie's waking cry caused both women to head for the bedroom door. "Mrs. Collins, you stay right there and finish your coffee. I can get to that baby girl."

"There's too much to do for me to sit around this morning. Willa Mae, I'll get Nanny Marie if you'll help Son put the eggs in the water glass."

Verna raised up Nanny Marie and gently paddled her bottom to send her to the kitchen before stripping the stained sheet. Verna hummed as she remade the bed with a clean but worn sheet she'd hemmed for her wedding chest years ago. Surveying the room to see if anything else needed straightening, Verna's glance paused at an off-focus picture of a fifteen-year-old girl dressed in a too-big white wedding gown. For a moment she felt again the panic she had this morning. Everyone kept leaving – walking out or dying, it didn't matter – they all left. She shook her head. "Willa Mae, I'm coming out. You're still there. Aren't you?"

# CHAPTER TWO

# EARLY MORNING

As Verna reentered the kitchen, she saw Willa Mae washing up the morning dishes. Verna knew that John had Willa Mae's boy in his jail for the night, but she was hesitant to tell Willa Mae, knowing how she fretted over that child. "Willa Mae..." Verna started and then stopped.

"Now you don't have to be telling me anything, Verna. I heard those men talking." Willa Mae looked at Son and cupped both her hands in back of her ears.

"Son, boy, go upstairs. See if you can find all the dirty clothes your sisters have just thrown around. Willa Mae and I will surprise them with clean undies when they come back." Verna smiled at Son, hoping to disarm his reluctance to leave the warming kitchen.

Willa Mae pulled a small wooden soldier, painted blue, out of her apron pocket. "And look what Mr. Judd made for you."

Son reached up to take the soldier, looking at his mother for permission.

"After you do your chores, Son. Now go." Verna smiled at Willa Mae, who didn't smile back.

"Now there's something bothering you, Willa Mae, and you just as well need to spit it out." Verna knew from the way Willa Mae avoided looking at her that Willa Mae was trying to hide her feelings.

"He oughtn't have put my boy in jail with Old Man Coulder, Mrs. Collins. Ain't right."

"What do you mean, Willa Mae?" Verna was puzzled. "You know John wouldn't do anything to hurt your boy. He's like a son to John."

"The sheriff ..." Verna noticed that Willa Mae was so mad she didn't trust herself to say John's name "... put three white boys and my boy in a cell together with a Hatfield and Deke Coulder. That Coulder's mean as they come. There's nothing he hates more than the likes of us."

Verna went up to Willa Mae to put her arms around her, only to feel Willa Mae tighten and draw back. "Mrs. Collins, my man's so mad. Just talkin' about it, he kept clenching and unclenching his fists."

"Why, Willa Mae, do you mean that Judd was fixing to swing at somebody?" Verna shivered. Judd was six inches taller and fifty pounds heavier than John.

Willa Mae's tongue was going now, propelled by her anxiety. "I seen Judd that mad only once before, in seventh grade when a white hill boy lit into Judd's younger brother. You know the one that's been crippled since birth. Boy called him a broken twig, not even good enough to be a nigger."

Verna had heard the story from John but pretended she didn't know, hoping that Willa Mae would be soothed by talking her anger out. "What happened, Willa Mae?"

"Well, I think you know, Verna." Willa Mae looked at Verna and a small smile slipped quickly through her face. "Your John jumped right in and pummeled that white boy. Almost killed him."

Verna felt the unspoken but always present racial barrier begin to come down again. Seemed each time she and Willa Mae got together they tested each other out.

Willa Mae took a sip of her coffee, cold now. "Oh, that's bitter, Mrs. Collins."

"You know where the sugar bowl is, Willa Mae. I'm not treating you like a guest." Verna smiled. The corners of Willa Mae's mouth began to wobble. She covered her mouth just in time to push back a giggle and stop the coffee from spurting out.

Verna began to giggle and both knew they were headed for a laughing jag. But Willa Mae held up her hand. "It's not funny, Mrs.

Collins. These are serious times. Sheriff Collins had no call putting my boy in jail with Old Man Coulder."

"Willa Mae, you don't want the boy growing up thinking he can get away with things." Verna felt that Willa Mae spoiled her oldest boy. "He and those two white boys, they got drunk and started shooting their rifles in town."

"Your skin's not black, Mrs. Collins."

"I've been poor, Willa Mae." Verna got angry when Willa Mae acted as if no white person had ever had troubles.

Willa Mae dismissed Verna with a wave of her hand. "They were shooting at bottles, Verna. Empty whiskey bottles. Boys do that." Willa Mae was starting into her story and once opened up she couldn't be stopped. "You know we moved to Middletown hoping they'd let us be. For a while it seemed that things might change, until about six years ago when the Devil's Day Law separated white and black children's schools. Now our children don't get to know each other like you and I did when we went to school together. Why, if my boy even said 'Hello' to your Ellen, I don't know what might happen to him. There's tension in this town."

"A little, Willa Mae – it's bad in other towns, but not in Berea. Besides, John put them in separate cells. He put your boy and his friends in one cell, Hatfield in another. And old man Coulder in another. He didn't put those boys in with Coulder."

Willa Mae took a deep breath and looked away. "Didn't have to put them in the same cell. Sheriff Collins put Deke Coulder in the jail at the same time he put my boy in there."

Verna knew that Willa Mae was poker-hot mad when she wouldn't look her in the eye. She decided to just listen and stop defending John.

"That old man's mean as they come. There's nothing he hates more than the likes of us. Except now maybe he hates the sheriff."

Willa Mae caught herself as she saw Verna's face blanch. Her anger hissed like a squeezed balloon. Willa Mae lowered her voice as if the Devil himself might be listening. "My Judd tells me they're riding again. Close to Berea."

"Who's riding?"

"The Klan."

"No! Not in John's county."

"They burnt our fields two nights ago. Before we could get all the tobacco in."

"Why didn't you tell me this before?"

"I'm telling you now."

"What does that have to do with Old Man Coulder?"

"He's one of them."

"How do you know?"

"Our community always knows these things. John used to know. Now he has to be told, and sometimes you just get tired of telling white folk what they ought to know."

Verna felt a tug on her dress. "I'm hungry, Ma." Son put his finger in his mouth and sucked.

"Well, of course you are." Verna gently removed his wet finger and put it in the bowl of sugar sitting on the kitchen table. "Lick this, Son."

"Verna, you know youse just spoiling that boy." Willa Mae frowned as she saw Son dip his finger again and again in the sugar bowl.

Verna laughed. "I'm sorry for your troubles, Willa Mae, and I will speak to John tonight. The town needs to stand behind all of you and we'll help. But now my boy's hungry and we need to get to the apple picking. Where has this day gone?"

Willa Mae went out to get more wood for the stove to keep the water boiling until all the apples cooked and Verna quickly fed the children. While they ate, Verna brought the jars she had boiled yesterday up from the cellar where they had been cooling, out of reach of Son's ever-inquisitive hands. Verna planned on putting up the best apples for the winter's pies and mashing the bruised apples for sauce. Willa Mae started cutting the bruise spots from the apples, knowing how fussy Verna was. She noticed Verna put out the sugar, butter, cloves, and a pie pan.

"What are you doing with that pie pan, Verna? We have barely time to make the applesauce." Willa Mae put her hands on her hips.

Verna pretended not to hear her as Willa Mae raised her voice higher. "Verna, now you know pies will have to wait for another day. Why, you haven't even put the onions in your garden yet. Mine have been in a week." Willa Mae's voice sounded cross, but Verna saw her eyes twinkling. Verna had seen Willa Mae eat an apple pie all by herself one day when she thought no one was looking.

Verna got out a second pie pan. "Well, you need to bring something home to that man of yours to show for all the help you've given me."

Verna didn't mention the dollar bill she had folded up to slip in Willa Mae's apron as she was leaving. Since John was elected sheriff, Verna paid Willa Mae for her help instead of giving her vegetables from the garden, but they never acknowledged the change in their relationship.

"Don't you be making me a pie; just look at these hips. I built a fire in the pit outside, Verna. If you have a mind to, you could put that bed sheet of yours in the kettle out there." Verna blushed. "Why, thank you, Willa Mae, I'll just do that."

Sweeping her undersized toddler up with one arm and two baskets for the apples in another, Verna yelled, "We'll race you, Son. Let's see who can pick the most." The three made an adventure of going to pick the last of the apples while the love-spotted sheet boiled atop a black, four-legged iron stove.

Mother and son, a squealing baby sister steps behind, raced around the orchard. Verna picked the remaining apples from the middle branches. At four feet, ten inches, with short arms, she could only look longingly at the clusters of shining apples toward the tops of the trees. Son quickly filled his basket to overflowing from the worm-holed remnants lying on the orchard's floor. "Son, you won. You always beat me." When each basket bulged with apples, they ran to the kitchen door and yelled, "Willa Mae, more, we have more."

Each time Willa Mae came out and said, "Well, my lands a gumption. That is sure a lot of apples." They put them carefully into a burlap bag to carry into the kitchen to peel, core, and deworm before placing them in boiling water. Verna and Son raced back to the orchard for more picking, with Nanny Marie squealing behind.

In moments like this Verna forgot she was thirty, a wife with four young children, and became a girl again, playing carelessly in the falling leaves of her apple trees on a beautiful, crisp Kentucky November morning. Watching Son and Nanny Marie run together to pick up apples from the orchard ground, Verna was struck with a memory. "Son, Nanny Marie, your uncle Grover and I would rush out to gather chestnuts in our orchard and then sell them for five cents a pint." Verna smiled at the memory.

All three held hands and skipped to the small brown-shingled barn. Son put two apples in the trough to welcome home Rex, their father's horse, and two apples in the stall with Willa Mae's horse. "Oh, Son and Nanny Marie, now we have to hurry."

By the time Verna and Willa Mae finished peeling, coring, deworming, cutting, and boiling the apples for the applesauce, it was after eleven. They filled over two dozen boiled clean jars and divided the morning's work evenly.

Willa Mae helped Verna clean the stove. While Willa Mae took off her apron, kissed Son on the forehead, and squeezed Nanny Marie, who squealed, Verna wrapped the now-filled twelve glass jars in old papers. They all walked Willa Mae to the barn and carefully stored the jars in saddlebags. Willa Mae mounted up and started down the County road to her home.

Verna put the root vegetables to soak, then peeled and sliced more apples quickly, unexpectedly nicking her pointing finger. She stopped to suck a small drop of blood.

While the vegetables soaked and the pie cooked and the bedsheet dried on the line, Verna took the children with her to pick up the parlor. Last night in the parlor, John told her about arresting a young Hatfield. His firm voice declared, "Verna, this is a law-abiding town. Those Hatfields might get mad enough to kill over a pig and keep the killing going for almost twenty years, but they aren't going to do it here." Wanting to change the subject, she told him about Nanny Marie's new word and Son's newest mischief. John read the paper and smoked a cigar. Verna hemmed Son's trousers and the evening passed. Until she bent over his chair to brush his lips and he pulled her down for a lingering kiss.

Breaking her reverie, Verna opened the front parlor window. The crisp Indian summer air shooed away the stale odor from John's evening cigar. As Verna picked up the *Berea Citizen*, she saw a three-inch headline about the war in France. But a foreign battle was too far away for her to really care about. Her eye stopped on a picture of three nurses carrying a stretcher. "What an adventure" sped through her thoughts. "Stop that, Verna." She smiled at her absurdity. She had a warm home, loving husband, fine children, and no intention of running off to be anything but a mother and wife.

# CHAPTER THREE

## LATE MORNING

In the late morning Verna began mixing the biscuits, smiling as she put in expensive baking powder and imagined John riding by the college, on his way home to her. She felt the dough start to rise. No more buggy flour and water, as in the desperately poor last years of her life with Granny. Verna pushed her hair back, as if shooing painful memories away. Her thoughts skipped like a stone in the creek – from biscuits, to the apples in the top branches needing to be picked for cider before a hard frost changed their tang, to John's brown eyes and early-morning lovemaking. Lost in her thoughts, she missed her older children's steps on the back porch and startled as Son yelled, "Darcine, come see my pies." Nanny Marie jumped up and ran to hug Ellen's knees.

"Oh, Ellen and Darcine, help me out while you tell me all about school."

"Ma, you know I want to meet Pa at the road." Ellen declared. Not wanting to fight with Ellen, Verna pretended she hadn't heard her eldest nor seen Ellen roll her eyes at her sister. Ellen's nagging voice persisted. "Ma, I knew you were running late again. The pie is steaming on the back porch ledge." Verna looked through the still open door and noticed the pie's trail of steam gently rising as if the recently bubbling apples were giving up their life heat to the air.

Verna heard Ellen slam down her books and slate and turned to see her oldest grab a glass of buttermilk with one hand and Nanny Marie's small hand with her other. As Ellen headed back out the kitchen door, Verna waited for the inevitable determined words.

"I'm going to wait for Pa outside."

Turning toward her middle daughter, Verna smiled as she watched Darcine give Son a hug and cheek- kiss before setting the table without being asked. Verna cut in the lard with two knives. "Darcine, how was school, honey?"

"Ma, I brought my slate home so you could see what my teacher said about my handwriting." Darcine beamed. Verna wanted to give her a hug but her hands were covered with flour. Verna's thoughts meandered again. This time to women who were too lazy to cut in the lard. "Darcine, don't forget when you make biscuits to always cut in the lard." Verna made an exaggerated gesture, clinking the two knifes against the clay bowl's bottom. "You can tell a lazy woman from her lumpy biscuits. Or those who are even lazier and just melt the lard and pour it in the batter." Verna scrunched her face in mock disgust. "Do they think people won't notice they didn't take the time to do it right?"

As Verna looked away from her biscuit-making to see if Darcine had heard this important lesson, she saw Son standing on a chair reaching into the flour canister. "Son, stop that, you hear. Your pa's just about home. He's not going to like it if you dump that on the floor. Give me the flour. How did you reach up here anyway?"

Verna smiled again at Darcine. "Darlin', watch Son, will you? You know how he is, and particularly when he knows his pa's coming home."

Darcine stopped setting the table and looked down on the floor where her brother was busily dumping the leftover flour and mixing it with water he had gotten from somewhere. Son had a way of finding whatever anyone left unattended. His pa would say, "He's just a boy, that's all."

Darcine's calm voice made Verna smile. "Look. Here's your top." Verna noticed how carefully Darcine handed Son the toy and wished that she could be as patient as her second oldest child.

Darcine continued encouraging Son. "Watch. Now, you try. You can do it. Just hold the string here. Wind it up again."

"I can't do it," Son whined. Verna started moving to help Son, afraid he would start getting angry if he failed. She stopped as she heard Darcine calmly saying, "Put your finger here.. Oh, that's so good. Ma, look. He's doing it."

Verna kept checking out the kitchen window, first to see if Ellen and Nanny Marie were fine, then squinting into the noon sun to see if John had topped the hill. No one else lived on their narrow, dirt hill road, far out of town. And because the new window held genuine glass without distortions, Verna could see clearly up to the top of the hill road.

Verna knew John liked to ride home from the jail by the hill road. Once when she asked him why he chose this longer way, she was surprised by the emotion in his answer. "Verna, it's so peaceful. There's no one about. A man can think and put the day behind him. As I reach the top of the hill, no one asks me, "Sheriff, why don't you stop that ornery Robinson from hitting his wife?" Or, "Sheriff Collins, who are you supporting for governor?"

Because she had the time with Darcine minding Son so well, Verna indulgently continued remembering John's sharing of his feelings. "From the time I turn onto the hill road, I'm back at nineteen, just me, free, with nothing to hear but Rex's whinny, his hoofs' clomping on the hard road and nothing to see but thick woods. You couldn't even spot a moose if it stood there ready to charge." She remembered he held her face between his hands while looking deeply in her eyes. "Verna, I don't care if it takes me longer. I need that time out of town and in the hills."

This November morning, Verna opened the kitchen window and stood on her tiptoes, leaning over her sink. She tried to catch a glimpse of John as he crested the hill. She checked on Ellen and Nanny as they waited patiently by the road. Verna smiled, feeling contented.

Looking out the window yet again, she could see Nanny Marie holding Ellen's hand, looking up the hill for her pa's arrival with her shoes somewhere between the kitchen door and the road. Beneath Nanny Marie's summer-browned legs, dusty toes wiggled free. Verna didn't understand her youngest child's enjoyment of being barefooted but bit her tongue to refrain from shouting out the window for Ellen to put her sister's shoes back on.

Then, instead of seeing Ellen in her freshly pressed new school dress standing by the hill road, Verna saw her eight-year-old self on a similar warm November day coming home from school. She felt again the tears running down her face, hearing the taunts, "Hillbilly, Hillbilly. You ain't got no shoes. You are just a poor hillbilly." She shook her head, whispering, "Stop that, Verna."

Verna began to wonder where John was. She knew he had to help his deputy get that Hatfield on the morning train, but today she thought he might have wanted to hurry home – just to see her. Maybe he had stopped by, but she blocked the thought. That lapse was in the past. They were starting anew.

# CHAPTER FOUR

# NOON

The noonday sun beamed boldly. Verna saw John ride Rex over the top of the hill and start down for home. Verna felt a surge of pride seeing John so straight in the saddle, his hat firmly on his head and his boots sticking out to the side. She didn't like to think about the guns on his hips. Each time Son asked his pa to show him how to shoot, John always gave his boy the same answer: "Guns are for men, Son; someday – when you're older." Verna saw Ellen squeeze Nanny Marie's hand tighter to stop her from running in front of her Pa's horse and heard her youngest daughter began to chant, "Pa, Pa."

The day was particularly bright. The sun struck John's badge and Verna saw a flash of light. A sack swung from his saddle and Verna figured he hadn't forgotten to pick up his new suit at Mason's Tailoring. Although she couldn't hear him, Verna knew he was humming. When they used to ride together, he always hummed as he got closer to home. She watched the suit sack swing and his gun bounce against his thigh. As the sun hit John's chest, Verna saw a flash from his gold badge. John had laughingly told Verna that putting a metal star over the heart started as a way to protect that body part without looking cowardly.

Verna watched as John's horse picked up speed, spraying the mud with his hoofs, anticipating the waiting oats and water. She stuck her arm out the window and saw John wave back to her and to his two jumping-with-excitement daughters. Verna heard two sharp bangs and looked for where the hunters might be. Then Rex began to speed down the hill. Verna yelled at Darcine, "Don't let Son out of this house. You hear me."

Darcine's voice quivered, "Ma, what's wrong? Ma!" Fear propelled Verna out the back door, leaving only the voice trail of her command. "Darcine, stay inside. Watch Son." A corner of her elbow sent the apple pie toppling, leaving flesh-like juices to seep in the earth. She watched helplessly as man and horse sped toward the bottom of the hill, John slumped over Rex's back, slipping to the right as Rex turned abruptly into the barn lane. She heard, as if through wax-plugged ears, Nanny Marie beginning to cry with disappointment. Verna screamed, "John," as a brownish-red stain spread over the right side of his back, pooled on the saddle, and then ran like tears down his pants, spattering droplets on the grass, while a small drop of blood lit on one of Nanny Marie's bare feet.

# CHAPTER FIVE

## AFTERNOON

Verna reached the children's side as Ellen turned to her mother, puzzled by her father's betrayal as he sped to the barn without reaching down to embrace her. Verna saw the blood on John's back. She commanded Ellen, who was paralyzed with shock, "Go to Mrs. Harrison's. Have her bring the doctor quick." Verna ran straight toward John, shouting back at Ellen, "First, take Nanny Marie inside, now."

"But, Ma." Ellen's voice quivered.

"Now!" Verna ordered without once taking her eyes off John's slumped, crimson-stained back. The horse's lowered head and crunching noises told Verna that Son's apples had stopped Rex's forward lunge into the small stall.

She grabbed a dry sheet off the clothesline, reaching John's side as he started to slip off the saddle. Adrenaline-powered arms enabled Verna's small hands to bring John's body to her chest, gently lowering him to the barn floor where she had dropped the boiled sheet and wooden spoon. Tears blurred her vision. She finished easing his body slowly and carefully, afraid each movement would harm him more.

"John, don't move. The doctor will be here soon." A groan escaped his lips, followed by a small crimson stream. She held his head on her lap, using her legs and stomach to keep his violated back off the floor, wiped his lips and pressed the sheet against flesh from which a seemingly endless stream of blood seeped.

Verna held John's perforated body, as if he were a newborn baby. "You'll be all right." She took a breath and leaned close to his ear. "I love you. Sleep until the doctor comes." Over and over, short sentences of love and reassurance, a still-warm body held in her fatigue-defying arms while unwiped tears ran down her cheeks. John's mouth moved as if trying to form words, but only blood left his lips.

Darcine, usually obedient, defiantly took Son and Nanny Marie into the parlor where children were never allowed without adults. After seating Son on the floor with his soldiers and Nanny Marie beside him with her dolls, she rushed to the open front window to see if Ellen had reached the Harrison's. She knew her father was badly hurt. She tried to hold back her tears so as not to frighten Son and Nanny. She thought about how her father had taken Ellen and her hunting with him just last week. He showed them how to aim the rifle and they watched silently, as ordered, when he spotted a deer and then shot it. Ellen closed her eyes. Her father looked on proudly as she ate the deer meat that night, while Ellen's "How can you!" reproached her.

The next day her pa let her shoot his gun. He set a can up on the back fence post, making sure Son and Nanny were in the house. John put Darcine's hand on the gun with his hand over hers with both their fingers on the trigger. "Pull." The sound hurt her ears, but she was also excited. Picking up the can from the ground, Pa said, "Nice shot." She could see the hole all the way through.

All the Collins children knew about guns. They grew up on stories of the Long Hunters. In their play, Daniel Boone, with his long rifle and coonskin hat, was captured by fierce howling Indians and then set free by friendly Indians; or like Mary Draper Ingles simply slipped away. Danger, fighting, guns, shooting, blood, enemies turned friends, friends turned enemies were part of their day-to-day make-believe world. Pa's wound seemed to Darcine part of that play world.

Ellen thought her heart would stop. She knew something was wrong with her pa. Fear replaced hurt and anger. Ma was not good at serious things. As her legs pumped, her mind filled with what Ma should have done. "Ma should have sent Darcine for Mrs. Harrison. Ma needs me to help Pa." Her legs were getting tired. She fell twice. Mrs. Harrison was out in front of her white frame single-story house when Ellen started yelling and waving, "Pa's hurt. Pa's hurt. He needs help. I think he's been shot."

Lillian Harrison became afraid instantly. Her family hadn't always lived in town. Like Verna, she grew up in the hills. She knew the suddenness of Kentucky violence. Like everyone else in this small foothill town, she knew John Collins had arrested Clem Hatfield. Like others, she felt it wasn't wise. She was afraid, afraid for John, afraid for Verna, who was in some ways still a child herself, afraid for their children, afraid for herself. But none of that showed as she calmly said, "I'll get the doctor, Ellen. Now go back home and help your Ma. My hired man can help me hitch up the wagon."

As Mrs. Harrison yelled for her hired man to rig the carriage, Ellen turned and ran back down the longest stretch of country road she'd ever seen. She heard Mrs. Harrison's measured adult-to-child voice carrying on the wind, "Now don't you worry, child. I'm sure your Pa will be all right."

As Ellen got closer to home, she cut through the side orchard and headed straight for the back door, thinking Ma had helped Pa inside the house by now. Rounding the corner of the house, she saw a leg sticking out of the barn door and heard her mother's voice. It sounded far away, farther than just the barn, and like none of her mother's voices. It wasn't the "Do it right now" voice, or the "Let's play" voice or even the "I think you're a fine girl" voice. It was like someone else was speaking through her mother's mouth. Ellen thought it was a good sign that her ma was talking to her pa, but she knew it meant he couldn't walk to the house. And if her pa couldn't walk, that meant he was hurt bad.

Ellen raced across the orchard feeling the smush of apples under her feet. She ran past Rex with the saddle still on his back and the reins hanging from his bent head as he grazed on half-rotten apples and orchard grass.

Verna didn't hear her daughter's steps. She didn't see Ellen's shadow cross John's body. She didn't feel the breeze from Ellen's entrance into the barn. Her ears didn't register the gasp or her daughter's tentative, "Ma?" Ellen knew what her ma at thirty would not believe – her pa was hurt real bad. She saw the crusted blood on the pink sheet. She saw the blood on her mother's hands. She saw her father's closed eyes. But she also saw his chest move and knew he was still alive. "Ma. Ma. I'm back. Mrs. Harrison is getting the doctor. Ma, is Pa …"

Verna looked at her with enlarged black pupils and seemed to unfreeze. "Oh, Ellen, honey. I need your help. Put the large kettle on to boil with as much water as you can put in it. The doctor will need it."

"Ma, is Pa ...?"

"Your pa will be fine. He's asleep. He needs his rest. When the doctor comes, he'll know what to do to fix him up." Verna went back to talking softly to John.

Ellen entered the back kitchen door and looked for Darcine and the younger children. Hearing voices in the parlor she went there, surprised to find her perfect sister sitting in her father's chair telling a story to Son while Nanny Marie slept in her arms. "I have to put some water on. Pa's hurt real bad. Ma's holding him until the doctor comes. Darcine, I'm so scared." Ellen began to cry, then Son began to cry. Nanny Marie woke up and she began a toddler whimper. Darcine let her emotions go for the first time that afternoon. Tears that had been eking out of corners left her eyes in gushes.

# CHAPTER SIX

## BEREA'S DOCTOR

D r. Benson ate his supper at his office desk. As usual he had worked into the early afternoon, and as usual his food was now cold. With absolute regularly his wife always brought the warm food into his attached office on the stroke of twelve. And just as regularly, he got involved with a patient or a medical article and forgot to eat until later. He never complained the food was cold.

His facial features, except for protruding ears, were indistinguishable and frequently hidden behind a large medical book. Behind his back, patients remarked about how his deep voice didn't fit with his short stature. A dedicated man, he had returned to Berea to practice medicine after receiving his degree from the Louisville Medical School. Like John, he fell in love with his wife while still in Berea's secondary school. Unlike John, he never strayed.

As he started to bite into a cold chicken leg, Millie Harrison came running in. "Tom, the Collins need you. I think John's hurt. Their oldest came running down the road. She thought he had been shot." As Mrs. Harrison talked, Dr. Benson began taking supplies out of his cabinet. After twenty years practicing in Berea, gunshot wounds had become routine for him. Guns came in all sizes in Berea. Holster guns for protection, rifles for birds, and shotguns for deer or moose. Maybe if John were lucky, someone used his turkey gun and went a little wild with the shot. He knew a gun used to bring down a moose could blow a hole the size of a melon in a man.

Tom Benson hurriedly packed medicines for life-threatening wounds, antiseptic, a sharp knife – in case the bullet was still embedded in John's flesh – two lots of sterilized packing gauze, enough to fix a Guernsey mistaken for a deer, needles and thread. He'd seen too many times the hole made by an old Civil War rifle or 10-gauge shotgun. Dr. Benson saw John as when he first met him, leaning against the railing outside the drugstore talking to the prettiest girl in town, Verna Gentry. He recalled the pang of jealousy because of the attention women gave John. Remembering John's vigor, he said to his nurse, "John's healthy. He won't be brought down." But his medical mind told him to be wary.

He alerted his nurse. "Melinda, we may need you to stay with the sheriff. Bring your overnight bag." Thirty-one years old, healthy but plain, Melinda knew she would never marry and dedicated herself to helping others. Four members of her family died from the influenza one winter because a doctor couldn't get through the snowdrifts to reach their cabin in the hills. Melinda witnessed her mother's painful gurgling and pink froth emerging from her mouth before she passed. Then her grandpa and two siblings. The baby's skin-covered skeleton and shrill cries through dry cracked lips continued to haunt her dreams. Melinda, her younger sister, and her father were the only ones alive when the doctor finally made it to their cabin. After that, her father just wandered away one day and never came back.

It seemed only natural for Melinda to attend the free nursing school at Berea College. Part of her training was working at Dr. Benson's home office. He needed help just as she was graduating and offered her a job. She liked his dedication to the poor and his willingness to do house calls no matter what sickness lay within the house or cabin.

Melinda would go into the hills to help with a difficult birth, a sick child, or the illness of an older person, since most hill patients wouldn't come to the doctor's office. She would plan on staying overnight, and if there were complications, a day or two. She was with Verna both times the babies died. She stayed after Dr. Benson gave Verna a sedative to stop her hysteria. Melinda treated Verna like a child and still thought of her as not quite grown up even though they were the same age. Being childish was part of Verna's charm. If John were as seriously wounded as Dr. Benson thought he might be, Nurse Melinda just didn't know how much help Verna would be.

Dr. Benson asked Mrs. Harrison's hired man to pack the stretcher in the wagon, just in case. He called the jail to let Clinton, Berea's deputy, know John was shot. Receiving no answer, he then called Dover, the college marshal, at his home. "Dover, I think someone shot the Sheriff Collins."

"Doc, I told John to stay away from those Hatfields."

"Dover, you're closer to the Collins' house than I am. Can you ride down there? Have no reason to think the family's not okay. But I'd feel better if you did."

"Of course, Jim. I'm leavin' right now." The marshal shook his head. "Damn, them Hatfields!" and yelled to his wife, "I'm off to the Collins." "No, nothing's wrong. Just want to talk with John about the Klan's restlessness. No, you and your damn intuition I said there's nothing wrong." As he was talking, he strapped two pistols on his belt and grabbed his rifle.

Dr. Benson told Melinda to call one of Verna's half-sisters. He heard her shouting into the phone, "Hazel, get yourself out to the Collins' place as fast as you can. Sheriff Collins been shot. No, Dr. Harrison hasn't seen him yet, so we don't know how badly." After ending the phone call, Melinda turned to him. "Now half the town knows. I kept hearing people picking up the party line."

The doctor soothed her concern about confidentiality. "It's all right. Word would get out soon enough, and Verna needs kin."

As they ran out of the office, Dr. Clark yelled at a man he knew on the street, "Tim, let the deputy know when he gets back in town that Sheriff Collins has been shot. We're going to his house now." Within minutes Dr. Benson, Melinda, Mrs. Harrison, and her hired man were heading for the Collins' house. The hired man drove Mrs. Harrison's wagon down the hard macadam surface of Chestnut Street and onto the county road. Silence settled in the wagon, as each person got lost in his or her thoughts.

# CHAPTER SEVEN

## LATE AFTERNOON

Ellen saw the wagon pass by the parlor window. She ran to the back door in time to see Dr. Benson, his nurse, Mrs. Harrison, and the handyman turn off the road and into the barn. "Darcine, please keep Son and Nanny Marie just a little longer. I have to go and help the doctor with Pa."

"Ellen, I want to go, too." Darcine's voice was muffled by the slamming back door.

Dr. Benson jumped off the wagon before it stopped, spooking the horse, which needed an extra firm "Whoa" from the hired man. The doctor ran over to John's unmoving body. "John, can you hear me? Verna, don't move yet. Wait 'til Rudy and I pick John up. We're going to put him in your kitchen. Melinda, go with Mrs. Harrison. Scrub down the table." While giving orders, Dr. Benson began a careful examination of John's wound.

Millie Harrison had envisioned John sitting up, smiling and saying, "Sorry to bother you all. It's just a shoulder, arm, leg graze..." The site of the wound kept changing in her mind's eye...a surface wound caused by a careless hunter. They would fix him up, have some of Verna's cooking, and go home. However, as Nurse Melinda ran to the kitchen, Millie Harrison froze, stunned to see Verna with blood covering her dress and John not moving. She saw John's crumpled body held tightly in Verna's arms, both frozen in a red-spattered moment. Her mouth opened involuntarily; she whispered "John." Her legs trembled as she moved dream-like toward his inert body. Until Dr. Benson's sharp command, "Stand back, everyone, give me room to work," penetrated her daze and she retreated.

The doctor immediately saw that John Collins was gravely wounded with an egg-sized exit wound on the left shoulder. From the gasping, gurgling sounds when John breathed, he knew a fragment had broken off, probably after hitting the shoulder bone, and punctured his right lung. The doctor observed John's paleness, with skin more gray than white. Upon touching him, he noted John's cool skin and fast, weak – very weak – pulse.

Dr. Benson muttered, "In shock, lost a lot of blood. Careful not to open up the wound as we move him. Coagulated. Good. Looks like it went clear through. Clean." Then he looked straight at Verna. "Verna, you did the best anyone could. But you can let go now. We've got him."

Verna didn't move and responded so quietly Dr. Benson had to strain to hear her. "Mrs. Roosevelt helped nurse her husband after he was shot and he lived."

Dr. Benson knew how shock affected people. He let Verna keep holding John while he packed both the back entry and front exit wounds to reduce the blood flow when they moved him. Calculating that after blood loss infection would be John's biggest enemy, Dr. Benson needed to get John off the barn floor. The doctor gently took him from Verna's numb arms. Together with the hired man, they lifted John onto the stretcher and carried him into the kitchen. For a brief moment Verna flashed on the picture in last night's paper of medics carrying the wounded off a battlefield in France. She felt Lillian Harrison's arms around her and knew Lillian was saying something but she couldn't understand what. Verna could hardly walk as her leaden arms hung uselessly and her circulation-deprived legs were too weak to carry her steadily. She leaned on her neighbor and felt the other woman's arms tremble.

Verna refused to leave the kitchen while the doctor thoroughly cleaned and repacked John's wounds. She vaguely recalled hearing Lillian Harrison say good-bye and something about her husband expecting her to be home when he arrived. The hired man stayed because the doctor needed him to help move John into the bedroom after his wounds were dressed properly. Ellen and Darcine, although told not to, took turns coming into the kitchen and just looking at their pa. Verna felt Darcine take her cold hand and try to warm it.

Verna refused to eat. She never took her eyes off John while the doctor worked on his wounds. She sat where told to and watched as a bullet was removed from John's back. The other had passed clean through. She was relieved to see her half-sister, Hazel, enter the kitchen. "Hazel. John's been shot."

"The deputy told me, Verna. How are you, darlin'?" Her sister's pale face and vein-popping hands aroused Hazel's protective feelings. She knew, from Dr. Benson's curt hello and the shake of his head that John's wound was critical. Hazel came immediately to Verna's side and began rubbing her sister's cold hands.

"Come sit down with me in the parlor, Verna." Verna shook her head while muttering "no". She let her trembling body be embraced by her older half-sister. Hazel stood even with Verna at four feet, ten inches, and like Verna, her creamy white skin aroused envy. Both had their father's green eyes and his thick brown hair. From the back they might be mistaken for twins.

Verna felt Hazel's warm arms soothe her shivering body. "Hazel, he'll be all right. Won't he?" Seeing the gravity of John's wounds, Hazel worried if Verna had the strength to withstand what seemed inevitable. Inseparable in their early teens after Verna's Granny died, the two half-sisters followed different life callings. Hazel, older than Verna, went to Berea College and became a teacher. Verna, when she turned fifteen, told Hazel that John had asked her to marry him. Hazel had tried to get Verna to wait until she was educated and could support herself if need be. Verna just looked at her and laughingly bragged, "What do I need education for? I have John."

Verna's mother, Sue Ellen Gabbard Gentry, walked out on her twin six -months-old babies, Verna and her brother, Grover, on a dark December day, Tuesday, 1885. She never looked back or even sent a postcard. There were no pictures. Sue Ellen evaporated and went with the morning mist from the hills, never to be spoken of again.

Verna's father, Curtis Gentry, hurt and angry, dropped off the infant twins with their maternal grandmother in a log cabin high in the Berea hills. Unlike Hazel's mother, Mr. Gentry's first wife, Curtis Gentry never sent support money to Granny Gabbard and never saw Verna and her brother again until Verna married John.

Although poor, Verna's granny filled her with pride. In the evening with the chores done, Verna and Grover would sit on Granny's rough-hewed wooden porch. Protected from the sun or rain by an overhang that stretched the length of the bark-intact log cabin, their granny would start each story with, "Remember to always hold yourself with pride because you come from strong roots." Then she would tell about when Daniel Boone and a small party of men came to Kentucky from Virginia. One of the men was Richard Gentry, and Granny always made sure to add, "So, don't forget. Them's your roots. You can hold your head as high as anyone."

Verna and her brother roamed hills shaped like humpback whales covered with a primal forest shrouded in moss-covered trunks. Oaks and hickories were so abundant; Verna learned to walk cautiously in the autumn to avoid the sting of falling fruit. Sycamores, ash, poplar, beech, maples, and walnut graced the foothills as the land swelled after the flatness of the northward bluegrass.

Verna looked up for a minute, cocking her head to see out the back window. Her beloved hills had given John's assassin cover, allowing him to lie in wait and then vanish, leaving only the pop of his rifle and the blood on John's shirt to attest to his presence. Verna heard Hazel's voice through the thickness of her dark reflections. "Verna, let's go see how the children are." Usually compliant with her older sister's requests, Verna defiantly replied, "Hazel, I'm staying here with John."

"Aunt Hazel, you're here." Darcine opened the kitchen door after hearing her aunt's voice. "I'm coming, darlin'. Stay there with the young ones." Hazel firmly added, "Don't let them come into the kitchen, Darcine." Putting her arm briefly around Verna's shoulder, Hazel turned and went to her nieces and nephew, torn between staying and knowing the children needed attention or they would all soon be in the kitchen. And they mustn't see their father like this.

# CHAPTER EIGHT

## CLINTON ARRIVES

Verna saw Clinton, John's deputy, ride into the barn lane in the back of the house. "Tom, Clinton's here." Verna's voice cracked as the words passed through her frozen throat.

Dr. Benson, thinking Verna probably needed something to do, kindly said, "Why don't you ask him to come in, Verna? I could use his help."

Verna walked stiffly to the door and opened it but didn't leave the kitchen. "We're in here, Clinton. Doc Benson says he can use your help." Verna in her daze started to shut the door and caught herself in time to stand politely until Clinton entered.

"How is he, Verna?" Clinton scanned her face and recognized shock at once. Touching her hand softly, he encouraged, "Never you mind taking care of me." He led her back into the kitchen and pulled up a chair. "Sit yourself down." He watched Verna awkwardly sit down as if she had forgotten how to bend her body.

Only after he knew Verna was safely seated did he look about and then at the men leaning over John. Steam filled the room from a large kettle on the stove. The kitchen resembled his uncle's slaughterhouse. Blood drops on the floor. Blood stains spreading across the table. He'd helped John cut the oak for that table. The doctor quietly said, "Come here, Clinton. I can use your help."

"How is he, Doc? I heard…"

Clinton saw the doctor raise a finger to his lips, silently signaling him to hush. Looking at Verna to see how closely she was paying attention, Tom Benson simply shook his head to let Clinton know John's survival was in doubt and asked, "Did you see the marshal as you rode up?"

"Yep. He's sitting on the back porch. Said we'd talk after I came in to see how John was doing."

Clinton moved over to the table and stood on the other side so as not to be in the doctor's way. John's face looked peaceful as if he were asleep, except his mouth was scrunched up. Clinton knew such a wound brought excruciating pain. Moving his eyes to John's body, Clinton saw blood still seeping slowly through the gauze.

The doctor leaned over and whispered in Clinton's ear. "John's lost a lot of blood. The wound's deep. I just don't know."

Clinton could see the weariness and sadness in the doctor's face. John and Tom Benson had become friends. Close friends. Each time the Collins had lost a baby the doctor had spent the night at their house, taking care of Verna's mind as well as her body. Then he kindly let his nurse stay for a few days until Verna was on her feet again.

Denial began to break down in Clinton as he absorbed Dr. Benson's sadness. "Does Verna know?"

"Sshush." Dr. Benson whispered harshly.

As Clinton looked at John again, his eyes moistened and his throat tightened. Determined to do his duty and blocking out his own feelings, he cleared his throat and asked, "Did he say who shot him?"

Still on edge, Dr. Benson in a barely audible voice impatiently answered, "Clinton, he's not spoken. Been out since I came. If he said something to Verna, she's in no place to let us know yet."

Clinton backed off, took a deep breath, and then came back to the table, looked down at John, touched his right hand, and turned to Dr. Benson. "Tom, you know I loved him, too."

Both men stopped for a moment and took stock of each other. The doctor's face softened. "Sorry, Clinton. I'm just… Well, you know."

Clinton slowly moved his head up and down.

Dr. Benson took a breath. "Clinton, if you can find out how far away the shooter was when he fired at John, I can tell you how tall a man he is."

"How can you do that, Doc?" Clinton was skeptical.

The doctor gently rolled over John's unwounded shoulder and pointed to an area of John's back. "He shot John at the top of the hill, which means he was standing in the woods up there on the same level as John. Here's where the bullet entered." The doctor looked at Verna and lowered his voice: "Measuring where it exited in the front, the slant of the bullet's flight, the distance between John and the shooter will tell us how tall he is."

"Well, I be darn. How did you know that?"

"Doesn't matter. You can't be of much help in here now, Clinton. Don't just stand around. I need the room." Dr. Benson wiped his eye as if something had gotten into it. Clinton felt his own chest constrict. He looked down at John's pale face one more time and thought, "I'll get the son of bitch that did this. I will."

Before leaving, Clinton automatically scanned the kitchen-operating room. He noticed Ellen standing in the corner out of the doctor's eye so she wouldn't be sent away. He won't tell on her. He'd seen his pa die and hated how his uncle tried to chase him away. They never found who killed his pa. Nobody bothered to ask a watchful ten-year-old who was stealing chickens from his pa's coop. When he had tried to talk about the chickens, the old sheriff just said, "Boy, nobody care who steals chickens in the hills. Maybe your pa took those chickens from somebody else."

Clinton had watched John for two months before asking for the deputy's job. He knew how John treated all equally – didn't matter if they were poor, didn't even matter what their skin color was or who their fathers were. Clinton, being good in school himself, admired how John had studied new ways of catching killers and thieves. Clinton worked hard learning from John how to look for evidence. Taking a last look at John's pale face, he placed a hand on Verna's quivering shoulder. "Verna, I'll be outside. You call out if you need me."

# CHAPTER NINE

## Late Afternoon

As Clinton left by the back door, Dover slipped out of the shadows, his rifle by his side but his pointing finger fully on the trigger. "Clinton, thought I should stand guard here. Heard rumors in town that they threatened the family." Dover's voice rumbled out of his dry throat as a Lucky Strike cigarette bobbled between cracked lips. "Sheriff Collins don't look good to me. But just in case that bastard's comin' back, thought I'd stay out here."

Clinton could think of no better man to stand guard on the Collins' place tonight. "Thanks, Dover." Clinton, feeling water gather in front of his eyes, turned his face away so the older man couldn't see him wipe them. Clinton took the cigarette Dover offered, lit it, and leaned back against the post.

"Think the Hatfields done it?"

Clinton just shook his head. "Probably. But old man Coulder was pretty mad at John this morning for making him stay in jail with Judd's boy. He was cursing all night about having to smell a nigger boy in the cell next to him. We let Judd's boy go at dawn when his pappy showed up. Gave him a head start. We let Coulder and your college boys go at the same time. 'Bout eleven, an hour before we took Clem Hatfield to make the noon train to Richmond. He would've had time to hide and ambush John. I won't put it past a Klansman to hide like a coward and shoot a man in the back."

Dover interrupted Clinton. "When I came, I asked Verna if she knew 'bout what time John was shot. She wasn't thinking too clear but she knew the sun was directly over the hill and that happens at noon."

Dover dropped his cigarette on the ground and spat the taste of the tobacco out of his mouth before replying, "I still favor the Hatfields."

Clinton, feeling his inexperience next to the older man's years of law-keeping, said, "Yeah, them Hatfields bad. John and me kept our guns readied as we walked that block to the train station. Walked the boy between us. John had one gun pointing out to the street and one gun at that boy's head."

Dover interrupted, "Clinton, them's nasty folks. If they'd done killed so many over a pig, no tellin' what they'd do to a sheriff that put one of them young'uns in jail."

Both men fell silent. Dover lit another cigarette. Clinton took a deep breath. "Remember how Simon fell out of that oak tree and woke up two weeks later?" Knowing Clinton's inexperience, Dover decided to stay silent. No point in reminding the deputy that just last year, the governor had received a similar wound as Sheriff Collins, and although treated right away, still died four days later.

"Dover, tomorrow at dawn, I'm going up that hill to look for evidence."

"Like what?" The marshal was skeptical.

"Like tracks, castings, just anything that tells something about who's low enough to shoot a man in the back."

"You know it's them Hatfields." The marshal didn't see why Clinton was making John's shooting harder to understand than it need be. Truth was he didn't much care for Sheriff Collins, although he never showed his dislike. After John beat him in the 1908 election, he had to settle for the College Marshal position. He thought folks made too much of John, but he'd learned to keep his mouth shut. Folks forgot and figured he felt the same way they did.

Clinton didn't notice Dover's irritation and earnestly tried to explain. "I'm gonna do it the way John taught me. Not the old way. Not the way where you catch a man, string him up, and then find the proof." The marshal went back to smoking his cigarette with fixed eyes long used to looking without seeing.

Inside the small house Hazel tried to get Verna to eat something or at least drink a little broth from the cooked vegetables. She refused a slice of chicken; the thought of food made her stomach churn. Picking her leaden body up, Verna walked slowly toward the parlor, with Hazel trailing behind her close as a shadow. Verna saw Ellen peeping out the door and felt such pain stabbing her body that she almost keeled over. She thought, "Those children, those poor children. How could I have forgotten them?"

Hazel took Ellen's hand. "Come, Ellen, let's go see how Son and Nanny Marie are."

"Ma, I want to stay here. Pa needs me." Ellen looked up at her mother with pleading eyes.

"Yes, yes, you do that, Ellen, that would be a good girl. He would like that." Verna didn't know where the words came from. It was as if her body, her legs, her arms, and her voice just did what they wanted and she didn't have to worry any more about telling them.

Hazel slipped into the parlor. She carefully shut the door so the younger children wouldn't see their father's body on the blood-drenched table. Darcine quietly requested, "Ma, can I go stand just outside the door with Ellen? Please, Ma."

"Don't be bothering the doctor, Darcine. Stay right by the parlor door." Seeing the children helped Verna come out of her daze. Although she wanted to rush back to John's side, she knew her children needed comforting. She remembered how the women let her watch as her Granny's body was dressed. "You're a big girl now. There's things you should know."

Hazel rocked Nanny Marie while Son curled into Verna's lap. "What's wrong with Pa?" Verna started to lie and then looked into his son's eyes, thinking, "No one ever told me the truth about my mother's leaving. I'll not do that to my children." Holding Son's face in her hands, she gently said, "He's hurt, Son. Your pa's hurt." She decided that one small lie would be all right. She leaned her mouth close to her boy's ear. "But he said to tell you that he loved you a lot and always to remember that."

Looking out the window she tousled his hair. "Look, Son." They watched as the washed-blue-jean sky faded to wispy white, exposing a half moon that in the daylight hung like a broken-off cloud. Hazel noticed Son's sleepy head fall gently against his mother's arm. She rose up and gently rested the sleeping toddler on her shoulder. "Son, take my hand. I'll tell you a story upstairs." As Hazel left the parlor with the sleepy children, she turned to Verna. "You sit a moment, Verna. I'll put these younglings to bed."

"Thank you, Hazel. It's time I get back to John." As Verna returned to the kitchen to check on John, Hazel helped the younger children into their beds in the loft. Ellen and Darcine stood just outside the parlor, with their arms around each other staring at the table where their father still lay.

Dr. Benson, seeing that Verna had recovered somewhat, knew it would be best to keep her busy. "Verna, I'd like to move John to the bedroom. Is that all right with you? "

"Of course, Tom. John will be more comfortable on the bed than this hard table." Dr. Benson asked the hired man to watch John for a minute and came over to look into Verna's eyes. "Verna, sit down here now. You're still in shock."

"No. I'm all right. I need to do something. Hazel's putting the young ones in bed for me." Verna's face tightened as she moved around lighting the kitchen lamps. After the doctor and the hired man carried John to the bedroom and put him carefully on the bed, Verna moved stiffly to the rocking chair in the bedroom. Ellen and Darcine went up to the loft and brought down their quilts to lie on the bedroom floor.

Lillian Harrison returned to Verna's house and picked up the apple pie tin as she entered the house through the kitchen door. She began to scrub down the kitchen table much as she scrubbed the pigpens after the fall slaughter. She looked out the kitchen window and up the hill road whispering, "John, will I ever see your smile again?"

# CHAPTER TEN

# Early Evening

The day passed and early evening began. Verna left John's bedside to relieve herself. Leaving for even a moment seemed a betrayal. As Verna stepped out the kitchen door, she looked once more up the hill road to where she last saw John alive. Swarms of shadow swallows circled in the fading pink twilight, their song an echo of the wail inside of Verna. She heard the clink of metal and startled.

"Evening, ma'am."

"Hey, Clinton, and you, too, Marshal Dover. Appreciate both of you being here. Know John does, too." Verna's words were appropriate but her voice barely made it out of her throat. Clinton had to lean forward to understand what she said. As he did, he saw the blank look in her eyes and recognized she was still in shock and moving on instinct alone. He'd seen that look before when a horse threw the young Kirkland boy and then trampled him to death while his ma and pa watched.

"We'll find who did this to John, Verna."

"You do that, Clinton. Yes, you do that." Verna walked slowly down the beaten path to the outhouse. The nurse came out, pushing the door so fast it snapped into Dover. "Sorry, Dover, didn't see you there. Where's Verna? She shouldn't be alone. She's not herself."

Melinda put her arm tightly around Verna to lead her down the outhouse path as if she were a blind woman.

Hearing voices, Darcine returned to the parlor and looked out the north window. She noticed people walking down the county road. She yelled into the bedroom door that opened in the parlor, "Ma, Aunt Hazel, there's folks coming. Should I ask them in, Ma?"

Verna was standing by John's shoulder, careful not to move the bed. "No, Darcine. Just let them be. They're here to stand watch on Pa." Verna looked out the bedroom window that overlooked the county road toward the town. In the lead were only a few, first in twos, then threes, then whole groups. She watched as they started to fill the side yard and stood still silently, waiting. Verna's manners overcame her inertia. "Hazel, find out who's here. Be sure they get something to eat." Clinton who had also been standing watch over John, quietly said, "I'll do that with you, Miss Gentry."

Once in the yard, even in the advancing shadows, Hazel and Clinton recognized almost everyone. Folks had came from all parts of the Gorge area – the college, the hills, Berea, and Middletown – black, white, well enough off, poor. Many of them family to John or Verna; others paying their respect to John for help he'd given them, Masons out of brotherhood, Baptists from his church, and town and hill folk he had helped.

The questions ranged from asking about John Collins to wondering who shot him. "How's the sheriff doing, Clinton?" "Who did this, deputy? I heard it was the Hatfields."

Clinton could feel the heat building. "Don't be hasty," he cautioned. Hearing raised voices, Clinton slipped through the side yard and starting making the rounds of the different groups. He listened, alert for the moment when crowd heat turns to boiling. He looked to see if anyone seemed pleased rather than worried.

Flashes of teeth, whites of eyes, and palms of hands flashed out in the encroaching darkness. "Hey, Clinton."

"Hey, Judd."

"I saw John just this morning. Warned him about the Klan riding again."

"John told me. Said you thought it might be a problem with Deke Coulder in jail with your boy."

"He's one of them, Clinton."

"I'll keep that in mind."

"I want to ride with you, Deputy, when you put together the posse. I know some folks won't cotton to that."

"Makes no mind with me, Judd. I'd be pleased to have your rifle riding with us."

"Deputy, you know John saved my boy from drownin'. I owe John the most a man can owe another man."

A few old men, shivering in the night air, picked up dried twigs from the apple orchard to start small fires. The deputy saw them squatting in groups of three or four toasting their hands. Hazel kept coffee and biscuits coming out to the mostly men folk crowd. Some brought blankets. The nurse would go out from time to time and tell the crowd about John's breathing, that he was still alive, and as long as he was still alive there was hope.

The minister said a prayer. Everyone, even those with other beliefs, hung their heads and said "Amen." Hazel asked the minister if he would stay the night. He slept in the parlor with his feet hanging off the carved wooden arms of the small horsehair sofa.

The mayor stopped by with members of the city council but didn't stay. He went inside and talked to the doctor, looked in on John, put his arm around Verna and said he'd be back in the morning. The nurse thought he might have wiped a tear from his eye as he left the bedroom. It was hard to see John's drained face and limp body without wanting to weep. One of John's brother Masons also asked to come in and see John. He told Verna, "Whatever he needs. Whatever you need." All the words evaporated like breath in the night.

# CHAPTER ELEVEN

# THE PROPER WAY

Dr. Benson returned to the Collins' house in the darkest part of the night to spell his nurse who refused to leave. Son and Nanny Marie were the only ones who slept. As John's breathing became shallower, the doctor stopped encouraging the rest of the family to try to sleep. Clinton kept watch in the kitchen as if the shooter might enter and slaughter the already diminished family.

Down the road Mrs. Harrison lay beside her husband, not sleeping but too afraid she might awaken him to move. Earlier that evening when she gave him the news, he seemed surprised to hear John was still alive. Mr. Harrison ate lustily, telling his wife, "Millie, there's nothing we can do. Come and eat."

She didn't ask this hard man, "Who do you think did it?" Silence settled over their house and in the town, as if talking might steal the air from John's lungs. Reverend Simms held a prayer vigil at the Collins' Baptist church. Over two hundred people came out of the hills and town to hold candles and ask their God to make the sheriff live, if it be His will.

The nurse changed John's dressings twice during the night. She noticed bubbles around his mouth. His breathing was labored as if a tree sat on his chest with its roots intertwined around his lungs. In a shaking voice she told Dr. Benson, who already knew, that red lines were extending from John's back wound. After the false dawn and before the sun reached the south bedroom window, John died. Ellen and Darcine saw the last of his chest movements, held each other, and wept. The doctor put quarters over John's eyes as mist gathered on his own. Verna, still in her blood-soaked dress, enfolded John's hands and kissed his white lips.

Verna gently released John's body. Only the dark sockets into which her dulled eyes had sunk broke the paleness of her expressionless face. Verna's body moved as if a puppet master pulled the strings on her legs and occasionally jerked her leaden arms. The voice emerging from her white lips belonged to an older woman. "Ellen and Darcine, your pa is gone, darlin's." She hugged them both, squatting down so they could rest their heads on her shoulders. "Hazel, please get Nanny Marie and Son before the others start arriving. I want them to have time with their pa."

"Verna, I'd rather stay with you. The nurse can get the children."

"I want them to be with you, Hazel." Verna turned to the doctor. Her inner voice admonished her to 'Mind your manners.' Taking a deep breath Verna raised her head and swallowed to stop her voice from cracking. "Thomas, we appreciate all you tried."

Hazel, the nurse, and Doctor Benson looked at each other, uncertain what to say. The doctor recognized shock. He'd seen it often, sudden death being no stranger to the Berea hills. He'd also seen a no-nonsense side of Verna before, although most often she deferred to John and any men folk around. After the Collins had a stillborn baby, he'd advised them not to have any more children. Verna had calmly and politely told him, "Thank you." She became pregnant less than one year later.

He tried one more time. "Verna, they're still asleep. Give yourself a little more time before waking them."

"They will be part of this, even Nanny Marie." All the time she was talking, Verna stroked John's hair and wiped his cheek with a cool rag just as she had all night. She held his hands as she sobbed, violent shakes racking her body. Darcine looked like a small mountain deer startled by the sight and sound of large unidentifiable shapes. Ellen stood on the other side of her pa, wishing her mother would move so she could touch his face.

The minister awoke on the couch and, hearing wailing, knew that

John had passed. He got up feeling stiffness in his legs and massaged the back of his neck. He tucked in his shirt, put his black coat on, and tied his shoes. Wishing he had time for a cup of coffee, he put on his solemn face and entered the bedroom. Moving first to the widow he put his stork-leg arms around Verna and then embraced the children.

Verna asked the minister to say a prayer, oblivious to Darcine's pulls on her dress just as she failed to see the quieter attempts to get her mother's eye. "Ma, why did God take Pa?"

"I don't know, Darcine. The reverend is going to talk to God now for us. Hush, child."

After the minister gave last rites and laid his hands on John, the doctor tried to regain control. Placing his gentle hand on Verna's shoulder, he attempted to raise her off the bed. "Verna, come away."

"No."

"Verna, I need to get John ready for the undertaker so he can take the body to the mortuary."

"He'll do what he must do, but he'll not show John in one of his fancy rooms. We'll say a proper good-bye, here in our home with his family and friends."

"Verna, people don't do that anymore."

"That's how we did when Granny died. That's how we'll do with John.

"It would be too hard on you. Think of the children."

"Thomas, you know more than I do about lots of things. But I just know I'm right on this. Hazel, you'll stay here and help me, won't you?"

"You know I will, Verna."

"And my brother and sisters will come. John loved this house. He would want to have the good-byes said here. You can call Mr. Welch to do what he must. But the respects will be paid here in this home."

Dr. Benson's head went back. He startled to hear this tone and firmness from Verna. Hazel lowered her voice and eyes to show respect. "You best not waste your breath arguing. Most things Verna leaves up to others, but if she speaks out, she's like an oak tree. The only way you'll move her is to chop her down."

Leaving to get Son and Nanny Marie, Hazel's footsteps sounded firmly on the wooden steps leading to the loft. Having gotten her way about the viewing being held in her home, Verna's demeanor became that of a hostess anxious about the proper tending of her guests. "Melinda, would you mind fixing some coffee and seeing if there's something for ya'll to eat? I figure there may be a heap of folks soon. Thomas, I'm sure you could use something before you start back to town."

"Verna." Dr. Benson's concern about her rapid mood changes showed in his parental voice.

"All last night I prayed John would live, but come this dawn I felt throughout my body his life leaving me. There will be time for grieving again when the work's done. When John's folks died, we didn't have money to properly bury them, so they are in a place in the hills. And when the baby ..." Verna drew in air to help her finish the sentence, "we buried him in the hills by Hiram and Beulah's because we couldn't buy a plot in the cemetery. Well, that's not going to happen with John. We promised each other that if anything happened we'd make it right. No matter what. I know what he wanted." She stopped. Whatever force entered her body a moment ago left her as suddenly as it came. She looked around confused again and grew silent. She flinched, as she felt the doctor's desire to put his arms around her.

Dr. Benson saw the automatic withdrawal of Verna's body like a child used to being smacked. He knew that for some, physical touch could be more frightening than helpful. He'd seen widows go crazy after their husbands died suddenly. Verna Collins looked right now just like Deke Wilson's wife after that cow kicked his brains out. His thoughts took over: "Mrs. Wilson was still in the county hospital. No one expected her to return home. Her oldest daughter moved back in and was trying to raise the kids but..." He stopped himself and redirected his attention to the present. "I'd better go get some sleep. Verna's not the only one who doesn't want to believe John's dead. I want to join that posse, and Hippocratic oath or no Hippocratic oath, I want to be there when they string that murderer up."

He could feel the salty, burning tears gather in the corner of his eyes. Pouring some water from the blue and white bedroom pitcher into a wash bowl, Dr. Benson submerged his cupped hands in the tepid liquid and tossed it on his aching face.

Hazel returned, holding Nanny Marie against her full bosom, and nuzzled the toddler's cheeks that started to glisten from her aunt's tears. Son held Hazel's hand. Both children rubbed their eyes and leaned against Hazel for support as they slowly gave up the comfort of sleep. Nanny Marie held out her arms to Verna. Hazel, seeing Verna's daze, gently shook Verna's arm. "Verna, hold this child. She needs her mother's warmth."

Verna looked at Nanny Marie and then at Hazel. "I don't think I can, Hazel. Not now. "

Hazel bent down and picked up the confused child and started swaying gently to soothe her. Nanny Marie whimpered softly, "Ma. Ma," then put her thumb in her mouth, which she hadn't done for six months.

Son looked at his mother, surprised she hadn't picked up Nanny Marie, but seeing that his mother wasn't going to answer his questions, he asked his sister, "Darcine, why's Pa still in bed?"

Darcine whimpered, "Pa died," and broke into full sobs.

Verna was still holding John's hand, which she had picked up after the doctor pronounced him dead. "Children, come now. Say good-bye to your Pa."

Darcine cried loudly and Son picked up her wail. Tears rolled down Ellen's face but no sound left her mouth. Nanny Marie began to cry as she heard her siblings' sorrow. The minister helped each child touch their father's hand and told them to pray for him each night.

Verna found her emotions swinging back and forth. She wanted to scream. She felt angry. Mad as the devil at whomever killed John. She clenched and unclenched her hands. The only time she raised her voice was when she saw Lillian Harrison start to enter the bedroom. "Hazel, keep her out. This is for family only."

Son felt his mother's anger and asked to be picked up. Verna had turned back to John's body and seemed in a daze. Hazel moved between Son and Verna, sat down in the bedroom chair, and took him on her lap. He curled up and sucked his thumb loudly. Nanny Marie seemed lost until Hazel reached out and raised her up also onto her lap. The bedroom clock chimed eight. Dr. Benson went over and felt Verna's pulse, and asked to look into her eyes. Deciding she would be all right for a bit, he slipped out the bedroom door and left the family to grieve. He asked Clinton to stand by the bedroom door and not let anyone else in until the family said it was all right.

During the early morning the women of the Berea Quilting joined their husbands in the vigil outside the Collins' home. Not waiting to be invited in, they came through the kitchen door and began serving the food they had brought. Hill women brought fall vegetables from their dry cellars. Town women had baked during the night after hearing John was shot. Food from cold cellars was quickly prepared and placed on the stove to cook. The women's work flowed like a conductor-less symphony. Wood was tossed into the black metal innards – biscuits made, bread sliced, and butter set out. Someone invited the men outside to help themselves to the water in the well for drinking and washing up. Extra dishes and silverware came out of covered baskets. One woman even brought needlepoint cloth napkins.

No one asked to see John yet. The conversation flowed quietly as if they were in church. "The family's with him in the bedroom." "How will Verna ever raise those four children?" "I've never known Verna without John." "My Jeff said he won't stop until he finds out who killed John." "Do you think it was the Hatfields, like they say?"

In the kitchen, amid the sizzling bacon and the popping eggs, someone mentioned, "I don't see Millie Harrison here. Isn't she Verna's neighbor?"

"She better not show up." The kitchen talk, like an old man's heart, stopped for a second and then picked up again.

"How are those eggs coming?" "Got enough here for a first run outside." "Put some of those old table cloths on the ground in front to put the food on."

Someone sighed and silence settled again. Flour-dusted hands wiped cheeks and crusted on faces wet with leaking eyes. To Verna the kitchen noises were muffled as if her grief had transformed into two cotton balls stuffed in her ears. She began to come out of her daze. "Hazel, would you help the children get dressed? I need to change. Can you see? Are there many people here? Are they getting enough to eat? Until Mr. Welch comes for John, we'll let folks say their goodbyes here in the bedroom. But give me a minute now. Oh, look at my hands. Oh, oh, oh, there's blood under my nails. Hazel, help me."

"Verna, look at me." Hazel gently commanded. "Oh, darling, you're shaking. It's too much. Verna, let Mr. Welch keep John in town. You can't do this."

"No, Hazel, I can. I must. Bring me some hot water, real hot. And the soap John uses after he's been working on the tractor. It's under the sink. Put it all in a bowl. I'll just soak my nails and everything will be all right."

When Hazel came back, Verna was still sitting there looking at the dried blood under her nails. Hazel brushed Verna's hair after putting her sister's hands in the water and watching it turn pink like a slapped cheek. "I'm all right now, Hazel. Better go back to the children. You know Son. Any minute now he could start up." Verna first dried and from habit started to buff her nails, then stopped. She hastily drew up her thick tangled hair and pinned it. She wiped her face with a damp cloth the nurse had left for her.

After rummaging through the clothes cupboard, Verna chose a long black skirt with a bustle and a black blouse with white collar and sleeve ruffles and ribbons for her widow's wear. Offended by yesterday's frills, Verna grabbed the nail-trimming scissors and impatiently cut the white ruffles and ribbons from the too-fancy blouse. After tucking a handkerchief up each sleeve, Verna turned to John as if expecting him to approve, then moved slowly to open the bedroom door, letting in the world for the first time in twenty-four hours.

As Verna walked into the parlor, she noticed the rumpled sofa where the minister had spent the night. She puffed up the pillows and smoothed the seat. Steeling her back, she opened the front door and saw groups of men, eating. She started walking among them and felt rough hands touch her skin. She saw the puzzled glance of moist eyes. She saw hats come off heads. She saw mouths move. She moved as the wind rippling summer wheat, an invisible force noticed only for its effect.

Verna went to each group, thanking them for being here, saying something about John to each. "He would be glad to know you came." "We'll always remember the help you were last summer." "The sheriff appreciated your riding with him in the parade." She moved from the front yard through the orchard while avoiding looking at the barn. The older children were playing Skip to My Lou while the younger ones sang out "Sugar or Tea." Ellen and Darcine joined the older group. Hazel stood with Nanny Marie in her arms while Son played. Verna was glad they all could be distracted for a little while.

One foot in front of the other, Verna made it around the side orchard to the kitchen door, stepping over the ants feasting on remnants of the fallen apple pie. "Oh, Lucy, how good of you to come. Brenda, with all you have to do with your family and sick ma." As she said something to each woman in the kitchen, they touched her arm or rubbed her back lightly. Some hugged her tightly and wept silently. Others touched her cheek or took her hands, squeezing the fingers gently. Each gesture spoke their concern and caring.

If the men had walked into the kitchen at this moment, they would not have understood what was happening. As the men talked and plotted about getting John's killer and avenging his death, these kitchen women silently pledged solidarity around this new widow; solidarity that would carry her and her family through the winter without having to cook a meal or worry about paying the grocer's bill. They couldn't keep Verna's bed warm but they could keep her children's stomachs full, and pledged to do so.

"What's wrong?" one woman asked, noticing that Verna stopped and looked as if she were seeing something no one else could see.

"Nothing, it's nothing." Verna wasn't about to tell them, even though they were some of her oldest friends, how she kept seeing John slumped over on Rex's mane with a growing red spot spreading out across his back. Why, they'd think she was crazy. Shaking her head and looking at the kitchen table to reassure herself that he wasn't still there, Verna went to find Hazel.

# CHAPTER TWELVE

## SOLIDARITY

Clinton watched the sun rise over the hills and thought, "It's time. The men have eaten. There's nothing more to be done here. No one would dare hurt this family with so many folks around." Gathering the four men he had picked during the night, he motioned them to slip away and meet him by the barn where the horses were tied up.

"Dover, Judd, Luke, Evert, we're heading up to old man Crawfield's place on Bernard's hill. John let him run that still as long as he was just making liquor for himself and kin. But when he let those Hatfields in, John decided he'd take a look. Best be prepared for a fight. I plan on bringing in those Hatfields. I'm not saying they did it. I don't want anyone taking the law in his own hands. We're just gonna bring them in and look around.

"Take their guns. All the guns. Evert, you look in the cabin and get all the guns and ammunition you can find. Dover and Luke, you round up their horses. I want to see what kind of prints they leave. Judd, you stay close to me. I think there are only two of them but with them darn Hatfields you never know. Two could be twelve or twenty."

The five men rode straight in the saddle. Rifles stuck out from the leather saddles of the two lawmen. Pistols cut into the waist rolls of the others. They headed up the hill road John came down on Friday. Instead of tracing his route to town they would head east out the Toll Road and then up Barkerfield Road until it became a wagon path and then a horse trail into the hills to the east of Berea, where men still didn't accept any laws, federal or state.

The deputy's men had been born in the hills. Clinton had picked them carefully. They knew the paths; they knew the land, and most important, they were known, except for Judd, and Clinton planned on watching his back. The Hatfields weren't from these parts. The posse knew that the hill folks' oath of silence didn't hold for Appalachian trash that killed Verna Gabbard Gentry Collins' husband. Hill folk would be grateful if the troubles were taken care of before that damn federal government came in.

As they reached the top of the hill, Clinton asked them all to get off their horses and be careful where they walked. "I don't want y'all riding over footprints and other evidence we might find. Just wait here in the middle of the road away from where we can see Rex's hoof prints. See, that circle of prints. That must have been where John was when the first shot was fired and Rex reared up."

While Clinton was looking at the hoof prints in the road, Dover gave his reins to Evert and walked over to the side of the road. Clinton yelled at him, "Do you see anything, Marshal?"

"Come take a look yourself, Clinton." Dover looked down at a spattered stained circle about the size of a man's fist, which turned a cluster of roadside weeds yellow. "That gall dern killer done come out to the edge of the road and pissed while he watched John dying." One of the men spat on the spot.

Clinton cussed the day for being so beautiful. He remembered how as a boy he would come to these woods and look for Shawnee arrowheads. Stones in the road sparkled like diamonds. Clouds drifted by, barely casting shadows. Leaf-bare saplings bent like naked children helpless before the wind's force. They reminded Clinton of the Collins children. The creek's movement was reduced to a fall-dry trickle. "And here's his casings," Dover snarled, getting angrier. During the night's vigilance his jealousy of John Collins melted like ice licked by a feverish cow. He was determined to get the man who would dare kill a fellow lawman. The two men found where the shooter had stood when he shot John and measured the distance from the footprints to where Rex had shied. Clinton wrote down the numbers and put the paper in his pocket until he could give it to Dr. Benson.

After gathering all the evidence at the site of the shooting, the men remounted and continued on. They met no one and kept their silence. The sharp clanks of cantering horses' hooves alerted turkeys, deer, and pheasants hidden in the denser roadside woods. With Clinton leading, five bodies bent forward, with jackets flapping behind, to blend into a solid projectile.

# CHAPTER THIRTEEN

# A FINE LAYING OUT

Saturday morning, a fine covered black wagon pulled by matching gray geldings and driven by a man in formal coat and top hat stopped in the Collins' backyard. Springing down from the high step, Berea's premier undertaker and one of her wealthiest citizens strolled to the back door. Tipping his hat to all the ladies, smiling as if pulled strings stretched from his large hairy ears to his yellowed teeth, Mr. Welch announced his arrival to the kitchen women.

"Where's Mrs. Collins? I was so sorry to hear about the sheriff. What a good man. We shall miss him terribly." Steel taps on his highly polished shoes clicked as he maneuvered around the battle-engrossed boys, cooed at Nanny Marie, and quickly pushed open the parlor door. Verna, watching his arrival, waited for him, Hazel by her side with a firm hand on the widow's arm.

"Oh, Mrs. Collins, it's just too terrible. My condolences. My sincere condolences. The sheriff was a fine man, a fine man. One of the best. We were fellow Rotarians, as you know. I will do the very best for him. The very best. Dr. Benson phoned me and asked me to come out. Said you wanted to have the laying-in at your home. Now, of course, we'll do whatever you want. But dear Verna, eh Mrs. Collins, it would be best if you would just let me take care of everything. We will have a fine laying out for John in town, a fine laying out. It will be lovely. Just what you would want for him. And of course you'll want our best room."

Verna felt the anger heat her body and burst out in blazes on her cheeks. When dressed like she was now, Verna looked like a gentle lady. Her soft lips adopted a slight smile as if pleased you were paying attention to her. Since marrying John fifteen years ago and moving to Berea, Verna practiced becoming a lady. With a tilt of the head, a slight indirect gaze, and a softened voice, she acquired the graces of a gentle, at times suppliant, wife.

Hazel knew better, aware of Verna's stubbornness. Standing there with that poor unsuspecting man, Hazel remembered the time when Verna was twelve and one of John's older friends told her that little girls didn't belong outside on the porch at dark. She smiled at him and drawled in an exaggerated, polite voice, "Thank you so much for saying that. I began worrying that you weren't knowing it was time to go."

"Mr. Welch, you are just so kind," Verna lowered her voice so the undertaken had to lean forward to hear her. "Why, everyone knows you think only of the wishes of the dead, and we wouldn't have anyone else but you looking out for John and us." From those words on, Hazel witnessed Mr. Welch's confused seduction.

Verna continued. "I'll be straight out with you. We don't have any money for a fancy laying out or an oak coffin – that is what John said he wanted if something happened to him. I know how the law requires now that a body be prepared, but I didn't think the law says a man has to do his last resting in a fancy room. Am I right?"

"Yes, Mrs. Collins. You're right. That is the law."

Verna leaned close to him as if they were the best of friends and a confidence needed to be shared. Her voice volume was barely above a whisper. "And if I'm not mistaken, as a fellow Rotarian, isn't there some code about watching out for families in case of hardship? Of course as a woman, I wouldn't know about that. But I could ask one of John's fellow Rotarians if that's true. Why, you know how it is when a family member dies. 'Cause we don't know who killed John. It must be dreadful for you when folks are reminded about that awful scandal. I just can't imagine how it would feel to have family kill family just for a woman." Verna, assuming her most innocent face, reminded Mr. Welch of the scandal that touched his family.

Waiting a long second, Verna took a breath and continued. "Let's don't talk about that. I don't think that should even come up again as we bury John. Don't you agree, Mr. Welch?"

In the end Mr. Welch wasn't sure when he made the commitment, but everyone heard it. Verna thanked him for his generosity. "You are a true Berea citizen, pledging to donate your services. It is truly generous of you to offer to give Sheriff Collins a fine laying out here in his home with a first-rate oak casket and satin lining. We accept your offer."

"Eh, Mrs. Collins, I will need to take John for a short while and prepare him for the laying out." Mr. Welch made a last effort to regain some control.

"Mr. Welch, gentleman that you are, I know I can count on you to have John back by Sunday after church so that friends and family can begin saying their good-byes."

"Certainly, Mrs. Collins. Of course, of course." With a butter-oozing biscuit in one hand and his top hat in the other, Mr. Welch, glad he could be of some comfort, backed out the parlor door with a slightly lopsided smile, bowing as he left the helpless, grieving widow.

With the help of some of John's friends, Mr. Welch wrapped the body in blood-stained sheets and carried it to the waiting wagon. Resting John gently in the covered back, the men looked on as one addressed the undertaker: "Burton, I heard you promise Verna he'd be back by noon Sunday after church. We'll be looking for you then."

"Of course, of course. The poor dear. I wouldn't make her wait another minute." With a slight tip of his hat the undertaker climbed up front with the hired man who had waited patiently and they departed. The wagon turned around, slowly descended the barn lane, to the end of the hill road, and entered the County road. Mr. Welch's departure signaled to all Sheriff Collins' passing. Each man took off his hat and held it over his heart while the women dabbed at the corners of their eyes as the hearse carrying John's body made its slow way to town.

Mrs. Harrison was standing outside watching Mr. Welch's wagon fade in the distance. She had heard the sound of wailing from the Collins home, drifting like smoke carried by the November wind. Reaching inside the door for her bonnet and shawl, she slipped out her front door. Out back Mr. Harrison was cleaning his Winchester rifle. She knew he would be mad she had gone.

Closing the front door quietly, she walked down the road cautiously as if there were a bull nearby who might charge her if alerted. She waved to a few of the men to get their attention, but they moved to the other side of the road, passing her silently. She wasn't willing to yell to them, afraid her husband would hear. Finally a family came by that she knew from her church. "Hey, can you tell me how Sheriff Collins is?"

"He died this morning."

"Oh." She placed her hand over her heart.

"Good-bye, Mrs. Harrison. We'll see you tomorrow in church."

"Yes. Tomorrow."

Just like on an idle summer afternoon, people started drifting off from the Collins home. Their voices spread out like lapping waves. "See you tonight." "Suppose Verna's brother and sister-in-law will be in by then?" "Gotta feed my stock." The children stopped their games.

Someone took a sleeping Nanny Marie up to the loft. Another admonished Son to "Hush, boy," then persuaded him, "You come home with me for a while. You and Will can play with our new wagon." Hazel informed Ellen and Darcine, while gently touching their faces, "Your mother needs her rest. There's nothing you can do for now." After protesting, the girls drifted off with families of their friends. The house and yard became as quiet as a churchyard on Monday morning. Hazel turned over the stained husk-stuffed mattress and put new sheets and pillowcases on the bed.

With flashes of John's bloody back distorting her vision, Verna sat motionless in the parlor until Hazel led her to the shade-darkened bedroom. Stripping off her clothes as if she were a newborn, Hazel gently rested the numb body on the cool sheet and touched her hair with a kiss. The afternoon passed.

# CHAPTER FOURTEEN

# BERNARD'S HILL

The posse neared where the Hatfields' new still was thought to be. Each man took the reins of his horse in one hand and readied his gun. Clinton motioned for them to be quiet. With the snorting of the horses, the request was as useless as asking hens to be quiet while you slipped into their house to take their unborn young'uns. Two of the men's guns slipped in their sweaty hands. They knew the Hatfields had no compunction about killing lawmen, particularly Kentucky lawmen. Didn't matter if they stole something of yours or if they stole something from a neighbor, if you were after them, it was their God-given right to shoot you dead.

Clinton led the way. He motioned for half the men to circle to the left and the others to follow him. He saw the new rough cabin in the clearing with jugs all around. "Come out. Hands up."

Clinton noticed the smokeless chimney. Motioning for two men to circle around back, Clinton dismounted from his horse and moved toward the cabin, running from the backside of one tree to another. He heard a mule bray and noticed the brown elderly critter standing by the idle still.

He and Dover hit the front door at about the same time, opening it quickly while flattening themselves against the cabin. Clinton felt the sticky sap on his cheek from the freshly cut logs. He entered blasting, hearing his shells shatter flimsy chairs and break pottery still resting on the table. "Boys. They've gone. Must have lit out in a hurry. Looks like they left everything here including their mule and jugs."

Feeling an acute ache, Clinton knew, with no authority outside of Richmond County, he wouldn't catch the men if they had set out for Anse Hatfield's home in West Virginia. One of the men disgustedly declared, "That proves it. One of these varmints did shoot John."

"It don't prove nothing. Except them is cowards and running back to Grandpa Hatfield," answered another.

Clinton asserted his newly acquired authority. "Let's go, boys. I need to ask the marshal in Richmond if we can get a posse to go after them. Right now just go home. I'll let you know what's next. Dover and me are gonna look around, see if we find anything."

Luke, Judd, and Evert rode out straight and tall in the saddle. As Clinton watched them go, he vowed to take all the time necessary to catch John's killer. He would walk in the woods all day, if that's what it took to get a turkey for a special occasion. He laid traps, checked them, and freshened the bait until he caught a possum. He knew the man who tried to rush didn't get what he sought.

Clinton and Dover began a slow, steady search of the cabin and the ground around the still. They picked up empty gun shells. They crudely measured footprints from heeled boots. They decided three men lived in that cabin. They saw the dried bloodstain where John took Clem Hatfield and the drag of his boots as the sheriff pulled him to his horse. Clinton saw that John had dismounted from his horse and walked right up to Clem, not hiding behind trees as they had. For a moment Clinton felt like a coward with leaden boots. After four hours of searching, Clinton and Dover desolately climbed back on their patient mounts and headed back to town.

# CHAPTER FIFTEEN

# THE GATHERING

At dawn Verna awoke, moaning and thrashing. She sat up, looked around, and barely stopped herself from screaming by jamming a reddened fist in her mouth. As she tried to raise her leaden, sweat-covered body, the effort exhausted her. She fell back into the rumpled, damp sheets. Sounds from the kitchen drifted through the walls, too muffled to understand. Dr. Clark had given her laudanum. At first she refused the drug but succumbed to the pleading look in Hazel's eyes. But now she hated this neither awake nor asleep state while John's bloody back flashed on and off, on and off in her mind.

She wondered about the time. When she looked last, the sky was still dark. Now dull light filtered through the heavy, drawn curtains. "What day is it? Sunday. Surely they don't expect me to go to church." Then, as if arguing with herself, "But I want to." She thought it might be comforting to sit in the back and listen to the hymns. She could talk to God about John. She could even tell Him things she didn't tell Hazel, like how angry she was. She could ask Him to help her remember how John loved her and not think about the times he wandered. Maybe God would put her mind to rest so she didn't see the blood, over and over.

Verna tried to pull her legs out from the covers. She noticed two extra blankets on her. Someone must have covered her during the night. She thought about the drafty cracks in the loft and how they must get fixed before winter or the children might get sick. John always recaulked the attic at this time of year. She tried to write a note to remind herself to ask Clinton if he'd fill the holes for her, but she couldn't find a pencil.

Thinking of the holes in the loft as eyes, she wondered if John watched her. "Can you see me? Please give me a sign. Are you with God yet or still traveling?" She tried talking to him, but as soon as she started tears flowed.

Verna got boiling mad. The anger felt familiar. Now she remembered. The same anger came on her yesterday, so strong that murderous thoughts sprang out of her mouth. After she said she could "just shoot the man who shot John," Dr. Benson gave her the sedative.

Verna heard voices in the kitchen, others beside Hazel. "Who could that be? Oh, my goodness. Nan's here. I must get up. Oh, thank the Lord. They're here." Racing into clothes carelessly thrown on the chair, Verna ran to the kitchen. Sitting at the oak table was her sturdy twin brother, Grover. Her brother-in-law, Hiram, stood at the kitchen sink, washing something dark off his hands. A tall willowy woman of indistinguishable age busily washed a sink full of soapy dishes. Another woman stirred a kettle steaming so it caused her to look away from the stove.

Tears of relief ran down Verna's checks as she felt her body relax. "Nan, Grover, Beulah, Hiram – oh, you're all here!" She threw her arms around Nan, a short, plump woman whose skin resembled wrinkled tractor tracks. Nan's eyes suddenly radiated like the sun freed from dark clouds.

Nan took her fragile sister-in-law into her arms, drawing Verna to a steam-warmed bosom. "Verna, darling, oh Verna." That's all she could say before the two collapsed, weeping in each other's arms.

Verna took her sister-in-law's face between her hands as if to make sure she would be heard. "I'm so glad you're here." Tears flowed from Verna's eyes while her voice quivered, "John's dead."

"I know, darling. Hazel wired us. I couldn't believe it." Nan took Verna in her arms and patted her head as if she were comforting a small child. Verna pulled away from Nan, wiped her eyes with the corner of her sleeve, and turned to her brother. "Grover, bless you for coming. All the way from Oklahoma. Beulah and Hiram, did you stop at Welch's and see John?"

"No, Verna, we came right here to be with you and the children." Beulah as usual did the talking for her and Hiram.

"Sis, I can't believe it. Not John." Grover bear-hugging his twin sister in his strong farmer arms, rubbed his mustache against her cheeks. "Clinton's been by. He told us what happened. Said you and the children saw John get shot. Ain't no real man that would shoot a man in the back." As Grover talked, his cheeks became increasingly red, puffing out toward the bags under his eyes. You'd never know they were twins. Folks used to say that Grover sucked all the fat out of his mother and Verna all the sweetness.

Almost six feet tall and two and fifty hundred pounds, Grover Gentry towered a foot over Verna. She couldn't catch her breath in the folds of his chest. "Did you see anything, Sis? Did you see who did this to John?" His voice boomed so loud and gruff that Darcine jumped and Nanny Marie started to cry. Feeling his wife's elbow in his side, he spoke softer, "Has Mr. Gentry been by?" Grover referred to their father as Mr. Gentry.

Nan sharply chastised her husband. "Grover, now you stop asking her those questions. You're scaring the children." Verna watched her sister-in-law pick up her namesake, Nanny Marie, soothing the child with a song older than anyone in the room.

Verna quickly answered her brother's questions and reassured him that their father had indeed made the proper call to the house, then turned to her sister-in-law.

"Nan, I remember Granny singing that song. Why, Nanny Marie's calmer. She belongs in your arms, like one of your own." Verna wanted to retrieve those thoughtless words before they reached Nan's ears. "I'm sorry, Nan, I wasn't thinking."

"It's all right, Verna. I'm gettin' more used to the idea that I'll never have my own. It doesn't hurt as much as it used to. Being in Oklahoma helps me look at my life differently. Darling, don't you worry about what comes out of your mouth. It's true. I do love Nanny Marie as if she were my own. I fell for that baby the minute I helped catch her coming out of your belly."

Verna felt safer than she had since John was shot. While they all got ready for church, she talked to her brother about her wishes for

John's funeral. "We never spoke of it. But I know John would want to be buried in the Berea Cemetery. It's only fitting."

Grover's gruff voice caused Nanny Marie to put her hands over her ears. "Verna, how are you going to pay for it? I'd like to help, but with the new farm in Oklahoma, God damn it, I don't have hardly any cash. Won't have until the harvest next year. And only then if we're lucky." Grover hung his head slightly. To admit he couldn't make a living in Kentucky had taken him a long time. Poverty during his childhood had affected him differently than Verna. Far from hiding his shame, he had fought anyone who dared taunt him for having no father or mother.

Verna looked at her children: "Now children, you are not to repeat this to anyone, you hear?" Turning back to her brother, she whispered as if the secret might be kept between just the two of them. "Grover, there's no money. We never put any aside. The town gave us this house rent free, for as long as John was sheriff. John got a little pay and he got to keep a part of the county taxes he collected. We were doing all right for the first time. But this year's taxes hadn't been collected yet. Now we won't even get that. I don't know how we're going to pay for food."

No one moved while Verna talked. Even the children stopped wiggling. She took a breath. "But I will get John a cemetery plot. He won't be buried on the land just anywhere."

Hiram, a farmer like Grover, didn't like to draw attention to himself. As tall as Grover, but half his width, Hiram had a face that was ugly, sharp and pointed like a rooster's, with yellowed teeth, and topped by thinning hair. Verna used to describe Hiram as "the nicest man there ever was. Dull as a rainy day and just as steady." His voice was as quiet as Grover's was loud. Seldom speaking, when he did, those around listened.

Hiram drew himself up, touched his mustache nervously, and looked at his wife as if she would say it for him if he didn't get started soon. "Verna, we're gonna go pick out a plot for John and make it big enough for you and the children, too."

"Hiram and Beulah, I can't ask that of y'all."

Beulah stepped in, knowing Hiram had said all he intended to say. "Verna, it's settled. We talked about it. Hiram and I are getting on. It's time we picked a spot for us, too."

Grover put his hand on Verna's arm as she started to protest again.

"Verna, you know Hiram wouldn't offer to buy the plot for John unless he'd thought through ever bit of it. Hiram won't say it, but you know he loved John as if he were his own son."

Verna didn't have the strength to fight Hiram any more on this. She wanted the cemetery plot and that took precedence over her concern about the obligation. "I swear I'll pay you back some day."

"You needn't do that, Verna."

"Oh, Hiram. Why did it have to be John who died? Why?" Verna's eyes and nose began to drip. She pulled a handkerchief from her sleeve. But the more she wiped the more the tears fell, until her lace cloth wouldn't absorb another drop. She didn't want to keep crying like this. Her eyes felt parched and stretched. Her eyeballs burned.

Darcine, wanting to comfort her mother, spoke up. "Ma, Uncle Hiram caulked the loft for us."

"Hiram, I do thank you. John was going to do that this Saturday." Verna swallowed, not wanting to stop the conversation until she'd made one more request. "I'd like to come with you to the cemetery to pick the site, Hiram, if that's all right."

"Of course, Verna." Beulah answered for her husband, who was becoming uncomfortable with all the attention.

Hazel broke into the awkward silence. "We'll be late for the service. Ellen and Darcine, go get yourselves ready for church. Nan, help me with the children. Verna, you just sit and have a cup of coffee until it's time to go."

Hiram and Grover went out to hitch up Rex. Beulah grabbed extra quilts so the children wouldn't get cold on the ride. Grover took it upon himself to tell everyone where to sit in the wagon. "Son, sit here beside me. You can help me with Rex's reins. Hiram, there's room for you and Beulah up here." Ellen and Darcine bounced into the wagon and immediately snuggled up on each side of Hazel as she asked them about school.

In the far rear seat Nan, singing softly, held Nanny Marie in her lap and patted the seat for Verna to sit beside her. The adults talked quietly about the weather and the war in Europe. Verna felt alone, in the midst of her family, irritated at the chatter about a war too far away to matter. She wanted to scream at them, "What's wrong with you?" But instead, she turned her head away from Nan and her child and stared at the passing countryside.

The Collins-Gentry-Gabbard family group arrived inside the church just as the deacon was clearing his throat. People made room so they could squeeze into overflowing pews. Verna looked at the altar, covered with fall flowers, the last vestiges of summer gardens. From habit she picked up the hymnal and followed as the choir sang "Onward Christian soldiers, onward to the fore. Raise the cross of Jesus..." As the words became militant, she regretted coming. This song about battles wasn't comforting her. People were going to get killed. She began to cry again and buried her head in the hymnal book with a handkerchief molded to her eyes. She saw the blood on John's back again. She heard shots and looked up in fright, expecting someone to drop over in front of her. She felt faint. Verna thought, "I'll never make it through the next days. I can't do this. I can't. I can't."

Finally the hymn stopped and the familiar litany began. The preacher spoke loving words about John. Verna's heart quieted. Afterward they thanked the preacher, received words of comfort and caring from friends, and invited all to the viewing that afternoon at the Collins home.

As Verna and her family walked down the steps of the church, two men she recognized as friends of John came up to her. "Good morning, Mr. Neiman and Mr. Hennesey."

Each man tipped his hat and greeted the widow and her family. "Mrs. Collins, we wanted to express our condolences again." Mr. Neiman leaned closer so that only Verna could hear. "When a fellow Mason dies, we take care of his family in need. We are here for you. Verna, whatever and whenever you need us."

# CHAPTER SIXTEEN

# THE INVESTIGATION PROCEEDS

On Monday, Deputy Clinton Blake and his horse again took the morning train from Berea to Richmond, Kentucky, arriving about eleven o'clock to see Clem Hatfield brought before the county marshal. Following custom, the law enforcement officers of Richmond County held court outside. Chairs were set under a big sycamore tree, waiting for the proceedings. Word of Clinton's arrival reached the courthouse faster than the Berea deputy's galloping gelding. As he arrived at the courthouse, his fellow lawmen and curious old men with nothing better to do on a Monday morning surrounded Clinton.

After a few "Hey, how you?" and "Too bad about John Collins" greetings, one old man slipped in the bad news. "They sprung Clem Hatfield about half an hour ago. You just missed 'em."

"I telegraphed I was coming over this morning for the hearing. What do you mean they let him go?" Clinton's voice, while controlled, snapped with irritation.

"His uncles came in town. Not acting like Hatfields at all. Nice as punch. Hats in hand. Guns in holsters. Asking what the charges was and why their nephew was bein' held. The county marshal had to let him go. With Sheriff Collins dead, there is no evidence that Clem Hatfield had anything to do with an illegal still in this county."

Another Richmond lawman jumped into the conversation as he

saw Clinton's face turn red. "I know what you're thinkin', Deputy. You're thinkin' that's a pretty good reason for a Hatfield to kill Sheriff Collins, who then can't testify against Clem Hatfield." Used to dealing with John Collins, these men didn't know what Clinton would do with his anger. Although sometimes Clinton came to Richmond with John, he was regarded as just a small-town deputy, someone they didn't have to pay much mind to.

One of the older Richmond deputies slurred over a plug of tobacco, "You may not like it, Deputy. But we are just as glad to get rid of them. Two other Hatfields rode down from Berea and arrived here early Friday afternoon. They had to have left Berea 'bout mid mornin'. From what we heard John Collins was shot shortly after noon. Those men were halfway to Richmond by then. They ain't the ones that killed the sheriff."

Clinton made a fist and hit his own hand, rubbing the two together to soothe the sting. "That's not right. You should've waited for me."

Another Richmond deputy spoke up. "We got a telegraph from the governor's office in Frankfort. 'Send Hatfields back to W. Virginia. Any trouble, put them in jail.'"

The older deputy jumped back into the conversation. "Look, Clinton, it may not be the way you would do it, but the governor's had enough of these Hatfields. All he wants is them out of the state."

Unused to the politicians John handled, Clinton's face turned red. He bit the side of his mouth to stop the angry words from coming. His hand automatically went to his gun holster as he clenched and unclenched his jaw. "That isn't right. It isn't right." He wanted to hit someone. A year ago he would have. John Collins taught him to hold his temper and use the steam from it to get even rather than blow it away.

"Whoa, there, Deputy."

Clinton took a deep breath, eased his hand off his pistol, and used it to rub his neck. "Okay. I'll think about what you said. But if it looks like they done it, I want your word that you and these others here in Richmond will join us and go after them, even over the state line."

"Clinton, if there's any proof at all that them trash killed John, you won't be able to breathe from the dust kicking out of my horse's back feet."

Clinton, believing him, felt calmer. He started thinking about John's killing from the beginning. Standing there under the marshal's tree, his mind went to the spot where he had found the piss stain. He reviewed everything else he saw, the tracks of one horse – not two. His anger turned on himself as he thought, "You stupid... You did the very thing John taught you not to do. You jumped for the easy one."

He began to think that the Hatfields might not have shot John. "It's not like them to go one on one. Them cowards would have been in the woods waiting for John. Damn. It was one man. One no-good stinkin' man. Now John's killer's probably sitting there in Berea laughin' at that dumb deputy riding off to Richmond after the Hatfields." Clinton was considering other possibilities when he became aware of someone speaking to him.

"Clinton, want to get a cup of coffee and something to go with it? I'd like to know what's going on in Berea and who besides the Hatfields might have had it in for John. John was a good man. If we let the killer get away with this, it could be any of us next time with a bullet in our backs."

Bob Sweeney, the Richmond deputy doing the talking, was old for a lawman. A hard fifty years showed in his deeply creased face. Most lawmen found safer work after they rounded forty, not wanting to get outdrawn by a younger man. Clinton knew Sweeney. Never said more than howdy to him before, but he remembered clearly John's telling of Sweeney's history.

They had come to Richmond for a trial and were sitting under the marshal's tree. John pointed out a man standing apart from the others. "That's old Bob Sweeney. Used to be a farmer. His wife walked off the same day the bank foreclosed on his bottom land. Tobacco company just rolled it right in with theirs, offering him a job as a hired hand. Doesn't look like much, but he'd always been handy with a gun. Never afraid of anything except his wife. So he went to the marshal and got himself appointed a deputy. To hear him tell it, life's no different. He's just turning over the bad side of men's lives instead of bad soil."

Clinton began to look forward to talking with Bob Sweeney. He could use some help sorting the ideas flipping round in his head like fireflies. One would light up and be gone before he caught it while another one, farther away and dimmer, lit up.

The two men went inside the fancy hotel across the street from the courthouse. Clinton realized as they slid into the bar that Bob wasn't really talking about drinking coffee. Didn't matter that it was not quite noon. Clinton, suddenly, wanted a drink worse than anything. It would be good to drink with someone rather than alone.

They threw a shot down, blew foam off a beer, wiggled horse-hardened butts into stools made for the soft behinds of businessmen, and began talking. Clinton hoped he wouldn't cry as Sweeney protested the cowardly way John was killed and then went out to question Clinton's blaming the Hatfields.

"You're right. I jumped the gun. I was there at the jail when Clem Hatfield threatened John. I jumped on the idea his uncles did it. I figured they done it again – killed another lawman. It doesn't make any difference for them."

"I give you that, Clinton. It don't make no difference to them who they kill if they're mad enough. Want another?" Sweeney signaled the bartender before Clinton answered.

"Sure, Bob." Clinton decided to trust this man. "I've been thinking. You might be right about it not being the Hatfields. At least not both of Clem's uncles. From boot prints I saw, there was one man and his horse on the hill where the shot was fired into John's back. That should have told me something right there. Them Hatfields don't do anything alone. As we were walking across the street, I was thinking of other possibilities. I'm gonna tell you some things that need to just stay here in this bar. Do you have any problem with that?"

"It depends." Bob Sweeney liked this young Berea deputy. He sure liked having drinking company, too, but he wasn't promising anything until he knew more.

"Nothing illegal. Just stuff people would like to gossip about and all."

"You'll just have to try me, Clinton."

"Well, John, he, well he...John liked women." Clinton turned a little red.

Bob started laughing. Not a big belly laugh, just an out-of-the-side-of-the-mouth, cough-like laugh. "I thought you were goin' tell me something, Clinton. Everyone knew that."

"How?"

"Don't matter. Tell your story." Bob picked up his second shot and tossed it down.

Clinton began feeling like Bob was someone he could talk to. He had missed just sitting and drinking with another man. "John's been flirting with his neighbor. Maybe more than flirting. I don't know for sure. I never could understand why he did it. First that waitress, Bette. Then this Mrs. Harrison. And he's got the best wife a man could ask for."

"Clinton, men like John don't have other women 'cause they have bad wives. They have other women 'cause they like women. That's why they get the best wives, too. But get on with your story. It's not going to be too long before they come and get me for one of the trials."

"Well, last week, Mr. Harrison, he's the husband of the woman I was telling you John had been flirting with." Clinton saw Bob's smirk. "The woman John's been messing with. Mr. Harrison came into the jail and threatened John if he didn't leave his wife alone. John pretended he didn't know what he was talking about. The man was definitely about to blow up. Seemed to feel he owned his wife."

Bob put his arm about Clinton's back. "I had a wife I owned once. When I lost her, I would'a blown out the brains of anyone I thought touched her. Man's not himself when he thinks someone's stole something from him. Sounds like that Mr. Harrison is worth looking into. Any other ideas? Anything else going on in that college town of yours?"

"No, it's pretty quiet. Night we put Clem Hatfield in jail we also bunked five college boys. Well, actually four college boys and one of their friends who used to go to school until the Day Law made the Negros go to their own schools. Anyway, those kids are harmless. Got drunk. Starting shooting their guns in town. John threw them in jail to sober up. Took their guns away. Oh, and yeah, there was an old pig farmer that night. Town's pretty quiet. You know we don't have much going on in Berea."

"I heard you were having some Klan trouble down that way. They's kicking up all over since that Simmons fellow got to leading them last year and started burnin' crosses in folks' yards." Sweeney thought how young Clinton was. He realized this Berea deputy hadn't been born when the Kentucky Klan was unchecked in their stringing up of black folks.

Intend on his story, Clinton didn't respond to Sweeney's comment. "Yesterday morning as I was leaving, I saw Judd Jackson. He's a Negro free holder. Family's owned land outside Berea for years. Got it for fighting with the Union during the War. Old friend of John's. He came to the jail to pick up his son. Told me their fields were burned the night before." Clinton stopped and took a large drink.

Bob Sweeney looked at Clinton with surprise. "Sounds like after the War when free Negro's fields were burned all over, even in Berea."

Again, Clinton just kept talking as if Sweeney hadn't interrupted: "Jackson said something was stirring folks up. Told me he had warned John. I didn't think much of it." With this final admission of his neglect, Clinton looked down. Sweeney let the silence stay.

The two men had one more round, patted each other on the back and vowed to arrest those murderers. Sliding off the barstool, Clinton slipped and almost fell. For a moment he felt ashamed before deciding, "Man's got a right to have a few when a friend dies."

# CHAPTER SEVENTEEN

# A RIDERLESS HORSE

The day of the funeral Verna woke late. She blinked her dry eyes to squint out tears to stop the stinging. She felt disoriented. What time was it? A feeling of tightness crept around her heart. Touching her left bosom, she felt her chest heaving while wondering if Mr. Welch had come for John. Muffled voices seeped through the bedroom walls from the parlor where John's body lay.

Verna's brother, Grover, and Hiram stood in the parlor watching over John's body. "Where's that sun today, Hiram, when we could use it?" Grover's mouth barely moved below his saddle-bag eyes that carried the load of sleepless nights.

The past days Grover had watched his sister closely, much the way he looked over his crops when the weather hit a bad spell. Stroking his mustache with a soothing touch, Grover confided in his brother-in-law, "Hiram, I don't think Verna's going to make it alone. She's walking around like she isn't awake. Bumping into furniture, looking at people as if she'd never seen them before. Even her hair. Nan had to brush it for her."

Hiram liked John Collins and loved Verna, but not her silly ideas about showing respect. Hiram didn't cotton to laying-ins and funerals. For him the old way was fine. Someone dies. You dig a deep hole so the animals don't get the body. Wrap it in a sheet – if there's one to spare – say a few words to the Lord, and shovel the dirt back in on top of the body. But they weren't gonna hear it from him. He noticed Grover still waiting for him to answer.

"Yep, Grover, she don't look so good." And Hiram went to make sure the animals were fed.

Verna wanted to say one more goodbye to John before Mr. Welch came to take his body away for the funeral service at the church. But she didn't want anyone else around at her final goodbye. Dr. Clark proved right. The ordeal of standing around inside the house greeting people, not being able to be alone with John, exhausted her.

Verna wasn't sure when she fainted last night. Awakened by a gentle slap on her face, she heard Hazel's dry voice: "You're fine, Verna. You just fainted, that's all." Verna wanted to scream at her sister, "I'm not fine. I'm dead. Let me be." If being numb all through your body was what being dead was, she was dead. She didn't want to live. How could she, without John? The children kept pulling at her and she just didn't know what to do. Poor things. They needed her but she had nothing to give.

She had stood by the oaken casket for two days, saying hello to people and thanking them for coming. A few made her smile. More made her cry, until she just couldn't cry anymore. Last night Dr. Benson had given her laudanum again, which made her sleep but not rest. Her mind was filled with dark passages that led nowhere. If she had the strength, she'd pick up John's body and put it on Rex, and they would ride away together like when they were teens. A smile briefly lit her face.

As if from the top of a hill Verna heard Beulah's nasal voice saying, "Time to go, Verna. Hazel and Nanny have helped the children get dressed. Dr. Benson will drive you, Grover, and Nanny in his carriage to the Union Church. Hiram, Hazel, and me will follow with the children in our wagon. Clinton came by this morning to get Rex. He'll meet us at the church and lead everyone to the cemetery after the service."

From the front pew of the Union church sanctuary, Verna stared at John's casket. Behind her came the buzz of people whispering, most well meaning, some simply curious. As she came in, many of the townfolk quietly said kind words, like, "I'm so sorry Verna. He was a good man." Verna accepted their well-intentioned words with a nod of her head, unable to trust her voice.

When Millie Harrison tried to give her condolences, Verna glanced up, surprised that her neighbor would dare to approach her. Standing beside Millie with his hat still on, Verna thought Mr. Harrison looked like he had a smirk on his face. Verna just put her head down and went forward without acknowledging either of them.

Baskets of asters, late-blooming roses, mums, and sprigs of colored berries softened the stone interior, filling the altar and tumbling down the two steps leading to the communion railing. Verna held Nanny Marie's hand as her toddler curled up into Nan's lap. Son, on Verna's other side, sucked his thumb, which he hadn't done since he was two. The children seemed far away as if at the end of a long tunnel. Verna noticed Ellen and Darcine held hands and then their images started to dissolve. She almost called out for someone to help put her children back together. She stopped herself and refocused on the sermon, something about killing being the gravest sin.

Coming out of Union Church after the ceremony, Verna was grateful that Hiram and Grover stood on both sides of her, holding her up. Two scores of black blanket–draped horses pulled rough wagons and fine carriages down Chestnut Street. Verna and the children were huddled in the lead carriage in back of John's horse, Rex. For a moment instead of John's horse, riderless with a black blanket and red roses draped over his back, Verna saw John. He was alive. And then, he slumped over, blood running down his back. She screamed. She felt someone push up the sleeve of her black dress, then pinch her upper arm, and the cold needle go in her flesh.

The cortege slowly traveled the two miles from the church to the Berea Cemetery. More than a hundred people rode or walked the road that afternoon. Many were weeping. Others were curious. One looked satisfied, almost smiling.

The sedative did its work again as it had the past several days. Verna stopped screaming and patted her children's hands. She felt Hazel and Beulah's arms around her shoulders. She asked them the still-unanswered questions, "Who did this?" "Who killed him?" "Why?"

The carriages and wagons were left at the cemetery gate, except for Mr. Welch's hearse bearing John's casket. The mourners walked past the large monuments of Berea's prominent families – Allens, Lewises, Galloways, Hayses – to the nearby spot Hiram and Verna picked for John. With effort Verna raised her head, looking around. She touched her hair under her black hat while re-experiencing a sense of pride. John was going to be buried in the section with Berea's oldest families and college dignitaries, just as she wanted.

It took a while for everyone to gather. The cemetery caretaker had placed chairs around for the family to sit for the graveside ceremony. Verna tried to avoid looking at the grave surrounded on three sides with mounds of brown dirt. But the minister took her hand, leading the family in front of the gaping hole. Turning to Hazel, Verna managed to whisper, "I feel faint."

"Don't look down at the ground, Verna. Look up at the beautiful tall oak over John's resting place."

Verna looked up, having chosen this site for the tree, and experienced comfort in the tree's presence. The burnt yellow leaves filtered the gray sky, making the day less dreary. The minister's words hummed on in the background. Verna heard creaking and looked down as Grover, Hiram, Clinton, and five other men lowered John's casket with strong ropes into the darkness.

The minister gave Verna a handful of dirt to throw into the grave. She let it sift like flour through her fingers. Others put in more dirt, flowers, and small mementos. Verna's ears involuntarily drew in each sound – scrape, plop, thud – the most painful noises she ever heard. A cataract of salty tears blinded her.

Eventually the ritual ended. Everyone left, bidding one more goodbye to the widow and offering sympathy. The bugler, who had been playing a mournful Irish tune, now extended each note as if his breath was leaking from his body. Verna whispered in Hazel's ear, "Please ask everyone to leave me here with John. They can wait by the gate. I need a little more time." Hazel hesitated a moment before rounding everyone up and reassuring the children "It's all right. Your ma just needs a little more time. She'll be with you soon. Come, I brought some biscuits."

Verna found the courage to ask the grave diggers to delay their dinner a little longer and move away so she could have the last moments with her husband. She knelt down, kissing the dirt placed over John's coffin. She began to tidy his grave, picking up small pieces of paper and cloth. Words swam up to her eyes: "Pa, I love you." Ellen's writing. "Pa, I miss you." in Darcine's block letters. "Come home, Pa." Darcine again. "We'll never forget you." Ellen. Shapeless scribbles, Nanny Marie's. Misspelled, large wiggly letters, "Bye, Pa." Son's. And amidst the letters of love, one toy soldier, gray.

# CHAPTER EIGHTEEN

# EARLY MORNING MONOLOGUE

"I know he's dead. Right this moment I know he's dead. But as soon as I look at one of the children or out the window, I forget. And when I remember again it's like a smack in the face. I don't want it to be true. It can't be true. He was so alive. He glowed. He walked into a room and all I wanted to do was look at him. If he came over to me, all I wanted him to do was touch me. Touch me on the shoulder or the arm. Touch me so everyone would know I was his and he was mine.

"I know he's dead. I knew it this January morning when I rolled over in bed to put my head on his shoulder and didn't stop until I felt his cold pillow. For a moment I thought he had gotten up to go outside and relieve himself. But then he didn't come back. I wanted to go asleep again and see if this time when I woke up he would be back and I could put my head on his shoulder.

"I know he's dead. But I still smell him. His smell is in his clothes that I won't let them give away, saying they will be good for Son when he grows up. He'll want something of his pa's. But I watched their eyes. They knew I wasn't ready yet to give up all his clothes. It was bad enough seeing him for the first time in his new dark brown suit in the coffin. He still wears clothes the same size as when we were married. Unlike me. I've put pounds on my middle but he remains trim and taut. But then, he didn't carry six children.

"I know he's dead. But I still talk to him each day. I ask him how can I manage: four children, no money, little schooling? Not even a house or a horse to my name. Everything belongs to the town. Sure, it was nice that they gave us a home to live in and a horse. But the sheriff is dead and his wife and children are living on charity.

"I know he's dead. But no God I could love would take him. He was only 34. That's not when people die. They die when they're old, 60 or so. They don't die when they are so handsome that women look out of the corner of their eyes to follow them down the street. They think I don't notice, but how can you help not notice when they practically fall down not looking where they're going?

"I know he's dead. But just for this morning, just for this minute, I'm going back to sleep. Ellen will get the children's breakfast and watch them so they don't run outside or turn something over. I'll get up later and maybe tonight I'll fix dinner rather than eating someone else's charity food. Maybe tonight.

Verna knew she was going crazy. She couldn't stop talking to herself. She'd tried. She felt like she was one of those tomatoes that just blew the top of the cooker one day when she was canning. She'd known loony Ben up in the hills and he, too, walked around all day talking to himself.

"Verna, get up. Get up now. Ya'll hear me? What are you doing letting these children take care of themselves! Throw this robe on. Tie the belt. Here, let me do it. Now put some shoes on. Your hair's a mess. After you get something to eat, I'll brush it for you." Hazel walked into the bedroom just as she had every morning since John died, alternating between bullying Verna and stroking her until she could get out of bed. She threw back the thick drapes, causing Verna to squint her crusted eyes.

"I'll get up in a little bit, Hazel. Just let me sleep some more."

"You know I've got to get to school. You could help a little, Verna. Ellen's out there gettin' em all something to eat. But after I take Ellen and Darcine with me to school, someone has to watch Nanny and Son."

"Can't Willa Mae come?"

"Not today. One of her boys is sick and she has to take care of her own. You know Willa Mae's got her own troubles."

"She didn't mention anything to me. She only said she was needed at home." Verna felt annoyed that Hazel acted as if she ought to know something about Willa Mae. And if the truth be told, she didn't want to know about Willa Mae's troubles.

"Verna, someone's been burning the Jacksons' fields down in Middletown. Trouble started down there the night before John died and it hasn't stopped yet. Some say it's the Klan riding again. You must've heard."

"Hazel, that doesn't happen here. Not anymore. Why, you know those Ohio abolishers picked Berea to build only the second college in the United States to educate Negroes. There had been bad times before, but it's been quiet since John was made sheriff." Verna looked off into the distance.

Hazel touched Verna's arm, saying, "We both remember that first time. We were eight or thereabouts, sitting in church, me with my Ma and you with your Granny. The whites and the Negroes together just like in the schools."

"I remember, Hazel. We heard noise in the back and Granny told me, 'Look down, child. Don't you look up until I tell you.' I had never heard her talk to me that way before, firm with no wiggle room for arguing. I heard men's voices shouting things like, 'You niggers better leave and not come back here.' Then the preacher yelled at them – "This is a house of God!" – and said they were welcome to worship with us and all kind of other stuff I don't remember. Then I looked out in the aisle. I recognized those shoes. Would have recognized them anywhere. My Uncle Grover's shoes and, above them, a white skirt down to his ankles. I punched you and you looked, too, and saw the white skirts. Then they left. First time I ever saw or heard any Ku Klux Klan men. To think my own uncle was one of them.

"I remember there was some burning back then and then again 'round the time they were trying to get that darn Day Law passed. I don't know what gets into folks. Is that what's going on now, Hazel? Is the Klan riding again?"

"I don't know, Verna. Seems so. People say they are especially picking on the Jacksons." Hazel felt Verna's energy for the first time in three months and thought, "Maybe she needed to worry about someone other than herself."

"Why the Jacksons? That doesn't make sense, Hazel. They never cause trouble."

"I don't know. Some say it's because they've got land and the Klan wants to take all the land the Negroes own in Middletown away from them."

"Oh, Hazel. That's awful. What are Willa Mae and Judd going to do?"

"Verna, I can't say. Just thought we should talk about it 'cause you shouldn't always count on Willa Mae. She's got her own to worry about these days. You need to be taking more care of these young chilluns yourself, Verna."

"I try, Hazel, but Son's too much for me. He still asks for his pa and then runs around looking for him. Yesterday I had to chase him all the way to the barn, and Nanny Marie followed him without any shoes on. There was snow on the ground, and her little toes turned red."

"Verna, he's only four. He misses his pa. That's all. He's not a bad boy. He's just missing John. Like we all do."

"Oh, Hazel, I just want to crawl into the earth with John. I just want to be in the everlasting with him. I went to the cemetery yesterday. Bundled up Son and Nanny Marie. It's so cold there, Hazel. I can't leave John alone. It's so cold."

"Verna, you stop talking like that, you hear. Stop it now. Get up. You're a Gentry, like me. We just keep moving on."

Verna felt her Granny in the room, reminding her she was a Gentry. As if being a Gentry meant you were something special. Verna didn't feel special. She just felt tired. But her body started moving. Her old habits just wouldn't stop. All her life, "Remember you're a Gentry" meant no matter what, you held your head up with pride. Even if your own mother walks out on you.

Verna put her feet on the floor, shuddering from the wintry air coming from the cellar through the floorboards' cracks. She wrapped herself in a knitted shawl, draped over the maple rocking chair. Walking a crooked path to the door on her tiptoes, she avoided the clothes, dirty nappies, toys, food remains, plates and cups, and papers scattered all over the room.

"Verna, the Quilting Society decided to meet in the church this afternoon after school. Blanche will come for you."

Verna stood up and looked at Hazel as if she was the crazy one. "I can't go, Hazel. I haven't been out of this house since Christmas services."

"You're coming, Verna. It's been decided. We're going to make a quilt remembering John. You're going to be one of us again."

"Hazel, I can't." As Verna began to panic, her voice raised to a crow's screech.

"Blanche'll be here at three o'clock. I want you to sort through John's clothes and decide which ones you want in the quilt."

"Hazel, I can't. You don't know what you're asking of me."

"Verna, all I know is after two months John's clothes still hang in your closet. The children need you. I need you. We all miss you."

"Hazel, you don't understand. I saw him shot." Verna looked down. "Besides, I'm saving those clothes for Son."

"Verna, you know I love you more than anything. Now come into the kitchen. Ellen, Darcine, and I have to go to school. Just make a start, Verna."

# CHAPTER NINETEEN

# A Remarkable Visitor

Around noon on Saturday Verna heard the sputters of an automobile pulling into her barn lane. Looking out the kitchen window she gasped and loudly laughed. Ellen startled, dropping the milk, to hear her mother laugh. Alighting from Berea's second motorized car was Mrs. Blanche Wellington Welch, the wife of Berea's wealthiest merchant and third cousin to the undertaker. She wore a hat bigger than her head, with red and violet ribbons tied under her chin as if she were trying to bring spring to the bleak winter day.

"Blanche, your car. It's wonderful. How on earth did you ever learn to drive?"

Verna felt full of curiosity and excitement. It seemed for a moment as if she were awake again. She looked around and seeing Nanny Marie smile, realized her baby was soon going to be two. Out of the corner of her eye she saw Son about ready to drop a handful of dough into his pockets. Feeling for a moment some of the old pleasure she used to get out of her boy's mischief, she gently admonished him. "Son, stop that."

"But, Ma, I want to give it to Rex."

"Horses don't like dough, Son. He likes apples."

"But we don't have any more apples."

"I know. Look at Mrs. Welch's car, Son."

Son ran outside and Verna warmed to see him throwing his arms around Mrs. Welch, who lifted Son up and put him into the driver's seat. Verna could hear Son, quiet since his father's death, through the open window as he mimicked Mrs. Welch's car. "Roar, roar, roar. Putt, putt, putt."

Blanche clamped Son under her arm and strode to the kitchen door before Verna could shut the window, much less open the door for her. Closed doors didn't stop Blanche Welch. Nothing stopped her. Used to wealth and having her way, since turning thirty Blanche walked into people's homes the way she walked through life, waiting for no one to give her permission.

Blanche was the leader of the Women's Suffrage Movement in Berea and Richmond County. She believed a woman should have the right to vote while Verna believed a woman's place was in the home. Despite her politics Blanche had a way of telling stories that made Verna laugh so hard that she would begin to hiccup.

"All right, young man. You will make a fine driver one day. Just keep your eye on the road and know where you want to go." Blanche dropped Son as abruptly as she'd picked him up. Quickly she kissed the older girls, imparting a cross-stitch saying for each. To Ellen she commanded, "Remember to be kind to your mother." While to Darcine, she declared, "Your smile is a gift." Turning her full attention to Verna, she erupted, "Are you ready? I don't see John's clothes for the quilt. They will be waiting for us."

"Blanche, I couldn't decide. I don't know if I can do this."

"Of course, you can do this. All you have to do is choose. Come. I'll help."

The two turned together. Verna was still putting down a spoon and looking bemused while Blanche plunged through the kitchen door and opened the bedroom door. "Come, Verna."

By the time Verna entered the bedroom, a pile of John's clothes covered the bed. "This would make a lovely piece for the quilt. What a delightful shade of blue."

"I can't use that. It's John's favorite shirt."

"It's perfect. You want his favorite. It will be with you forever. Better than collecting dust in this closet. And that suit and these two flannel shirts. Now we're done. Don't you agree, Verna?" Blanche handed the clothes to her, not waiting for Verna's answer.

Verna, as she did every morning and at least twice nightly, put her face into John's shirt and drank deeply of his smell. Her eyes filled. She even lost the sense of Blanche Welch's presence until her friend's voice cut through Verna's consuming memories. "Verna, it's time to go."

On the way to the church, Blanche kept up her usual chatter. She and her new car sounded the same, "putt, putt, spat, spat." Both huffing and puffing with a combination of exuberance and power. Blanche had been trying to recruit Verna for over a year for the Kentucky Women's Suffrage Union.

"You saw what happened this year with the governor's election. We can't always let the men settle these things. Why, I got active after reading Jane Addams's speech at the Bull Moose Convention. She showed us how to speak up. I know how John felt about the saloons. Now he's not here to vote anymore, you don't have a vote for your family. It's not right. Join us, Verna. It would be good for you and we need every woman we can get."

"Blanche, I've been telling you all along. Politics don't interest me. John would ask my opinion on issues and I liked that. But I've got no need to be out there holding a sign for women's rights. When the time is right, we'll be able to vote in all the elections. But right now it's good enough for me that I can vote on school issues."

Blanche lit right into Verna's soft spot like a butterfly landing on the most delicate flower. "Verna, wouldn't John want you to vote in his place? We've just got to keep this county saloon-free. Why, I wouldn't be surprised if it weren't one of those big liquor companies that..."

Verna interrupted her, "Blanche, I know you mean well but I can't stand talking about John now. I just think about him and lose whatever strength I've mustered. I don't want to walk in there with all those women and my eyes all red. I'll think about what you said."

Blanche could never leave well enough alone. "Verna, with the war in Europe and men striking in the coal mines, the politicians are ignoring us women. We can't let this go on. Look what's happening at the White House. Treating women like their only purpose was procreating. Putting women in jail and forcing food down their throats. We're smart as they are, Verna, and you know it. Why, you're smarter than most men I know, much as you hide it when the men are around."

Just as Blanche turned quickly from the County road up Chestnut

Street, she changed the subject. "I've been talking to Hazel. We think you should get yourself back to school. You could go to Berea College. Get yourself a degree. Then you could support those children."

Verna felt awake. She noticed the cool air seeping into the car. "Blanche, if I let you, you'd tell me everything I should do from the time I got up until I went to bed again. Now how on earth could I go to school, study, and still take care of those children of mine? It's hard enough taking them when I clean houses. I'm not like you. I like to read. But I'm too old to go back to school."

"Verna, you don't fool me. I've watched you talking to the best of them. Behind that smile and tilt of your head, I've seen the spark when someone said something stupid. You just didn't want to stand out or cause trouble for John, which is why you hid. But that's what I've been talking about. Women don't have to hide how smart they are anymore. They need to stand up and say, 'I want to vote. I got the right.'"

"Blanche, watch that horse. You almost scared him to death. Now let's just enjoy this afternoon. I can't believe how quickly we made it to town."

# CHAPTER TWENTY

## BEREA'S QUILTING SOCIETY

All the members of the Women's Quilting Society of the Baptist Church of Berea, Kentucky, met for the first time since early November. People came to Berea from throughout the region to admire and buy these women's handiwork at the College craft store. They sat in the church basement on chairs around a large rectangular frame. Various-sized sewing bags, overflowing with multicolored skeins of yarn, scissors, and hooks carpeted the wooden floor.

The conversation was muted. Several women looked up guiltily when Verna and Blanche entered the room. Verna heard Lillian Harrison's name linger in the room. She knew John found Lillian attractive. She had watched him eye her. She didn't want to know anymore than that. Not now. Verna whispered to Blanche. "Take me home, please."

"No."

Blanche's refusal acted like a shove to Verna's back and she continued forward into the room. Walking as she had practiced after she married John – back straight, eyes forward, head lilting to the left, and a slight smile on her lips.

She placed a hand on Blanche, stopping their forward movement, and whispered. "When I was eight, two bees began buzzing a molasses-covered turkey leg my Granny made 'specially for me. I first said, gently, 'Shoo, shoo.' Except one made me so mad with his buzz, buzz, buzzing, I swatted right at him. I don't know who jumped more but he lit out and didn't bother me again."

To take a swat at the buzzing women bees, Verna stepped forward, smiled sweetly, looked straight at one of the talkers, and drawled, "Why, honey, don't you worry. There's no need to hush. John and I talked many a time about Lillian Harrison. So don't you worry none that there's something you might say I don't know already."

Blanche squeezed Verna's hand and whispered in her ear, "Welcome back, honey."

The rest of the early afternoon was spent putting the cotton-backing base on the quilt frame, deciding the basic outline, and talking about what people remembered most about John that should be in the quilt. Someone suggested they cut dark material in the shape of liquor bottles to represent how he hated the bootleggers coming into the hills around Berea. One woman wanted to have a section of black and white squares to show how John was fair to all people. Verna was asked to bring pictures of her children so they could be traced onto the quilt.

With a voice barely above a whisper, feeling the safety of friends, one woman released her private fear: "My Johnny went missing today. He wasn't at the table for breakfast. Lord knows how that boy loves to eat. One of his friends came by as I was leaving to come here. Said Johnny lit out with Edgar Whitten to go fight in that foreign war." Her voice trembled. Verna strained to hear the ending. "He's so young."

An older woman who knew all their children and was considered wise spoke up: "Your boy's been wandering off since he was five and walked to town 'cause he wanted to see the circus. President Wilson's promised we wouldn't get into this foreign war. Don't get me wrong, I never trusted a Democrat yet. But mark my words, Jamey'll be home for supper."

Several women nodded. They wanted to believe Jamey would come home. But a sense of pessimism prevailed since the sheriff's murder months ago and still no one arrested. Verna rose from her place around the frame to hug her friend with the missing son.

"Verna, what does Clinton tell you about who..." An awkward silence fell as the woman questioner realized she didn't want to say the word "killed."

Blanche held Verna's hand, then answered the question herself to relieve Verna of the pain of responding. "Verna told me Clinton has some good leads. He found evidence on the hill. Soon he'll have John's killer in jail. But she's not allowed to say anything."

Another woman whose daughter was Ellen and Darcine's friend spoke up. "Verna, if there's anything more I can do to help with the children, you know all you have to do is holler."

Verna welcomed the chance to share with her friends about the children and ask their advice. "Breaks my heart to hear them talk about their pa. I don't know what to tell them. How do you explain death to an almost two-year-old? And Son still asks, 'Is Pa coming home tonight?'"

Several women gave Verna advice, but mainly they shared words of comfort. A prayer was said for John and his family. Then conversation went back to gossip and deciding about the quilt. Verna managed to laugh once.

"What are you going to do, Verna?" spilled from the lips of the youngest woman there, who also had four young children.

"I don't know. I just don't know." Verna hung her head as stomach contractions made her queasy. Sweat gathered on her palms until she wiped them dry on her dress.

Blanche put her arm around Verna, squeezing her tight. "She'll be fine. Verna's going back to school."

Verna caught her breath. "Blanche!" She sputtered.

"She's thinking about it." Blanche backpedaled. "Now let's eat. I'm hungry from all this work and talk."

The women drank tea and cider and feasted on pies and molasses cookies left over from Christmas until someone said, "Oh, Lordy. It's three o'clock. My Hugh will be coming home and there's no supper."

Verna's head snapped back as she drew in a quick breath. Touching Verna's arm, Blanche signaled she understood the pain Verna might feel from this thoughtless reminder of her husbandless home. One of Granny's stories slipped into Verna's mind. Rebecca Boone, Daniel Boone's daughter, had gone canoeing on the Kentucky River with some friends soon after settling in Boonesville. The peaceful afternoon turned into a terrifying encounter with hostile Indians. Granny ended the story with a lesson: "Becky should have stayed in the fort where the men could protect her."

Verna thought, "How can I go to school, or anywhere for that matter, with no man to care for me?"

# CHAPTER TWENTY-ONE

# THE INVESTIGATION HEATS UP

On his way back to the hill where John was shot, Clinton stopped at the college marshal's office to talk with Dover. Seeing Clinton dismount, Dover lit a cigarette and left his office feeling closed in by the shortened winter days. After Clinton tied up his horse, the two men leaned against the railing as a January light snow began to fall.

"Bob, I'm no further along finding who killed John than two months ago, on the day after his murder. Doc told me our man's about five eight, but hell, that fits three quarters of the men in this town. Talked to Mr. Harrison; he claimed he was out of town that night. Said a friend of his would back him up. Went to see the friend, who said they were drinking a jug in his cabin. Not sure I believe him, but can't prove different. I've followed every rumor. Seems all the feuding families in the hills have a different person to tell me a tale about. I've run them all down."

"Been hearing about that, Clinton. Heard tell most folks told you a pretty good story about they own doings. Seems everyone knows exactly where they were and what they were a doin' at noon on Friday, November the 8th. Told you before, Clinton, it's them Hatfields. If you ride out to get them, count me in." Dover pushed his battered hat back as he stuck his chest out.

"In fact, I decided this morning to go to West Virginia and talk with Anse himself. Good to know you're with me, Dover." Clinton, swinging back on his horse, settled in to complete the same route that John Collins took the last day of his life.

Two, three times a week Clinton went to the wooded area where the shooter hid. He would squat on his haunches trying to think like a killer. He even walked down the hill following the path he thought John's horse had taken to the barn. He sought a clue about the coward who shot John in the back. With no formal training, Clinton's limited knowledge of solving crimes came from John's book, *Robinson's History and Organization of Criminal Statistics of the United States*. About two weeks after John's death he called the federal marshal in Richmond for help. The marshal suggested Clinton look for the bullet that shot John and then send it to Washington for identification.

Four weeks after John died on a particularly bright day, just three days after he had been appointed acting sheriff, Clinton walked about halfway down the hill. The sun lit a shiny object in the middle of the road. He stooped and barely recognized the smashed and twisted piece of metal as one of the bullets that shot John. Surprised he'd even noticed the bullet, Clinton pushed away images of what that bullet did to John's chest wall to emerge so twisted. Wrapping the deadly metal in his cloth neckpiece before sliding it in his left front pocket, Clinton marked the spot.

Now, a month later, he was still waiting to hear about the bullet he had sent off in December. From habit he dismounted at the top of the hill to search the killer's hiding place yet again. Snow covered the ground, obliterating any remaining evidence. He could see the smoke from Verna's home.

Clinton often talked to himself. A habit he developed after his father died and his mother picked at the details of his life until he retreated into one-word answers. Now he needed to hear his thoughts aloud to think through this problem. "It's cold. Time to stop looking for what's not here." He started to get back on his horse when another thought needed saying. "You come to see Verna, not the hill. For two months, every day, you've been finding an excuse to visit with the widow of your best friend." Shaking his head, he remounted and rode down to the Collins place.

After taking the bit off, so his horse could nibble on oats with Rex, he knocked before opening the kitchen door. There was a hot cup of coffee and biscuits sitting on the table.

"Morning, Verna."

"Come in, Clinton. Rest a while." Seeing Clinton in the doorway, Verna touched her hair and moved a wandering wisp back in place, automatically responding to his presence. As she found herself leaning toward him, she stopped quickly, giving a little shake of her head.

"Sure it's no bother?" Clinton asked as always.

"It's no bother." She looked him straight in the eye, unaware of her tilted head and slight smile.

"Wanted to tell you, Verna, I'm going to West Virginia. I gotta talk to those Hatfields myself. Tried to go back in November, but Anse hid those boys of his and that grandkid out in Tennessee while the fever was on strong about John's death. Something's not right. What do those federal marshals know about talking to a hill man? All they know is busting 'shiners. Maybe those Hatfields didn't do it. But I just got an itch that they know something. I was sitting up on the hill just now..."

As Verna sensed Clinton wanted to touch her, she became cautious. She'd always known when men were interested in her, as natural as knowing when the churning butter was set. But she wasn't ready yet for any man, as comforting as Clinton's deep voice and musk smell were. "Clinton, how can you sit up there? Knowing that was where the – knowing that was where he stood to shoot John."

"Verna, I can feel him there. Each time I go, I feel him stronger. It's as if I can smell him. And he smells real bad. Real bad. Bad like rotten food."

"Clinton, I took Rex and went for a ride yesterday. First time I just rode with no place special to go."

"Good, Verna. Cooped up here all day. Only going out to clean other people's homes. I hate to see you do that, clean for other folks."

"I don't want to hear from you again about that. I'm lucky people are kind enough to give me work. A little sewing never hurt anyone. And the cleaning. If I close the drapes and no one can look in, I don't mind. It's something I can do and still watch Son and Nanny Marie while Ellen and Darcine are in school."

Verna looked at Clinton, not sure if she should share gossip about John with him. "I went back to the quilting circle at our church. They want to do a quilt remembering John. As I was coming in, they were gossiping. Don't suppose I'm telling you anything when I say ladies gossip. One of them, not meaning any harm, was talking 'bout Lillian and John."

Verna started to cry. Clinton wanted to get up and put his arms around her, but he'd learned better. One morning while she was crying so hard that he thought his heart would stop, he put his arm around her to comfort her. Verna jumped as if attacked by a wasp.

They didn't talk about the embrace, although Clinton resisted touching Verna, but the wanting to hold her got stronger. He kept his hands busy, either around a cup of coffee or in his pockets. His palms inched to feel her softness, to touch her face and look in her eyes. But since that day, Clinton placed himself three feet away from Verna. Once when she walked toward him, he startled and touched the stovepipe. On the back of his scorched hand, skin peeled away to expose bleeding flesh. He hid the wound from Verna, not wanting her to think him clumsy.

Verna wiped her eyes with the sleeve of her blouse. She'd forgotten a handkerchief and continued talking about John's unfaithfulness. "Clinton, "I'm all right. Each time he strayed I knew. Didn't always know their names but I knew. I knew he had someone new. I didn't want to know more. You might think me weak. It wasn't what he did. It was what he didn't do.

Clinton saw Verna's cheeks redden. She dropped her eyes to the front before continuing. "Knowing his heat was for someone else was as much as I could bear. I knew about the woman before her and the woman before her. Sure, he came home every day. Always polite, like I was a distant relative who cooked his food and took care of his children. Then one day, he'd be laughing and hugging me and I knew it was over. I know I sound weak. Maybe I am, but as long as he didn't throw the women in my face, I pretended I didn't know."

Now that Verna had shared her secret with Clinton, she couldn't seem to stop talking. "What I didn't tell John, didn't tell anyone, not even Hazel – Mr. Harrison came by one day 'round noon – just a few days before John died. Nanny Marie and Son were napping. The table was spread with the last of the green beans I was putting up and the butter churn stood full by the back door, when there he was at the kitchen screen door. Like to scare me to death.

"He looked like that old bull when you try to cross McCormick's field, snorting through his nose the better to butt you aside. I asked him in, of course, although I wanted to just slam that kitchen screen right in his red face. You could smell the whiskey clear across the room."

Clinton, getting uncomfortable, put his hand up as if to stop a child from walking in front of a carriage. "Verna, you don't have to tell me this if you'd rather not."

She continued as if he hadn't spoken, the words propelled by pent-up anger, "He bellowed, 'Mrs. Collins, do you know where your husband is right now!'

"I think I just stared at him. Of course I knew where John was. He was at the jail where he usually was, or out making the rounds checking up on folks. He used to go by some of the older folks' homes just to make sure they were fine and no one's been bothering them. But you know that."

# CHAPTER TWENTY-TWO

## INTO THE DARKNESS

Except for Wednesday afternoons at the Women's Quilting Bee, Verna's outlook became darker and darker. When Clinton left for West Virginia, she was surprised to find she missed his daily visits. With Willa Mae coming less and Ellen complaining more, Verna's isolation grew. She avoided the mirror over her dresser, rarely combed her hair, and never brushed it. She couldn't even take an interest in the January seed catalog.

She stopped dusting her house, neglected to air the bedding, and even stopped bathing. Hazel complained about her odor and sometimes forced her to at least wash her face. Hazel's concern annoyed Verna.

Verna's unfocused eyes gazed off into space. She rarely spoke except to tell Son to be good or Nanny Marie not to cry. Sometimes after her daily visit to the cemetery, Ellen would have to remind her to wash the dirt out from under her fingernails. Hazel heard Verna muttering, "Oh, the blood. The blood. The blood." When Hazel asked, "What blood?" Verna looked at her sister blankly.

As the days darkened, Verna became suspicious of Hazel's intentions.

Finally Verna let out the thought festering inside her. "I know you think I'm going crazy, like Bill Thompson's wife." Mrs. Thompson had been found wandering nude about town after both her twins drowned in Slippery Creek. "Send me away. Go ahead. I know you want to."

Despite Verna's increasing silences, Hazel kept expecting Verna to wake up one day and be her old self. Verna's anger came as a surprise and hurt Hazel, who loved her sister. "No, Verna. I'm never gonna do that, because nobody comes back from there. One day you're going to be yourself again."

"You're like everyone else." Verna spat the words out at Hazel, turned her back, and retreated into the bedroom. Feeling abandoned by her sister, who always knew what Verna felt even before she said it, Verna considered going back in the kitchen and yelling at Hazel, "I don't even want to live anymore!" Instead she lay down on the bed, wrapped the musty quilts around her cold body, and tried to fall asleep.

The next day at one of her regular cleaning jobs, Verna slipped on the icy grass while shaking Mrs. Duggan's rug out in the backyard – victim to the impotent winter sun's failure to melt the morning's frost. Embarrassed and looking to see if a neighbor had noticed, Verna picked up the damp rug and hurried back inside.

"Ma, are you all right? I saw you fall."

"Son, what are you doing watching me? You're supposed to watch Nanny Marie. Where is she?" Verna panicked. She didn't see Nanny Marie, who had been sitting at the kitchen table, busy drawing with broken crayons on the back side of box lids. Verna raised her hand in anger, striking Son, and started to shake him, but stopped as she heard Nanny Marie's singsong voice from the Duggans' parlor. She'd hit Son a few times since John died. Something she swore she'd never do. Each time she'd hug the sobbing child, bring him into her bosom, and wet his hair with her tears.

Relieved at finding Nanny Marie safe and the parlor free of crayon marks, Verna tightly held both children's hands. "Son, Nanny Marie, help your Ma. Mrs. Duggan's coming home soon. I promised to have her house sparkling clean before she returned. Son, wipe the table for me with this cloth." Verna gave him a small piece from the worn muslin sheet used for dusting. "Nanny Marie, put the spoons away. Here, stand on this chair." With the children so occupied, Verna studied Son's reddened check. Her face flushed from embarrassment at her loss of control.

She finished Mrs. Duggan's place, locked up, and slipped the key back under the second flowerpot before putting the children in the wagon to head for Hazel's. Self-conscious about cleaning someone else's house, she avoided people. Verna reluctantly headed Rex up Chestnut Street toward Hazel's place and away from the large homes surrounding the college. Rex, sensing Verna's ambivalence by the way she held the reins too loose, began a faster trot. Still uncomfortable after the confrontation with Hazel last night, Verna started to give him his head to go home but remembered her promise to stop by Hazel's.

Verna knew Hazel's daily evening visits were well-intended, but she wished her sister would just let her be. Last evening Verna had bitten her tongue when Hazel gave Son an extra spoonful of gravy. But when Nanny Marie played with a green bean, swinging it in a circle, Hazel ignored it. Verna took the vegetable away only to have Nanny Marie begin to cry. Then Verna silently seethed as Hazel soothed the small child. Verna thought about how John never let the children behave so badly, but she felt too tired to keep reminding her sister not to spoil them.

Verna bristled when remembering how after letting the children misbehave, Hazel had criticized her. The words still stuck in her mind. "Verna, stop moving your food around your plate and eat."

Perhaps realizing she had gone too far, Hazel offered, "How about I roast a chicken for y'all tomorrow?"

With shame Verna remembered how snidely she dismissed Hazel's offer. "Hazel, unlike you, we have to save our chickens for their eggs. John wouldn't like it if I wasted a chicken in that way. "

Verna took her eye off the horse for a moment and looked down at her body. She had lost so much weight her clothes hung from her shoulders and needed to be tied around her waist with a rope. Even her shoes slipped off her feet.

As she looked up again, she remembered Hazel's next words. "Verna, darling, I know it's hard, but honey, John's dead. You've got to go on living, Verna."

She could hear herself as she screamed, "Stop it, Hazel, I don't care if I die." Then all the children began to cry as Verna ran out of the kitchen and flung herself across her bed. Her cheeks flushed with the memory.

Verna was determined to keep control today. She practiced what she would say to her sister. "Hazel, I thank you for your help, but I don't need your pity."

Before Verna finished tying Rex's reins to a tree in Hazel's front yard, Nanny Marie and Son ran toward their aunt. Hazel skipped down the front steps of her large white porch, hugging both children simultaneously.

"I made molasses cookies just for you. Son, don't swing on the door. Go play with the train." Hazel's father wanted a son. He tolerated her older sister, Beulah, while trying to pretend affection for Hazel by giving her trains, soldiers, and bats and balls until he left to marry Verna's mother. Finally, reconciled to her father's abandonment, Hazel enjoyed the irony of Verna's boy child playing with her childhood toys.

Hazel brought a plate of cookies into the parlor, hoping the train would distract the children while she and Verna talked. "Verna, come into the kitchen. We can talk private there while the children play."

Verna took off her hat, shaking a few snowflakes from her black cape. "I could use a cup of tea, Hazel." It was cold riding in the open wagon even with quilts piled around them. Verna rubbed her bright red ears with cracked hands.

She couldn't look at Hazel. She didn't want to talk about their fight last night. She didn't want to talk about anything. She began to relax in the comfort of Hazel's kitchen with the heat from the stove filling the room.

"Verna, you've got to tell me what's on your mind. I know you miss John something bad."

"You say you know, Hazel. But you don't know. You can't." Verna didn't mean to be snippy, but she was beginning to wish she hadn't promised Hazel she'd stop by.

"Then tell me, Verna." Hazel leaned back, picking up a small, delicate bone china cup that looked too fragile to be held safely by a working woman's hands.

"I keep seeing him, Hazel." Verna looked straight at her sister.

"Of course. You miss him, Verna." Hazel's placating voice irritated Verna. Instead of sitting across the table from her sister, Hazel sat beside her so she could touch her if Verna started to become upset.

"I'm not talking about feelings, Hazel. I see him. I see his back."

Hazel put the cup down to listen better. "What do you mean, Verna, you see him?"

"I see him. I see his back. I see the blood running down his back."

Tears started down Verna's face. Choking sobs bubbled from her mouth. She covered her eyes. "Hazel, the blood, it's everywhere."

Verna couldn't sit still in the kitchen and ran into Hazel's back bedroom, flinging herself across the old quilt. Hazel followed her. Verna yelled, desperate to keep her sister at a distance. "Hazel, if you don't leave me alone, I'll never speak to you again. Never, you hear me? Never!"

"Verna, I'm your sister. I love you with all my heart and I'm not going away." Hazel's calm but firm voice reminded her sister. "Verna, you have to be strong for the children's sake."

Verna crumbled onto the bed, pleading. "Hazel, you can't understand. I just want to be with John. Why did he leave me?" Verna couldn't stop the words from rushing out. They'd been bouncing around in her brain for months and it took too much effort to keep them inside any longer. "I just want to be with him. I pray God will take me, too."

Hazel sat down on the bed and began rubbing her sister's back, determined not to let Verna's scary words drive her away. "Verna, you've got to think about the children. There'll be better times again. Why, you could go back to school. Be a teacher like I am. You're good with children. Maybe now that you're not married anymore they won't count your dropping out against you." Hazel was shocked that these cruel words slipped out of her mouth.

But Verna acted as if she hadn't heard. She shook off her sister's talk of the future. She couldn't see beyond the darkening night. Verna whispered, "It's not fair. He loved life so. Nothing good will ever happen again.'

Hazel tried to reassure Verna. "You're an attractive woman, Verna. You'll find someone else."

Verna kept talking as if her sister hadn't spoken. "I'll never marry again. There's never been anyone for me but John. You know, I never had a mother or a father to speak of. She ups and goes before Grover and I are even one year old. And then, my father just ups and leaves one day, just like he left you. Only one I could ever trust was Granny and then she died and now John. He promised he'd never leave." Verna paused and looked right into Hazel's eyes. "I might as well be dead."

"Oh, baby." Verna felt Hazel's hand touch her hair.

"Hazel, I wish I could cry again like I did when he first died. But

I feel dried up inside." Tearless sobs shook Verna's body. Her body felt so empty without John's love, she feared if the shell of her skin peeled off, nothing would be inside. After a while Verna stopped shaking.

She felt the bed move as Hazel got up and threw a quilt over her. When the bedroom door opened, she was aware of Ellen's voice whispering, "Is Ma all right?" And Hazel's response, "Shush child, your ma just needs to sleep." Verna was relieved when Hazel followed Ellen out of the bedroom. She slipped deeper under the quilt until only the top of her hair remained exposed. She heard whispered voices in the kitchen but was too exhausted to move.

Sometime later she felt Hazel's arms around her shoulders. Hazel held her most of the night. It was the first night since John's death that she slept without violent nightmares.

# CHAPTER TWENTY-THREE

## THE POSSE RIDES

The posse left Berea on a cold January day, riding the better part of every day and some nights to reach the Hatfields' place in the Eastern Appalachian Mountains. Clinton noted his backside ached more than the time his pa whupped him for sneaking out at night. His ears tingled; he rubbed them when he could take a hand off the reins. By the end of the first day Clinton was sorry he had promised himself not to drink whiskey until they got back.

They breakfasted in Estill County and lunched in Lee; the riding became rough approaching the mountains. The posse stopped only long enough to rest the horses and swap news with the sheriffs and deputies in the counties they passed. Clinton was proud of their determination.

They didn't talk much, which suited Clinton. Once Bob Sweeney asked him, "How's the widow Collins getting along?"

Clinton muttered back, "About what you'd expect," not wanting to talk about Verna and his growing feelings for her. He saw one of the Berea men pull Bob Sweeney aside. Clinton's cheeks reddened as he wondered if the men talked about his visits to Verna. But he didn't ask.

"Boys, I figured we'd stop at Rand'l McCoy's at Tug Fork. No one better than Bud McCoy and his boys to tell us how to move up on Anse Hatfield's place.

The posse easily found old man McCoy and one of his sons outside the saloon in Tug Fork, apparently waiting for the Berea posse. Clinton figured the word must have gone out on the wire even before they crossed the Madison County line.

"Hear you Berea boys let those Hatfields get away with murder in your parts," Bud McCoy taunted Clinton and his boys. "Can't even keep your sheriff alive. How you expect to come out of West Virginia without holes clean through you?"

"Well, Mr. McCoy. We figured you were a good one to help us do just that. Reckon you could tell us about how many boys Devil Anse has over at his place these days. And what mood they be in."

Bud McCoy practically wet his pants laughing at the sight of six sorry posse men thinking they could just ride into Anse Hatfields' place and have a go at his boys. "Oh, Deputy, I reckon he's got four or five of his around the place these days. Heard most of them were still down in Tennessee, not due back for a while."

Bud McCoy wanted nothing less than to use this soft Berea posse to pull a whole pack of federal men on those Hatfields. Raised on stories of the Hatfield's massacre of his Uncle Randolph McCoy's family in '88, Bud wanted revenge. If he could fool the deputy into underestimating the strength of the Hatfields, the posse might try to bring the Hatfield boy back to Berea. McCoy knew Anse would never let a lawman come peacefully on his land and take one of his kin away. He bet Anse couldn't resist fighting back. With all those Hatfields, at least one of the lawmen was apt to get killed. If he could rile up this deputy, then the federal marshals would have to come back in and finally bring Anse Hatfield to the justice he deserved.

He decided to sweeten the jug: "Fellow told me one of Anse's boys bragged how they shot that sheriff of yours in the back. Then fooled everyone by saying they left early for the ride down to Richmond. Ain't no Hatfield gonna let one of theirs get taken. Shooting in the back's just their style. But guess you boys' mothers never taught you to tell a liar from a sweet talker."

Clinton could feel his heart pump. From the rustle of the horses he knew he wasn't the only one pulling harder on the reins. Talking himself down like John taught him, Clinton started slow. "Reckon you're right, Mr. McCoy. Good of you to help us think straight on this one. What do you reckon we should do? "

Even nearsighted Luke could see the smirk on Bud McCoy's face. "Why, the best and only way to talk to Anse Hatfield is to slip up in back of his cabin with your guns drawn and shoot the right hand of any man who starts to pull his gun. Except watch his oldest boy; it's his left hand that will get you first. After you take their guns, then the talking can start."

After a little more talk about the weather and the coldness of this January, the men moved on. As they were crossing Tug Fork River, Clinton turned to his men and quietly said, "That was the biggest whopper I ever heard. He must think we are Estill county boys who will believe anything.

"I talked to the Tug Fork sheriff before I left. He said that the minute Devil Hatfield heard we were riding he called all of his clan together. They've been coming into town for the last week. I figure old Bud McCoy was setting us up for a killing, all right. Ours.

"But we did learn one thing. Don't draw your guns. Don't be the first to take your guns out of your holsters. Bud McCoy didn't mean to tell us but he might as well have written on the slate. Old Anse is gonna have men hidden in the woods around his place. Drawing our guns would give him reason to shoot us all dead." The men muttered their assent with Clinton's assessment.

After a while Clinton leaned over to talk softly to his boys. "I think we're getting close. Smell the hams smoking and see the smoke rising off to the left. That's about where the sheriff told me Anse's cabin is. Judd, ride into the woods on our right. Luke, take the woods to the left. Walk your horses quiet as you can. We'll make noise to hide your movements. Look for his boys and get behind them. If you don't come back, we'll know Anse has some of his boys surrounding us. When we get there, Evert, drop back and keep an eye on our backs."

They reached a small clearing. The meanest-looking bunch of men Clinton ever saw stood as if posing for a picture. Must have been twenty Hatfields lined up in front of Old Anse's cabin. Some of them sitting in chairs, others standing, leaning against the logs. And right in front, Old Anse himself. Next to him, just like the Tug Fork sheriff said she would be, Levicy Hatfield.

At first Clinton couldn't tell her from the men; her hat and gun matched theirs. She sat as straight-backed as the men, a pipe stuck out of her mouth. Clinton later wondered how she held that pipe, because her laugh revealed but only two or three teeth left in her mouth. Clinton couldn't tell her age – could be fifty or eighty.

No one smiled. Every Hatfield held at least one gun of some sort. Most rested their right second finger on the trigger. A few, including old Anse himself, nonchalantly stood the gun upright, close by his hand.

Clinton called out to him, "Mr. Hatfield, tell your boys to put their guns away. We didn't come to make trouble. Your sheriff promised us you had something to tell if I came by nice like. We aim on doing that."

"Deputy, since I found the Lord four years ago, you're as safe here as in your mother's arms." An "Amen" followed Anse's proclamation.

In the long ride to West Virginia six disparate men had molded into a single-minded posse, intent on revenging John's death. Clinton knew his men were just waiting to shoot some lead into those sneering Hatfields. Then he felt the air change as it does at the end of January when a thaw comes suddenly. Clinton figured Anse, after proclaiming his conversion, must have made some sign, because his boys, one by one, took their fingers off triggers, rested their small guns in their laps, and placed their rifles or shotguns straight up in front of them, leaning on their long legs.

Clinton heard one of the younger boys give his pa a hard time about putting down his gun. Fast as a bull charge, old Anse smacked him across the mouth so hard that Clinton thought they could hear the sound all the way back in Berea. Blood squirted out, like when the local butcher pulled out his father's decayed wisdom tooth. But the disciplined man never made a sound.

"Mr. Hatfield, before we put our guns away, tell your men to come out of the woods and ride up front beside you." Clinton used the most respectful voice he could muster, trying not to anger the old man.

"What makes you think there's more men than you can see right here?" Anse challenged Clinton.

Clinton maintained his respectful manner, not wanting to anger the Hatfields, who outnumbered them, four to one. "Doesn't matter how I know. Just have them come out so we can have our talk."

Anse nudged the man next to him, who slipped around the side of the cabin. A cloud moved over the sun, darkening the clearing.

Clinton felt trapped. Hearing the crackle of dry leaves, he wanted to draw his gun but thought that might be just the excuse Anse needed to justify slaughtering this Berea posse.

Judd's voice boomed out from his side of the winter-darkened woods. "We're coming out." On each side of the clearing Hatfields emerged, walking toward Anse and joining their brothers, uncles, and cousins. Clinton heard them grumbling but couldn't distinguish what they said. Judd and Luke rejoined the posse.

The Berea men put their guns back in their holsters and slowly moved the horses forward until they could smell all the Hatfields, not just the Missus's pipe. Having exposed the old man's deviousness, Clinton needed to restore Anse's dignity in front of his family for the safety of the posse. He got off his horse, removed his hat, and stood before Anse, like a supplicant asking the president of the United States for a favor.

Facing close to two dozen men, Clinton thought every Hatfield in West Virginia not in jail was sitting in front of the cabin --- sons, son-in-laws, grandsons, and Mrs. Hatfield. Not another woman appeared that whole afternoon. Anse told one of his older boys, Johnse, a man about fifty, to come forward and speak for them.

Clinton nodded as he listened to the first part, information he already knew. John did go up into the hills all by himself even though he knew better. He did arrest Clem Hatfield when Clem was drunk.

Clem Hatfield's pa was telling the story. Clinton could tell he didn't take kindly to his son's arrest by the Berea sheriff. Clinton watched the father's hands as they started waving. Then he was shaking a finger at Clinton. In a voice loud enough that the man next to him stepped aside, he hollered. "I didn't raise a son so lazy some dumb Kentucky sheriff could outdraw him."

Clinton balled his fists. The urge to strike the man started in his belly. Standing up in the stirrups and raising his voice so even the smaller Hatfield children playing behind the grown-ups could hear, Clinton shouted, "Sheriff John Collins made the hills safe even for the likes of you. He's a better man than all of you together."

Dwight, who had seen men provoked into unwinnable fights through deliberate insults, cautioned, "Steady, Clinton. He's trying to get under your skin. John won't want you to die out here for an insult that's too stupid to be taken seriously." Clinton sat back in his saddle, releasing his fists until they dropped back to his side.

Clem Hatfield's father started again in a more respectful tone, "Deputy, we didn't kill your sheriff. We were on our way to Richmond same time as you put my boy on the train. We came by the jail, saw the sheriff and you walking down the street with my boy, Clem. Truth is I wanted to take a shot at you, but my brother, Cap, stayed my hand. He was afraid you might hurt Clem if we missed. If we wanted to shoot you, we could have had you both, right there on the street in Berea.

"After you put Clem on the train, we brought two tickets right quick, and rode with our horses in the cattle car. We didn't follow directly behind you from the train. We knew where you were going. One of the men hanging around said you was drinking at the salon so we just waited until you left Richmond.

Clinton felt foolish that he and John hadn't thought to check the cattle car. He looked around at his men. Two had lit up cigarettes. He scolded them, whispering, "Keep watch." Clinton's mind wandered as the Hatfields talked about how the Richmond lawmen found out about John being shot and then dying the next day. When Clinton's attention returned, Hatfield was winding up.

"Clem was let out of jail soon after word came Sheriff Collins died. There weren't no case anymore. And we sure as hell hadn't done it 'cause we was standing there in Richmond right in front of their eyes. We headed straight for West Virginia." Clem's father turned around and looked at Anse before taking his place in the back row of men who were having trouble standing still.

Anse raised his voice, "There's one more thing, Deputy." Turning to his grandson and slightly throwing his head back, he directed Clem to step forward and say his piece. Clinton, seeing hatred in the young man's eyes for being embarrassed in front of his kin, knew he better not turn his back on him. Clem swaggered forward. "You know that old man Sheriff Collins arrested because his pigs was running in the streets? When you stepped out to say goodbye to the sheriff, he went berserk at that colored kid. I don't much like colored myself..." Clem looked at Judd, "... but he was like he was touched in the head. He told me he was goin' kill the sheriff for putting him in jail with a nigger."

Clinton told Anse he wanted to talk to his men privately but they would keep their hands in view. Judd and Dwight kept their eyes on the Hatfields and their hands close to their holsters as Clinton polled the posse. "I think the story's straight. They might have wanted to kill John but I don't think they did."

Bob Sweeney came in, "It all fits with what I saw and heard. Men at the courthouse saw them coming from the way of the train station not long after you put Clem in the courthouse jail. While you and I were drinking and talking at the hotel bar, two men were seen hanging around the marshal's tree, acting like they were part of the crowd in town for a hearing. The men were pointed out to me when I got back. That man who talked just now was one and I seen the other in the back row. Clinton, I think we better put this dog to rest."

Several other of the posse shook their heads in agreement. They looked at Judd, who quietly remarked, "Looks like the Klan man might have taken his hatred out at John."

Clinton put his hand on Judd's shoulder and squeezed it tightly.

The posse accepted water and corn porn from Mrs. Hatfield before remounting and heading back to Berea. Clinton felt let down and uneasy. Conversion or no conversion, Hatfields didn't help the law unless there was something in it for them. He knew standing in front of those Hatfields that he had come to shoot somebody, and his arms and hands twitched from the restraint.

# CHAPTER TWENTY-FOUR

# HAUNTED BY DEATH

Verna heard the horse clopping down the hill road. She ran out bare-footed, not feeling the February snow underneath.

"John, you're back."

Clinton saw a ghost before him – white face, wild hair blowing in the wind, dirty gray nightgown billowing out as if to give the apparition flight. "Verna! It's me, Clinton." He jumped off his horse, not thinking a minute before enfolding her in his arms.

"Oh, darling! Oh, Verna. It's too cold to be out here." He lifted her up in his arms, startled at how light she was. Just a slip of the woman she used to be. Getting her into the warmth of the kitchen and rubbing her reddened feet became his only thought.

As he opened the kitchen door, no warmth greeted him. This Saturday he'd expected the children to be sitting in the kitchen with baking smells and the pot stove heating the room so a man perspired if he sat too close.

Motionless as the outside air, silence filled the seemingly childless home. Clinton recoiled. He remembered his mother's command, "I want you to be quiet as a tomb." No toys cluttered the kitchen floor. No food cooked on the stove or sat ready to eat on the table.

"Verna, where are the children?"

By now Verna realized it wasn't John but Clinton who rode into her barn lane. Conscious of her dirty gown, she grabbed a shawl to wrap around her shoulders while trying to tuck tangled hair in back of her ears. But it wouldn't stay. Her ears were too small to hold a month of oily strands.

"Verna, where are the children?" Clinton repeated, getting frightened. He had the wild idea that she had gotten rid of them somehow. Maybe gone crazy enough to kill them. Clinton couldn't believe his thoughts. Gentle, loving, prideful Verna. Had grief stolen her soul?

While Clinton mused privately, Verna gradually returned from the world she retreated into while he was gone. She began to feel her body again. Her feet were cold. She looked down, startled to see a nightgown rather than clothes and bare feet without shoes. She heard his voice asking where the children were. She had to think for a moment as the idea slogged through her disconnected brain.

"Clinton. I thought you were John. I look a sight. Let me clean up, then I'll fix you some coffee. Do you mind getting some water? I haven't had time this morning to do that."

"No, Verna. Of course I don't mind. But..."

Clinton heard footsteps on the loft stairs. Some running, some light as if on tiptoe. The children burst into the kitchen, stopping when they saw their mother in her nightgown standing close to Clinton.

"Ma, what are you doing? You look terrible." Ellen scowled. Verna drew herself away from Clinton, knowing once again she had displeased her eldest child. It was getting harder and harder to do anything that Ellen approved of, except the quilt.

"Deputy Barry's come back. I need to get cleaned up. Darcine, be a dear and help get the stove going. I'm afraid I let it go out again."

"Of course, Ma. We didn't hear you up so we just stayed in bed like you told us to."

"You're a good girl. Clinton will get us some water. We'll all clean up and have something to eat and coffee."

"Ma, you know you don't have any coffee. You ran out a week ago." Ellen was feeling a lump of anger inside her belly that wouldn't go away until she had thrown up just the right number of words.

Verna touched her hair. "Ellen, I've got to get dressed and do my hair. We've got company. Help make Mr. Barry comfortable. Go see if the parlor's set."

Clinton interrupted the growing tension between Verna and her oldest daughter. "Verna, you know not to treat me like company. I've got some coffee in my saddlebags. I'll go get the water and the coffee. I shot us a rabbit on my way over." Turning to the children and holding Nanny Marie in his arms, Clinton gently said, "Then I want to hear what you've been doing while I was gone."

Ellen didn't leave the room, instead challenging her mother. "Ma, I want to hear what he learned about who killed Pa."

"Ellen!" Shocked at her daughter's demand, Verna wondered how she had lost control of her children's manners.

"You know who killed my daddy?" Son's voice quivered.

Clinton wanted to reach down and pick the boy up into his arms, but he knew Son didn't want to be treated like a baby. "Well, Son. I sure know more than I did. But a story needs telling when the work's been done. Right now we must get some water and wood. Your stove needs lighting. This house needs warming and the rabbit needs cooking. Maybe if we do it just right, your ma will make us some biscuits with butter."

"We ain't got butter."

"The biscuits your ma makes don't really need butter. But let's get our work done first and then the stories." Clinton started out the door with Nanny Marie in his arms and noticed Son silently watching. "How 'bout you? Wanna come too?" Without waiting for Son's nod, Clinton gently placed both children on a hip and strode out the back door.

Verna left the kitchen. Looking in her bedroom mirror she attempted to brush through hair that refused to yield without pain. She hummed between the "ouches" while her thoughts sprang out, glad to be released. Good to have Clinton back again! How'd I let myself get like this? Fighting with Ellen as if she were a grown woman.

These days she'd only washed on Wednesdays, right before Blanche picked her up for the quilting. She thought, "Verna, you got to get ahold of yourself. Not even getting wood for the fire. Instead, telling the children they have to stay in bed to be warm. Can't help if there's no food except what's left over from the charity supper, but that's no cause to let go of yourself." She looked in the mirror and began to see a trace of her former face emerge.

# CHAPTER TWENTY-FIVE

## CLINTON'S STORY

Verna smelled the coffee all the way into the bedroom. She hadn't smelled fresh coffee for a week at least. The smell reminded her of the first time she begged for a sip yet recoiled from the bitter taste, almost dropping Granny's heavy mug. Not wanting to confess she hated it, she forced herself to drink until the mug was empty. Now again Verna felt she needed to force herself to swallow something bitter.

Upon reentering the kitchen, she saw Clinton surrounded by children. The two young ones perched on his lap while the older girls poured coffee and gave him the cold remains of last night's supper. "Tell us now, Deputy Barry. Ma's here." Verna sighed, relieved that Clinton was back, but reluctant to push away the protective clouds that dimmed her awareness of John's death.

Before beginning Clinton looked at Verna for permission. Her hand covered her mouth as she nodded slightly. "Verna, children." Clinton began, noticing Verna stood as if ready to run back into the bedroom. He wanted to reassure the family that John's killer would be found, but he wasn't used to talking with small children about death and murder. He leaned forward and everyone hushed expectantly.

"We rode straight through the hills. Close by where your ma grew up. Each night we stopped. The hills aren't safe to ride when it's dark." Clinton paused and looked at each child.

"Did you stay with your mother?" Son asked.

Clinton held back a smile and answered Son as seriously as he could, "No, we slept on hard ground." Next he described the trick the McCoys tried. When the children praised him for not getting fooled, he smiled. "Verna, you'll tell me if I'm not saying it right for the children, won't you?"

"You're doing fine, Clinton. We like it that you rode out to set things right for John." Verna smiled fleetingly at him. Clinton was encouraged that she remained in the room listening.

He liked telling them about how Mrs. Hatfield looked like a man and that Anse Hatfield tried to fool them by having men in the woods where they couldn't be seen. Clinton puffed up a little as he told the children how he sent two of the posse to scout the woods and foiled the Hatfield ambush.

As Clinton came to the part where the Hatfield told about Deke Coulder threatening John, his guilt returned. On duty that night, he hadn't thought a fig about putting young Jackson, a Negro man, and Deke, a white man, together in jail. Riding back from the Hatfields, he became increasingly guilty.

Since John died, Clinton kept going over the details, looking for what he did that caused his murder. He should have ridden home with John that day. He should have told John to stay in town until he came back from Richmond and they could ride home together. He should have made John come with him to Richmond. He couldn't tell Verna this part. She would know his carelessness caused John to be killed. He should have known not to put Deke Coulder in the jail with a Negro, even in separate cells. Just because he was raised not to think of the color of a man's skin didn't mean that he shouldn't have thought of it that night.

"Verna, children...this is a hard part to tell. Deke Coulder – he's a man your father arrested because he broke the new law about pigs staying off the town streets. Well, according to Clem Hatfield, when old man Coulder realized he was in jail with a Negro man, he just went berserk."

Clinton couldn't go on. "That's the end of the story. We found out what we went to find. Those Hatfields didn't have anything to do with, with... They didn't have anything to do with your pa's death.

Now we're looking into where Deke Coulder went after he was let out of jail and what kind of gun he has."

"Who was the boy in jail that made him so mad, Clinton?" Verna asked.

"Willa Mae's oldest boy."

"The Jacksons' boy. He's such a nice young man." Verna shook her head in disgust.

Clinton couldn't look Verna in the eye. "Judd's boy had been drinking with some Berea College friends. John and I arrested all of them for shooting it up in the streets and threw them in jail to sober up. I didn't think anything about it except how mad Judd would be to learn his boy couldn't hold his liquor."

Caught up in the story Verna interrupted, "I can just imagine Judd getting angry at his boy, Clinton. Why, the Jacksons are harder on their young'uns than most others I know." Verna remembered how John used to say, "I hope we raise our children as good as the Jacksons'." She shared her thoughts aloud. "Those boys have the best manners of anybody around. You know, children, your pa saved that oldest boy's life."

Ellen said, "I never knew Pa saved Justin's life, Ma. But Willa Mae is always – I mean always – saying, 'I owe your pa more than you'll ever know.' Ma, what happened? How did Pa do it?"

"Your pa had gone into the hills to hunt some turkey for his own ma. It was before we married and Grandpa wasn't doing well enough to do the hunting any more. On the way back, your pa decided to stop by the west meadow creek to cool off. Somehow that baby Jackson wandered away from his ma, Willa Mae, while she was picking berries. He fell into a part of the creek where the water whirls 'round and 'round." Verna motioned with her hand the strong circular movement of the creek's eddy. "It sucked him under. Your pa says you couldn't see even the top of his head. Not so good a swimmer himself, your pa dove into the twirling water and pulled that boy out by his hair."

Clinton looked at Ellen and saw her eyes sparkle with the pleasure of hearing about her father's bravery. "That explains something I heard before I dozed off the night I was watching the prisoners. The Jackson boy told his friends, 'Sheriff Collins is good folks,' when they were fussing about being locked up and how mad their pas would be. Oh, and I just remembered something else Clem Hatfield said."

Clinton sipped his cooling coffee before beginning again, taking his time to settle back into the story. "Well, Clem Hatfield started mocking old Mr. Coulder, how he must sleep with his pigs 'cause he smells so bad. Then we all heard Clem make a voice that sounded just like that ignorant Coulder: 'I'm gonna get that sorry-ass sheriff.' That's the way he said it. 'I'm gonna get that sorry...'" Clinton paused, unwillingly to say in front of the children exactly what Coulder said. He continued, "He said something not nice about your father and then he used bad words to say how mad he was to be in the jail with a Negro."

Verna was stunned. She never imagined Deke Coulder shooting John. Every time she flashed on a shadowy figure standing in the road in back of John, drawing a rifle up to his shoulder, bringing his head down to sight the bullet's path, the figure was tall and robust. Like an oak tree, not a scrub pine.

"That pathetic old man. Clinton, do you really think that could be true? Could Deke Coulder kill my John, just because he was put in jail with another man whose skin was black?"

"Verna, I don't know what I think at this point. Maybe those Hatfields were just makin' mischief. But something about it rings right with me. It would fit with the trouble the Jacksons had right before John died and have continued to be having." Clinton looked seriously at each child. "Now you are all swore in as assistant law keepers to me. What you've heard tonight you mustn't tell anyone; all the men with me took a vow of silence."

Clinton looked at each child and had them hold up their hands and say, "I swear to not tell anyone what I've heard tonight." Clinton knew that Ellen and Darcine could be trusted and that Verna had not let Son or Nanny Marie out of her sight since John was killed. He also knew that speculation about the Klan's involvement in John's death was already running wild in the town.

Verna began crying a little. Not the recent dry, gasping crying. But a comforting cry that brought a little relief. Nanny Marie went back to playing with her doll, not really understanding Clinton's story but enjoying people sitting at the table and talking, instead of silence. Son pointed his finger and pretended to shoot, until Clinton whispered in his ear, "Don't do that, Son. It upsets your mother."

"I started thinking about what you told me right before I left." Clinton didn't want to talk about Verna's neighbors, the Harrisons, in front of the children. He certainly didn't want the children to know their father had been carrying on with Lillian Harrison. "Whoever killed John, it was personal. Someone hated him enough to stand on the hill and wait for him – somebody cowardly enough to shoot him in the back."

"Clinton, I think that's enough. Maybe I shouldn't have let you talk so much with the children here. What will the children make of this talk of killing and hating 'cause of people's color? Why, John and I have told the children how the town Berea was started by some white men from Ohio just to educate Negros and how proud we all are to be in a town that treats white and colored folks the same."

Ellen had been listening intently to Clinton's story. A couple of times she blinked back tears, but mainly she found herself becoming angrier. Finally she burst out, "You mean some dirty pig man killed Pa because he didn't like Darrel Jackson? We wouldn't have half the food we have if it weren't for the Jacksons. Mr. Jackson and his brother came each spring and plowed the garden for Ma, and Willa Mae has come 'bout every day since Pa got killed 'cause Ma needs her help. You mean some stinky, dirty..."

"Shush, child. Now, you shush right now." Verna found that she couldn't take Ellen's anger on top of what she had just heard. "Enough of this talk. Clinton, I appreciate your coming by, and a rabbit for supper's a treat these days. But maybe I should've stopped you from telling all the story. This is just too much to take in right now. I don't know what to think. It's just too much."

# CHAPTER TWENTY-SIX

## SPRING AWAKENING

Next Wednesday, on the first day of March 1916, Verna awoke to a cardinal in the spruce tree outside her window. She noticed tiny hay spouts in the fields. She put purple crocuses in the old cream pitcher and daffodils in the parlor. Returning birds, gone all winter, competed for her attention. Two blue jays squawked so loud that Verna missed hearing Clinton's horse in the barn lane. She even missed his knock. Suddenly he stood before her in the kitchen.

During the winter Verna's life had narrowed. As she did the chores, her mind jumped around, like popping corn. Sadness made her body feel heavy and awkward. The future seemed unpromising and the present unbearably dull. She missed John's love and knew she would never again be held or kissed so hard that her blood rushed through her body.

Kind friends still brought food every afternoon, leaving it by her back door and scooting off before she could thank the donor. Often she knew the Good Samaritan by the pot. With spring and Clinton's return, her mood changed. She tasted food again, felt its texture in her mouth. Like sap in the maple trees, her blood moved faster in her veins. She set a coffee cup on the table in the morning for him.

He came by every day now, only in the mornings, and never stayed long. He wanted to avoid gossip to protect Verna. With tension like summer heat lightning filling the kitchen, both avoided acknowledging their growing feelings for each other. But there were signs.

Verna put on lipstick one morning. Clinton had his hair cut. They would move their chairs closer together, pretending their conversation was too important for others to hear. Even though the only "others" around were two small children who mainly noticed the candy Clinton hid in his pockets. Once their shoulders touched and both jumped back. After that, they seemed to bump into each other more often.

They talked about John and the investigation. Verna spoke about the quilt and Blanche Welch's attempts to make her a suffragette. And Hazel's suggestion she study at Berea College to become a teacher. They both were disappointed when the word came from Washington that the bullet Clinton found came from an old Civil War rifle. Clinton knew that both Harrison and Deke Coulder had those kinds of rifles (as did half the men in the hills). Learning the type of bullet was not helpful.

They talked about how the Jackson's fields weren't being set on fire anymore. Some said the county Klan stopped trying to drive the Negroes out because they didn't want the federal government to get riled up and start investigating the sheriff's death. But Clinton wasn't crossing Deke off his list of suspects that easily. He knew the Klan's cowardly way of riding and burning the Negroes' homes, barns, and fields where they felt safe and hiding when it suited them.

Time began moving faster. The seductive March light awoke the lethargic widow. Verna relinquished her dark wishes for death and began planning small acts of living. She hitched Rex to the plow and planted a small patch of potatoes.

In her blackest days she stopped reading the family bible and instead asked Ellen to read a passage to the children before they went to sleep. Instead of listening, her mind's eye would wander to the cemetery. She stopped going each day to John's grave and went only on Sundays. Each time she'd stop on the way back and pick greens. Looking for wild lettuce, shepherd's spouts, and mustard reminded her of better times. Now that she was feeling better she was more conscious of not worrying the children. .

With April only a week away, Verna asked Clinton to bring her Berea's newspaper. Pleased to see her interest, he brought the weekly

*Berea Citizen*, the daily *Louisville Chronicle*, and the spring Sears and Roebuck catalog.

She didn't read the recipes. She wasn't sure why they no longer interested her – maybe because she wasn't cooking. First, she read the serialized episodes of love and loss in the *Berea Citizen*. The next day she noticed ads for hats and dresses in the catalog. Finally, on the last day of March she began to read the front-page news stories from the *Louisville Courier*. She was attracted to news of the foreign war.

She looked for stories of women. Most were about women helping their husbands or doing charity work, except for the Suffragettes in Washington picketing for the vote. As she remembered seeing picture of nurses carrying wounded men the night before John was shot, an idea began to pick at her brain. Maybe, just maybe, she could be a nurse.

# CHAPTER TWENTY- SEVEN

# RESOLVE

Rays of April sun peeped into Verna's bedroom, awaking her. She tied back the muslin drapes, drawing cool mountain air to her face. Mist floated out of the dales. She sprang to her toes as if flying out the window to catch a rope of mist. She breathed deeply, seized with a desire to run into the hills as she had when a child.

Looking in the mirror, she recoiled at the wild mane atop her head. Using her hairbrush as a weapon, she attacked her hair, starting at the ends. The side locks gave in to the brush, but the thick hair on the back of her head refused to release week-old knots. Verna pulled harder, clenching her teeth against the hurt. Some thick, tangled strands stubbornly broke off into the horsehair of the brush. Twenty, twenty-one, twenty-two. She began to sing, "Johnny, where are you?"

Answering in a deeper voice. "Gone. Gone."

"Will you come home to me?"

"Not until forever comes."

After finishing she looked in the mirror. Satisfied that her hair would do, she rubbed her cheeks red. Quickly putting on her black dress, Verna sailed into the kitchen. Noticing the stacked wood beside the stove, she silently thanked Ellen for taking care of a chore that had been John's. After starting a fire, she drew water for the coffee and took butter from the icebox to soften. For the first time in six months, Verna made biscuits and hummed. She heard steps coming down the loft stairs. Quick toe prances halfway down, than slower heavy steps.

"Morning, Ellen."

Verna noticed Ellen's too-small nightgown covered a body that bulged with new curves. She made a note to talk to Ellen about binding her breasts until they could afford new clothes. Should she tell her daughter about the monthly bleeding? She wished John were here so they could talk about Ellen's new development and decide what to do.

"Would you like some milk? It's still cool from last night. I surely do appreciate the wood for the stove."

"Sure, Ma. I mean, yes, ma'am. You're welcome."

"There'll be some biscuits soon. Ellen, would you like to get washed before the little ones come down? You might want to put a sweater on." Oblivious to the confusion on her child's face, Verna went back to humming, determined not to fight with her eldest this morning.

"Remember I told you Mrs. Welch is coming by this morning to take me to church. The quilt is done today and I want to see it. I'll be back real soon. I appreciate you and Darcine caring for Son and Nanny Marie."

"Ma," Ellen started. She wanted to go and see the quilt but knew Son would raise Cain. Then Nanny Marie would cry because she was being left behind, and they couldn't all fit in Mrs. Welch's car. "Never mind."

Verna heard Blanche's automobile coming onto Hill Street and hurriedly kissed Ellen goodbye before stepping out the back door.

Blanche Wellington Welch turned into the barn lane, yelling out over the engine's roar. "Verna, I can't believe it! Here you are, up and dressed and ready for me." Verna smiled. Some of the birds, gone all winter, competed for her ears' attention. Two blue jays made enough racket for Verna to hear them over the motor of Blanche's car.

"Ma," yelled Son, who raced out the kitchen door despite Ellen's calls for him to come back. "May I sit in Mrs. Welch's car?"

"For just a minute. Then Mrs. Welch and I must hurry."

Listening to Blanche's hearty welcome for Son and her jolly laugh, Verna decided to share with Blanche her secret thoughts. Her skin tingled with anticipation of Blanche's reaction. Waving to her friend, Verna strode to the topless car. Blanche attempted to regain control of her watermelon-sized hat as Son sat on her lap, vigorously steering the motor car. Taking Son off Blanche's lap, heading him toward the kitchen, and giving his bottom a pat, Verna gently commanded, "Mind what Ellen says. I'll be back soon."

"Blanche, do you suppose we could pull out on the County Road and then just sit a spell before we head for the church? The quilt's almost done. I don't think it would hurt to be a little late."

Blanche, although accustomed to the indirectness of southern women, recognized the unusualness of Verna's request and decided to be blunt. "Verna, sounds important to you. Of course we could be a little late. Your eyes are lit like I haven't seen them in months. Come."

After Verna took her seat, Blanche quickly drove the car to a quiet spot just off the County Road. "This car makes a wonderful place for telling secrets. I think you have a secret to tell me, Verna Collins."

"Blanche, since Clinton came back from West Virginia he's been visiting with us most days."

"I knew it. It's a man. Verna, you will never change! You always did light up the most when a man paid you some attention. It didn't matter his age – fifteen or fifty."

"Blanche, that's not fair. No, it's not about Clinton...exactly." Verna's animated voice softened her words. The women laughed together. The sound of their laughter made them laugh even more. Before Blanche could get her handkerchief out of her side pocket, she almost sprayed her friend. Then Verna, whose first tentative laughs sounded more like coughing than glee, began to cackle. She put her hand over her mouth, self-conscious about the sounds coming from her lips.

"Is it your children? Not being a mother myself, I'm probably not the best to help you with them. But I think sometimes Ellen needs more softness from you. You're hard on that girl, Verna."

Verna didn't want to be sidetracked into talking about the children. She quickly acknowledged, "I wish I could be softer with Ellen. Her father spoiled her. But that's not what I wanted to talk with you about." Verna wiggled in the seat to get more comfortable and turned to watch her friend's eyes.

"When Clinton came back from West Virginia, the Hatfields

hinted that Deke Coulder killed John. Clinton told me bluntly that he still leans toward Mr. Harrison, although the killer could be someone he hasn't considered yet. When Clinton found out from Washington the information about the bullet being too common to help find the killer's gun, something popped inside of me.

"Clinton's determined to find John's killer. I believe he will – someday. Without meaning to, I've been holding my breath, waiting to hear the name of John's killer. I can't wait anymore to restart my life. It's like I thought life stopped and then woke up to find it was still going on and leaving me behind."

Blanche's head shook in support of Verna, "You're right! I've been doing it too. Thinking that knowing who killed John would make a difference."

"I don't know if I can talk about the rest of it." Verna began to look away from Blanche and straightened her skirt.

"Verna, you can't do this. Teasing me with a wiggly worm and after you hook me throwing me back in the creek." Blanche's tone admonished her friend to continue.

"Blanche, I've been sad for so long I kind of forgot what it felt like to get mad. I know this sounds silly, so please don't laugh. I'm mad that everyone seems to be moving on while I'm supposed to stay the grieving widow. I'm supposed to remember John all my life, wear black, and take care of my children." Verna put her chin up like she used to when she was in her early teens. Her granny, recognizing the signs of Verna's stubbornness, would caution, "Don't you get too big for your britches."

"Blanche, I want to do something with my life. I'm getting afraid I'm gonna be like my mother. Up and run away one of these days. Blanche, I can't do that. I need your help. Please don't think I'm bad. But I'm beginning to get squirmy. Like I got pinworms."

"Verna, how can I help? You're not bad. You're just feeling like a lot of us women these days."

Verna grew stronger hearing Blanche's words of support. "I don't know anybody else I can ask. If I ask Hazel, she'll just tell me again to be a teacher. And Beulah would worry I've gone crazy and tell me to leave everything just the way it is." Unused to talking about her sisters outside the family, Verna shifted in the car seat before continuing.

"Blanche, I woke up this morning and I watched Ellen and Darcine go off to school. I thought..." Verna paused. She looked at Blanche. She felt afraid but had gone too far to stop. "I want to go to back to college. Now I know that's kind of crazy, but I figured of all people you wouldn't laugh at me. I just had to tell someone."

Blanche cocked her head to the side and looked straight into Verna's eyes. "Verna, I've seen women in the movement go through this change – wanting more, but not being clear what the 'more' is. Those that could afford it or had families who supported their notion frequently did return for more education. Others got jobs. This is an important moment for you. Dear Verna. You are awakening."

"I could see me sitting in a class like at the college. I used to like learning. Granny encouraged me. I remember you saying, 'Women can do anything these days.'" Verna eyes focused on her hands in her lap. "I just stopped having dreams when John died. He always said I could go back to school someday. It was my idea to stop when I got pregnant with Ellen – only eighteen and thinking I knew all I needed to know."

Blanche patted Verna's knee and then impulsively leaned over to give her friend a cheek kiss. "Verna, you surprise me. Guess a little girl not afraid to swat a bee can grow into a woman unafraid to swat a few ideas about 'a mother's place.' Going back to college. Well, why not! As my friend Madeline Breckinridge says, 'Kentucky women are not idiots even though they are closely related to Kentucky men.'" With that Blanche retied the ribbons of her red hat and started her car. As the motor went bang, bang, spat, spat, Blanche honked her horn as if geese waddled in her way that better scatter fast.

# CHAPTER TWENTY-EIGHT

## THE QUILT IS DONE

Verna, still wearing her widow's black, and Blanche, head to toe in red, lightly ran into the church room holding their hats on their heads. They were greeted by each of the nine women sitting on assorted wooden chairs around the sides of the quilting table. Verna's compassion for others had returned and expanded over the last two months. When one of the younger women's baby contracted whooping cough and the doctor thought she might die, Verna went to help out. When Johnny's ma brought his postcard for all to see – "Ma and Pa, I enlisted. Leave for England soon for the War" – Verna enfolded the weeping mother in her arms.

On this final quilting day, the buzz of contentment in the room resembled that of a family after a satisfying meal. Two of the older women's glasses slipped down their noses as they bent over to complete stitches. One woman brought her youngest child, who played with bits of yarn at her mother's feet. Two women touched hands under the table out of tenderness for the group's memorial to John. Rivalry over the daintiness of stitches dissolved.

During the months of working on the quilt, Verna often couldn't bear to touch John's clothes that were being cut, reshaped, and sewn. She narrowed her focus to her own stitches on the double wedding ring section of the quilt – not once stepping back to regard the totality of the work. Today Blanche stopped her evasion by lightly touching her arm and commanding, "Look, Verna."

The quilt was magnificent. "Oh, it's beautiful. The satin border, Hazel, you're right, it's just the right choice." As her fingers touched the blue satin Verna noticed how perfectly the white cross-stitching followed the border. Verna allowed herself the painful pleasure of slowly touching each section – John's blue flannel shirt as sky, parts of his brown pants as the rounded peaks surrounding Berea. The tailor's wife, who helped sew John's burial suit, held her breath while Verna touched the pants. Verna bent over and kissed her cheek, and the tailor's wife exhaled.

Her eyes moving on, Verna appraised the green embroidery and yellow cotton matting that created rows of growing crops in freshly turned earth. Despite initial concerns, the women experimented with selective embroidering and even coloring with crayons. The success of their risk fit into the pattern of Verna's evolving plans. She hugged each of the younger women who had added abstract shapes of material to somehow create the illusion of a town nestled in the hills. Then she noticed how some stitches looked like brown roads curving through the town. Even without labels she could follow the curves of Chestnut Street. Her fingers touched the quilt where a single red thread interrupted an otherwise undistinguished road's course.

Finally Verna's eyes rested on four abstract figures, running children, whose variegated sizes resembled the sepia images from Verna's parlor walls. Lastly, Verna touched the pieces of small stones from the road, carefully stitched into the fabric and cushioned so as not to cause discomfort to a sleeping body. Verna looked around the room and quietly declared, "I do thank you."

As Verna took her place, the room grew hushed, not in discomfort but as in church during the blessing of the wine and bread. One woman handed Verna a piece of silver material for her to place in the blue sky over the hill everyone recognized as Kissy Mountain. While Verna held steady a small five-pointed star, Hazel quickly stitched it on John's transformed shirt. Verna buried her face in a corner of the quilt.

"It's done, Verna."

One of the women touched Verna on the shoulder gently. "Let go now, honey. I'll take it home to wash and block. When it's ready, we'll bring it over."

"Yes," Verna said. "It's done."

In the early evening Verna rode home in silence. Blanche tried to start a conversation and then gave up, instead singing loud enough to hear herself over the engine. Upon arriving at the Collins home, Blanche quickly kissed Verna's cheek.

"Are you all right, honey?" Blanche wondered if seeing the finished quilt had pushed Verna back into lethargy. The women's work was painfully beautiful. Not one to give false reassurances, Blanche patted Verna's hand and waited patiently.

Slowly unfolding herself from the car, Verna picked up her sewing bag from the backseat without looking up the hill road to see if John were coming home. She took a few tentative steps toward her house. She heard Rex neigh and in the distance a dog barking. She looked at the barn floor. John wasn't lying there, bleeding. The pigs grunted over their evening feed.

"Verna!" Blanche yelled above the engine's noise.

Realizing she hadn't said goodbye to her friend, she turned quickly and yelled, "Bye, Blanche. I'll be fine." Only then did Blanche put her car in gear, backing into Hill Road and blowing Verna a kiss. As the sound of the engine receded, Verna turned. No longer buoyed by her friend's cheeriness, Verna felt herself slipping again into lethargy. Steam from the family's dinner, placed – as always since John's death – by her back door trailed into the growing dusk. Without much thought she balanced the dishes in one hand and opened the kitchen door.

"Ellen, Darcine, I'm home. Get Son and Nanny Marie ready for supper."

Without Clinton's attention to buoy her spirits, Verna withered within her home. Spontaneity vanished, replaced by the safety of monotony. Even after Verna began to slip a small flower into a buttonhole of her widow's dress when she went out, inside her home, she lived in silent routines.

Mechanically she placed the warm food on the table. Exactly as she always had, she set the table. Crockery plates, metal knives, forks, and spoons for two adults and three children, all but Nanny who still had a bowl and a spoon. Verna set the butter in the center. After carefully placing the jelly glasses for the children and mugs for her and John, she filled each with milk taken from their cow.

The children came in quietly, reluctant to share the day's

adventures with their silent mother. Ellen looked furtively to assess her mother's mood, while Darcine slipped her hand in Verna's. Verna bent down automatically for a cheek kiss.

"Son, were you good for Ellen this afternoon?"

"Yes, ma'am." At home, even Son faded into silence.

Verna lowered her head and in a monotone delivered the blessing, ending with a whispered, "Amen."

Ellen decided to risk her mother flaring into anger or running from the table in tears. "Ma, is the quilt done?"

"Yes, Ellen, it is."

"When will we see it? Is the star there for Pa like Aunt Hazel said it would be?"

Verna raised her head. She looked first at Ellen. Then Verna, instead of her usual avoidance for the past six months, looked there. She saw no one. Just an empty chair. At the end of the table John's place was set as it had been since his death – an empty plate surrounded by a knife, fork, and spoon, and, off slightly to the side, a large mug.

In this moment of startling clarity, she said aloud as if talking to a mirror, "Verna, you silly goose. He's dead."

# CHAPTER TWENTY-NINE

## RETURNING TO SCHOOL

"Ma, these shoes hurt."

"Son, here, put some paper around your toes. You look very handsome in your new suit."

"Ma, it's not new."

"Yes, it is."

"It's Jimmy Tyler's suit, Ma."

"It's new to you, Son."

"I hate it. I hate Jimmy Tyler."

"I told you, Son. There's no money for new clothes. Just hold your head up. Don't let others know how you feel."

Inside Verna felt the same child-like anger as Son, grateful to her friends for their handouts but bitter with the taste of wounded pride. Giving him the same advice her grandmother had given her, Verna silently vowed her children would not suffer the taunts of others as she had. Verna smoothed the shoulders of Nanny Marie's dress,

"Do you like your dress, Nanny Marie?"

Nanny Marie jumped up on her toes and ran to look in her mother's mirror at her blue garment, previously Darcine's secondhand dress, passed down from Ellen.

"Are we going to church, Ma?" asked Son.

"First we're going to talk to a nice woman at Berea College.

Then I'm going to look for work." Her brain swirled constantly with thoughts of money – for clothes, for the church offering, for Ellen and Darcine's books – money, money, money.

Verna sold the pigs first, then the chickens, and now she might have to sell the cow. Clinton offered to help out. But Verna knew the first years of a deputy's salary were barely enough to support one person.

All her life she thought about, dreamed about, worried about money, except for those brief years after John had been elected sheriff. Then they just went month to month, spending every penny he made. Verna once laughed as she said to John, "Why, we can't put money away for a rainy day; we need it now. If it rains, we'll just go out in the drops and play."

John teased her back that day. "Verna, where's that girl who would say she'd never be poor again and used to be all over me about money?" In truth Verna was never easy about money, when she thought about it. But after John was made sheriff and she accidentally found out about his first affair, she decided she just wouldn't think about money anymore. She started buying clothes for herself out of the better catalogs. She still made a lot of clothes, but she used softer materials and didn't worry so much that they would wear out sooner.

Now she had a quarter left in the jar and nothing coming from her sewing or housecleaning for at least a week. Some of those people for whom she had rushed to finish the sewing for an event they said was "so important" hadn't paid her. She was beginning to wonder if they ever would.

Same with cleaning houses. There weren't that many people anyway who hired a woman to clean their house. Since they were rich, you would think they would pay the minute she finished the job. But oh no. It was, "Verna, I can't believe it but (Henry, Joseph, George) forgot to leave me the money for you today. We'll bring it by later." Later and later and later.

Anger and the fear of further humiliation rekindled her suppressed desires to be educated. Putting Nanny Marie and Son into the wagon, she sang, "Off to school we go, school we go, school we go. Hi dee ho." Soon all three were laughing and singing, "Hi dee ho. Hi dee ho."

Nanny Marie, missing the warmth of her mother's body, snuggled up as Verna held the reins. She nestled so close that Verna feared, as she encouraged Rex to go faster, her pumping elbow would knock her daughter's chin. Still, lacking the heart to push Nanny Marie away, Verna placed the child on her lap. Son waved to all they passed as Verna heard the warm greetings: "Mrs. Collins, it's so nice to see you out." "Verna, drop by soon. We've missed you." Verna's cheeks began to take on color from the rushing air.

About a mile up Chestnut Street, the campus came into view. Verna experienced her usual awe at the beauty of the red brick buildings. Set in enough land to make scores of families into wealthy farmers, each building was separated from the next by a cornfield length of green grass. Towering sycamore trees provided shade and grandeur. Verna never ceased to feel proud of Berea College. She knew there weren't many colleges that took as their calling educating poor hill people like herself, providing work opportunities in the college's industries to pay for their tuition.

As Rex completed the final push up the hill, Verna said to Son and Nanny Marie just what her granny had shared with her. "You can go to this college. You don't have to be rich. Just study hard. Work at your lessons."

Pulling up in front of the registration office, Verna noticed more cars on Chestnut Street than she had remembered. "Nanny Marie, Son, be careful getting down. Don't get in front of Rex. With all these autos around, he might spook. Remember when we go in, you are both to be quiet and polite. If asked anything, you say, 'Yes, ma'am. No, ma'am.' Nothing else. Son, no matter what you hear me say, you are not to say anything, anything at all. Is that clear? I know you will be good children, but I want you to be quiet also. It's not anybody else's business how we are doing. If asked, you say, 'Just fine, ma'am.'"

Son giggled. "Yes, ma'am."

Nanny Marie slipped her hand in her older brother's hand, looking to him for guidance as she always looked to Ellen. If Verna had bothered to glance at her youngest child's face, she would have seen calm acceptance. Anything her mother wanted to do was all right with Nanny Marie. She was with her mother. That's all that counted.

# CHAPTER THIRTY

# THE INTERVIEW

Verna opened the door marked "Director, Berea College School of Nursing," finding a woman with gray streaked hair piled high on her head and large pins sticking out in every direction, typing furiously like a reporter on deadline. Her glasses slipped down her nose and her head bobbed up and down. Acting surprised to see Verna with her children, she asked them to wait a moment. "I must finish this report for President Frost. Please take a seat."

Verna felt confused. Her appointment was at 11:00 a.m. She could hear the college bell chiming, nine, ten, eleven. She remembered how John used to hate writing reports to send to the courthouse. A few times when she came by the jail during the day, he would be sitting at his desk and slowly, with one finger, he would hit the typewriter keys. He would cuss and cuss, pulling out paper after paper when he hit too many wrong keys.

"Ma, Ma, can I play with my soldiers?" Son's request brought Verna back from her reverie. The child's small voice pricked the conscience of the typist, who suddenly realized she was being rude and didn't need to finish this report now after all. She stood up to greet Verna. "Nice to see you again, Mrs. Collins. These must be your children."

"Director Hays, this is Grover and Nanny Marie. I couldn't find anyone to keep them today. But they are good children and will play quietly while we talk."

"No need. I have a student assistant from the teaching program who will take them to the nursery school to play while we complete the interview."

A slightly plump young woman, about eighteen years old, got up from her seat in the corner of the room and reached out her fleshy hand to Son and Nanny Marie. "Hello, I'm Marjorie. Come. Let me show you the nursery school. You can play with some of the other children. There's slides and swings."

Clearly excited to play, Son quickly gripped Marjorie's warm hand. As the student reached out to Nanny Marie, the toddler yelled, reached toward her mother, and began crying as if struck by a bolt of heat lightning. "No, no." Her cries melted the hearts of the Berea College student while Verna's embarrassment turned to anger. "Nanny Marie, this is a nice young woman who simply wants to take you to play."

"Ma, no, no, no." Large tears fell down Nanny Marie's tiny face. Verna hadn't expected this reaction, assuming her children would be excited to be in a new place where they could play.

Clearly annoyed by the episode, Miss Hays put her handkerchief to her nose as if Nanny Marie smelled as bad as she sounded. "That's all right. We can talk with her here." Turning to the flustered scholarship student, Miss Hays's voice registered disapproval. "Just take the boy while his mother and I talk."

Verna got out a rag doll from her pocket and, placing Nanny Marie upon her lap, began the interview that would change her life. The words tumbled out. "Miss, Director Hays, I would like to enroll in the Nursing School at Berea College. I've thought about it a lot. As you know from the last time we talked, I was a student in the general college course here for six months before I got pregnant with my first child and had to stop. My grades were good. I know I can do the work. I've kept up with my reading. And I'm a hard worker."

"Mrs. Collins, it's not about your qualifications. The last time we met, I asked you to think about the children. Our nursing program lasts two years. You will be in classes, at the hospital, or in the infirmary working for ten to twelve hours a day. Our nursery school opens for only six hours a day. Who will watch over your children the rest of the time?"

Miss Hays spoke with the arrogant tone of a Lexington matron that she unconsciously adopted when feeling out of control, "You should consider going back to the general course of study. Maybe taking our weaving classes. Many women from the hills are learning to make a living with their quilts and homespun garments. It's desirable for some women these days to be independent.

"But there are restrictions. You know women who marry aren't allowed to be teachers. I wanted to be a teacher, so I never married. Some of us made choices. Mrs. Collins, you have four children and you might marry again. Even today, when I specifically said that you must come alone for this interview, you brought your children. That simply will not do."

"I'm sorry. I do understand."

"Mrs. Collins, I'm not sure you do. But our college was founded with the purpose of helping those whom society doesn't. Our first president made our college special – the first in the South to accept Negro persons. Now that the state has foolishly ruled that black and white can't be educated together, we've changed our mission to helping poor mountain folks like you used to be. But our students are younger and unmarried, Mrs. Collins. The nursing school curriculum is very demanding."

Verna wanted to cry, but imagining her granny's face and summoning her pride, held back the tears. Sucking in a deep breath, Verna looked at the wall rather than Miss Hays. "I'll work it out about the children and finding time to study." Verna clamped her lips shut to stop herself from adding "Somehow."

"I'll be truthful with you, Mrs. Collins, I think it would be a mistake for you to enroll in the nursing program. I talked with President Frost as to your request for admittance here. He told me he thought highly of your husband's work on several town issues. Also, Dr. Benson spoke favorably to Dr. Frost in favor of your application for the nursing school. Would you consider waiting a year or two and then reapplying? The children would be older, and it's so soon after your husband's tragic death."

Verna thought, "You mean, my husband's murder." Instead she asked, "What was President Frost's decision about my application?"

Miss Hays hesitated, clearly reluctant to proceed. "President Frost asked me to tell you – if you insisted on enrolling this year – we would accept your request to register at the college. But you must find someone to care for your little ones. You can't bring them to class or to the hospital."

"Oh, Director Hays, thank you." Verna could feel herself wanting to cry from relief. Then she recognized a strong urge to speak her mind. The words grew in Verna's mind: "Miss Hays, you're just an old maid." Taking two deep breaths and swallowing each, Verna instead gave her practiced, "I'm a Gentry" smile, and said, "Thank you, ma'am. Please thank Dr. Frost for giving me an opportunity. He won't be sorry."

Verna continued, her confidence building from knowing that the president of the college had interceded on her behalf. "Director Hays, as I told you in our first interview, I didn't come to this decision easily. After I decided to return to school so I could support my children, I talked with one of my sisters and a good friend you might know, Mrs. Blanche Welch."

The director's eyes lit up. Indeed she knew Mrs. Welch. Mrs. Welch and her husband had given the school a great deal of money, specifically to educate poor women.

Verna, caught up in her own words, didn't notice the director's reaction. "Both of them encouraged me. I thought about nursing and the thought kept getting bigger and bigger until it took over. Since then, and even more so since the first time I met you and talked about the nursing training program, that's all I've thought about. I want to be a nurse. I'll do anything to be a nurse. To go out in the hills or even across the ocean to help people in their illnesses and their suffering. If I had been a nurse, my husband might be alive today. It's now clear to me."

Verna's words touched a vulnerable spot within the stern director, a place where dreams of doing important work, work few women were allowed to do, were hidden safely from ridicule. Miss Hays graduated from the college's nursing program, also to help the hill people, except she never had a husband killed. She had instead watched her sister die of typhoid. But she stopped, reining in her thoughts and afraid of her emotions.

Looking into the eyes of the earnest widow before her, she softened. "You can start this July. Let's go over some of the rules and next steps." Miss Hays hadn't planned on telling Verna what she told her next, but her heart had softened toward this determined woman. "We just found out...I don't think it need make a difference but..."

Once she began, Miss Hays wanted Verna to have all the facts. "The legislature just enacted a new state registration code for nurses. The State Nursing Organization has been working on it for ever so long. It allows a certificate to be given to certain nursing graduates who can then practice independently. Unfortunately, our Berea College nursing students won't be eligible to be certified because we are a two-year, not a three-year, program."

Verna wondered what registration had to do with her. "I don't understand."

"Three of our recent graduates tried to volunteer for nursing assignments in France, in the war over there with the Florence Nightingale division. They were turned down for not graduating from a three-year nursing program. I'm sure you don't want to go to the war front since you have four children to tend, so it doesn't really apply to you. But I just thought you should know."

Verna felt her body become limp and her mind turn to mush, like days-old oatmeal. She knew she needed to talk to Hazel and Beulah. Her sisters would help her sort out this new information. She wasn't going to spend two years working hard to be a nurse and then not have the same rights and privileges as three-year graduates.

Again Verna thanked Miss Hays, and asked her to thank President Frost for his consideration. "Don't bother showing me out. I know where the nursery school is." As Verna took Nanny Marie's hand and turned to leave, she noticed a picture of a young pretty woman. Miss Hays was touching the frame. Verna remembered after Miss Hays's sister died, the nursing director had broken an engagement to stay with her grieving mother.

Verna turned back. Before opening the door, she added softly, "Thank you for telling me about the registration."

# CHAPTER THIRTY-ONE

# THE MASONS

Her mind spinning, Verna gathered up Son and placed the children on either side of her in the wagon while they headed up Chestnut Street toward the business section of town. She had promised Clinton she would stop by the jail after her interview. She had to hold the reins tight as the street overflowed with carriages and cars. Verna noticed the college girls' skirts seemed a little shorter than she remembered. She could even see ankles. She imagined Miss Hays clicking her teeth at the sight.

May, the month in the mountains that cracks open the coldest heart. Roses bloomed everywhere. Their scent hung in the air, clogging the nostrils, disguising the manure on the side of the road. Verna waved to people she knew from church, imagining after she passed their whispering to each other, "That's the widow Collins, poor dear."

As Verna guided Rex down Chestnut Street toward the jail, she needed to hold tighter to the reins to stop Rex from breaking into a fast trot. Verna noticed several men talking in front of the crossed-saber sign of the Masonic Lodge. John had joined the Masons after his election as sheriff. Two men, whom he identified as "brothers," came to the house.

John asked her and the children to remain in the kitchen while the men retired to the parlor to speak confidentially. Afterward he told her in somber tones, "To be a Mason means some things are secret even from our loved ones. You need to respect this, Verna. When a Mason gives his word of silence, the trust is never broken."

Son pulled on her dress. "Don't wiggle, Son."

"Ma, that man is waving at us. I think he wants us to stop." Sid Neiman, one of John's closest friends, waved her over to the side of the road under the eaves of the brick-faced lodge. Verna tightened her lips, determined to hide her emotions. "Be good, children." She guided Rex to the curb and pulled the reins for him to stop.

"Hello, Mrs. Collins. Lovely day to be out." Mr. Neiman tipped his hat to Verna and the children.

"Why, hey, Mr. Neiman." Verna tugged at her dress, which had crept up her ankles.

"Still can't believe John's not with us." Verna thought he looked genuinely sad. With formalities over, Verna waited to see why Sid had waved them over. Sid looked earnestly at Verna. "Have you talked to Clinton yet, Verna?"

Verna was embarrassed that Sid would ask about Clinton and wondered if the whole town was gossiping about them. "No, haven't talked to anybody but Miss Hays at the college. As I told you at church, I've decided to go to nursing school and my interview was this morning. Clinton asked us to stop by afterward and tell him how it went."

Sid figured he'd let Clinton tell Verna about last night's arrest. Looking at her face, he could tell she didn't know and he had other business with the widow before she went on her way. "Do you remember what I said at John's lying-in? How the lodge helps families of its fallen brothers?" Sid asked as he ruffled Son's hair.

"I do, Sid. All your words comforted us." An awkward silence started to develop.

Sid crushed his cigarette out before looking at Verna again. "We have a special fund for widows and children. If you're ready, Verna, I could find time tomorrow to talk with you. Reverend Simmons wants to be with us. He said we could meet in his study."

"I'm ready, Sid." Verna lowered her head, humiliated by her need. "What will I do with the children? Hazel has to teach. Hiram isn't feeling well and until the doctor knows what he has we're keeping the children away.

"The reverend's wife said she would enjoy looking after your children. But only if you're ready." Sid respected the wounded pride of folks who fell on hard times.

Verna found herself looking into Mr. Neiman's sympathetic eyes. At first she felt comforted by his obvious concern. Then she realized she missed the twinkle in the eye, the slight smile, and the head tilt of a man flirting. "Having Reverend Simmons there would add God's comfort and blessing. Would eight-thirty, after Ellen and Darcine leave for school, be too early?"

"Eight-thirty it is." He tipped his hat, smiling soulfully as if his duties with John's widow prohibited the corners of his mouth from reaching up to his cheeks. Verna continued her journey up Chestnut Street to the jail. "Son and Nanny Marie, want to go to Aunt Hazel's house and sit on her porch?"

"I thought Mr. Blake wanted us all to come by Pa's jail?"

"You're right, Son. Maybe another day."

"Look, Ma, Mr. Welch is waving at us." Son started to wave back and Nanny Marie imitated her brother. Verna shouted above the street noises, greeting the undertaker like a best friend. "Good morning, Mr. Welch." Verna forgave him for trying to take advantage of her mourning and Mr. Welch forgave Verna for getting the best of the deal. He still didn't know how she outfoxed him, conceding the hidden cleverness of the innocent-looking widow. Mr. Welch chuckled as he saw Verna turn down Buffe Street. Like others, he enjoyed the gossip about Clinton's feelings for Verna and speculated that the deputy was waiting until it was proper to declare his intentions. As Verna approached the jail, Clinton tried again to get through the phone line to Richmond. When he called before to let them know he had arrested John's murderer and was bringing him in on the three o'clock train, the only response he got was "About time." Now he wanted to make sure Bob Sweeney would be waiting for him at the Richmond station. "Hey, Bob. Clinton, here. Got that no-good coward last night just as we planned."

# CHAPTER THIRTY-TWO

# AN ARREST

The night before as they rode out of town about 2:00 a.m., Clinton ordered his men, "Stay in back of me and keep your horses quiet. Just in case this rotter has a friend, I don't want anyone letting him know there's a posse riding tonight."

"Clinton, let me lead tonight." Luke's voice sounded like a small boy. Clinton knew how John helped him during his teen years when Luke's father beat him regularly. John just went up to Luke's father and said, "In this town while I'm sheriff, there'll be no beating of children by men. If I hear that you so much as put a hand on that child's face or a whip on his back, I'll put you in jail so fast you'll think that time blinked. Then the feds will find out how you've been making illegal liquor."

Clinton let Luke lead them down Chestnut Street and turn onto Hill Road. The men were silent as they passed the place where John had been shot. They leaned over and comforted their horses so they won't snort a greeting to Rex as they turned the corner in front of the Collins home and headed back down the County road toward town.

When they got to the edge of the apple orchard, Clinton signaled for each man to get off and tie up his horse. The tender spring grass would keep the horses quiet while the men silently crept into the Harrisons' home.

The men spread out. Luke hid by the front door. Judd waited outside the first-story bedroom window. Clem waited in the driveway on the other side of the house. The back door was unlocked just as Millie promised. Clinton and Dwight entered, immediately hearing Mr. Harrison's snores, loud as logs roaring down the Kentucky River to the sawmills.

Millie Harrison had kept her promise to get her husband good and drunk, make sure he stayed in the house, and then leave herself just before midnight. Clinton shivered in the warm night under the filtered light of a cloud-covered moon. The two men tiptoeing in the house would not have fooled their mothers, but the drunken man slept on as if this weren't his last hour of freedom. Clinton followed the noise to the bedroom. Clinton and Dwight slipped through the door left ajar. Dwight went to the foot of the four-poster bed. Clinton went to the head where the sleeping man had thrown off the covers and lay buck-naked. Clinton silently drew his gun, cocked the trigger, and put the muzzle to Mr. Harrison's temple. "Don't move or you're a dead man. Believe me, I'd like nothing more than to put this bullet and five more like it through your rotten brain."

Mr. Harrison's eyes sprang open. Seeing Clinton's face within two inches of his own and feeling the gun at his temple, he rolled over to the left and vomited on Clinton's best boots

# CHAPTER THIRTY-THREE

## KNOWING

Verna tied Rex securely to the hitching post outside the jail. Once, when in a hurry, she loosely threw the reins over the post. Rex had wandered off to munch the grass on the hill in back of the jail. He hadn't gone far but Verna felt too tired after her morning at the college and conversation with Mr. Neiman to walk up even a slight hill to bring down a hungry horse. She hadn't been on so many errands outside her home since November. She could feel it in her feet and in her burning eyes.

Nanny Marie leaned against her mother and whined, refusing to get down from the wagon. Her first defiant act since her father died. Verna remembered Nanny Marie hadn't eaten since early morning. As they left the college, Verna had wiped a red remnant of currant pie from Son's mouth and chin. Now four hours since Nanny Marie's last meal, she only whimpered, "no." Verna experienced a moment of guilt; "Whatever have I done to this child that she can be so good?"

Yesterday over coffee, Clinton asked Verna to come by the jail after her interview at the college, stressing the importance of her coming straight there and not stopping to talk with anyone else. He explained. "There's something I want you to hear first from me." She wondered if he wanted to ask permission to court her. The thought brought color to her cheeks.

Clinton came out the door of the jail and gently took Nanny Marie from Verna's arms. She was grateful for the lifting of the burden. "Come along, Son."

"Ma, I want to stay outside."

"Just stay by Rex. Don't be wandering off, Son."

"I won't, Ma," said Son smiling as Clinton ruffled his hair.

Verna confided to Clinton. "That's one I'll never have to worry about speaking up for himself." Son began throwing rocks against the jail wall. The noise increased Clinton's nervousness.

"Verna, let's go down to Bette's. The children can get something to eat while we talk. I could use a cup of coffee and maybe a sandwich before I leave."

"Where are you going, Clinton?" Verna felt confused. He stressed last night the importance of her coming by the jail before noon. Now he acted like what he had to say could be said publicly.

"I have a prisoner I need to take to Richmond. Just let me tell Luke." Clinton had hired the young man to help him out at the jail after seeing the way he handled himself with the Hatfields and at the Harrisons last night.

"You put the children in the wagon. I'll be right back." He'd first thought he would tell her in the privacy of the jail. Clinton realized that with the children here and Mr. Harrison locked up in one of the cells, he didn't want to risk Harrison saying something hurtful. He figured Verna had enough hurt. What was the harm in a little lying, if he could make this easier for Verna?

"Clinton, where are you? I swear you just went somewhere where no one was going to find you. Nanny Marie's been pulling on your ear."

"Sorry, Verna. I got a lot on my mind but that's no reason to be rude."

While Verna lifted the children back in the wagon, Clinton went inside the jail. "Luke, Verna's here now. I want to tell her about Harrison before she hears it all over town. We'll be at Bette's if something comes up."

They took the corner table at Bette's that looked down the street to the train station. With a pad in her left hand and pencil in her right, Bette readied to take their order. She shuddered slightly seeing the

Widow Collins and her two youngest children. As Verna laughed at something Clinton said, Bette could feel the emotion between them.

"We've got some wonderful rhubarb pie today. Made it myself." Bette looked at Clinton first but he refused to meet her eyes.

"Verna, what would the children like?" They went back and forth like a couple familiar with each other, finally settling on the meat loaf, mashed potatoes, and green beans for everyone. Clinton began to relax. John had reassured him Verna didn't know about Bette, but Clinton no longer respected John's judgment about his personal life. If there had been any other place close to take Verna and the children for lunch, he would have. Looking around, he saw two men deeply involved in a conversation. Otherwise, the café was empty.

"Bette, do you think you could take Son and Nanny Marie out back to see your colt? There's something important I need to talk about with Mrs. Collins." Clinton asked the waitress-owner. He then turned to Verna, "It's about John. It'll be all over town before we leave Bette's. I want you to hear it first from me."

"Clinton, the children can hear what you have to say. My grandparents kept news of my mother from me. I won't do that to my children. What could be worse than seeing their father die?"

Clinton respected Verna's decision. "Bette, you best leave us alone a minute. Then we'll order." Turning back to the family, Clinton's face looked somber. "Verna, Son, Nanny Marie --- we've arrested the man who shot your father." Clinton waited for Verna's reaction. He knew learning who killed a loved one was like the beginning of a snowstorm. If the news came softly and gently, one flake at a time it could be absorbed and appreciated. But if the sky opened up and the news came out too fast, it could panic the family who felt vulnerable in the deluge.

Verna gasped. Not knowing who killed John had become like an abscessed tooth, the pain considered part of life. In March, she decided to stop asking Clinton about John's killer. Once when pestering her grandparents about her mother, her grandfather had angrily yelled, "Your mother's in Cincinnati, Ohio, 'cross the river." He warned her never to ask again.

Her mind wandered so it wouldn't have to hear more. She didn't want to know who killed John. She felt that somehow knowing who killed him made his death more real. At times now the pain hurt less. She pretended his work took him to the next county and he would be home soon. The thought comforted for the moment it flitted through her mind.

"I have him in jail right now, Verna. I'll going to be taking him to Richmond on the one o'clock train."

Bette brought their order by and Son took a bite of the meatloaf while Verna fed Nanny Marie some mashed potatoes. Son seeing that his mother wasn't asking questions jumped in, "Who killed my Pa, Mr. Blake?"

"Well, Son. Not a nice man."

Son looked squarely at Clinton, "Mr. Blake, what's the man's name?"

Over these past six months, as Clinton learned Verna habits, he discovered she pretended something hadn't been said, if she didn't like what she heard. He recognized the changes in her smile. Later she would apologize, "Oh, I must have wandered off for a little bit. Please, forgive me, Clinton." She did that when he tried talking about his growing feelings for her.

"Verna, I know you don't want to hear this. And I don't blame you. No one should have to hear the name of her husband's murderer. But the whole town is going to be talking in just an hour 'cause someone's going to see me walk him to the train station. You know how this town gossips. Someone at the station is going to tell one of their relations and with the party lines it won't be two o'clock before everyone in town will know. Even folks in the hills without phones, like your sister Belula and Hiram, will know by suppertime."

Verna looked at him like a deer caught in the gun sights while Bette hung back but close enough to hear.

"It was Isiah Harrison."

"Mr. Harrison? Millie's husband. Oh, no. Was it because ....? Did he know?" Verna stopped. She caught herself and looked at the children. "It was over. I know it was over."

"Verna, we have all the proof we need. You know his gun fit the bullet I told you about. He had motive. Wasn't just the personal issues. Mr. Harrison was Klan. So we've been watching him. I saw him talking with Deke Coulder in front of the jail. Turns out Coulder heard John talking to me about picking up his new suit at Mason's Tailoring on Chestnut and then taking the Hill Road home rather than the County Road. 'Course Harrison knew where to stand to be hidden. They cooked it up together."

"Mr. Blake, how did Mr. Harrison's cooking kill my pa?" Son looked puzzled.

"Son, Mr. Blake meant that Mr. Harrison's planned what he did to your pa." Verna was torn between stopping Clinton's story because of the children's presence and needing to hear all of it. "Clinton, please finish the telling."

"Harrison wanted the Jackson's good land and thought, with John out of the way, they'd be scared enough to sell. You know the Klan isn't strong around here any more, not like in other places. But Harrison got some of his Klan friends to put on white sheets and burn the Jackson's fields at night." Clinton slammed his fist on the table. "Cowards. Dirty rotten cowards."

Verna put her hand on his fist and he relaxed. "Tell me the end of it, Clinton. How did you find out?"

"Harrison began to boast. He'd get drunk and say things like, 'Well, guess that sheriff got what was coming to him. Serves him right sticking up for ni ....'" Clinton stopped himself just in time. He blushed.

"Verna, Harrison started drinking more and more, and talking, bragging. One time his brother came to the house. Brother's as bad as he is. The two of them got dead drunk. Millie cleared out of their way in the kitchen 'cause their mean talk scared her.

"She stood outside the door and listened. He told his brother all about ...." Clinton lowered his voice, "....about waiting on the Hill Road for John. Verna, Millie told me details that no one but the murderer would have known. Exactly where John was hit. And...." Clinton stopped himself. He could feel Son's eyes on him.

"Verna, it's true. After we brought him in last night. After some persuasion, "Clinton stopped, not wanting to tell Verna all they had done to get Harrison's confession," and our telling him all the details we knew about his part in John's death. He denied it. But we've got the evidence. Verna. Now John can be at peace." Clinton sighed.

Bette who had been standing back listening to the entire conversation, thought, "It's the good men that die."

"I hope they keep Mr. Harrison in jail forever and ever." Son declared loudly and banged his fist on the table.

Verna wiped her eyes. "Clinton, it's good to know the truth finally." Fearing the anger simmering inside her, she wanted to be alone. Avoiding Clinton's eyes and his outstretched hand, Verna barely restrained her impulse to run out of the restaurant. She hadn't eaten anything, only moved her food around the plate. "Clinton, I want to talk to Millie." "Son, Nanny Marie, finish your food."

"But Ma, you haven't!" Son declared.

"Mind your manners now. " Verna turned to Nanny Marie and fed her a few more bites. "Clinton, I think we better be going now." Verna's voice caught as she struggled not to cry.

Clinton quickly paid Bette, rounded up the children, and escorted the family out into the blinding sunshine before answering. "No, Verna, you can't talk to Mrs. Harrision."

"I want to hear Millie say why her husband killed John." Verna's eyes flashed.

"She left town for her own safety. Moved to Madison with kin. The Klan's laying low. There's been no more burning of fields." Clinton took Verna's hand. "Verna, I'll have Luke drive you and the children home. He can stay with you until I can come over tonight. You shouldn't be alone now."

# CHAPTER THIRTY-FOUR

## A PLACE FOR THE CHILDREN

For a week Verna stayed inside her home leaving only for the cemetery to talk with John. She had Hazel cancel her meeting with Sid and the preacher. Verna even kept Ellen and Darcine home from school, waiting for the gossip about John and Millie to run its course. She prayed the focus of the town would be on the evil doings of the Klan. Hazel and Clinton came out to the Collins' home to help receive those who came to express solidarity. Blanche, blunter than Hazel, confirmed Verna's suspicion that some still talked about John's relationship with Millie Harrison as part of the motive.

At the end of the week, Verna sent word to Sid Neiman that she wanted to meet with him about the Masons' offer to help. She got Willa Mae to watch the younger children while they talked, not wanting to risk their overhearing talk of the orphanage. On the ride to town, the rain beating down on the roof of Sid's car made conversation difficult. Holding a parasol over her head as they both ran into the minister's study at the back of the church, Verna stepped into a puddle, spraying her dress.

Her long black dress absorbed the late spring rain, making her legs feel sticky. Verna removed a handkerchief from her right sleeve, and mopped perspiration from her brow.

"Hello, Sid. Good morning, Reverend. Good of you to let us meet here." Verna politely acknowledged the two standing men.

"Verna, come sit with me. The minister dressed in his black officiating suit, patted a gray horsehair settee. Tightly holding the bulb of his carved ivory cane, he gently lowered his body to protect his arthritic knee.

Sid Neiman's thin six-foot frame looked out of place in the minister's study. Before starting the difficult conversation, he placed his bowler on a hat rack that also held the minister's collection of canes "Verna, as I mentioned last week the Masons' fund for widows and children was begun after the Civil War to help families whose husbands died."

"Sid, John told me, if anything should happen to him, the Masons will take care of me. I never asked him what that meant." Verna poured a cup of tea from the steaming China pot for herself and Mr. Neiman, thankful for something to do with her hands. The minister refused her offer.

"What the Klan did is against God's word and we won't stand for it. Verna dear, Hiram let us know you've done the best you can, but now with the money gone, you need our help."

"Oh, I do." Relieved that Sid Neiman knew her financial situation, Verna's worries spilled out. "Reverend Simmons, your sermons about the evil of the Klan and bigotry have reminded us all of why Berea was founded. And members of the congregation have been so helpful, bringing food and even clothes for the children. They do grow so fast." Verna remembered with pain Ellen's embarrassment at how the chances in her body were exposed by her too tight Sunday dress.

"I'm ever so grateful. But I can't do it anymore. I haven't any money. Not for shoes or books. We live on food given to us by others." Verna began to cry softly.

The men's quiet acceptance encouraged her to continue. "I want to support my family by becoming a nurse. I considered returning to Berea College but their program is limited."

The minister held Verna's hand and looked in her eyes as he attempted to ease her nervousness. "Verna, we know. From the first time you went to see Miss Hays, people speculated. Dr. Benson's nurse overheard him talk to Dr. Frost about you. She told her sister and then the news just spread."

Verna continued sharing her dilemma with the two men whose

quiet acceptance emboldened her. "Miss Hays told me the Berea program didn't qualify nursing graduates for the new state registration. She also told me that they would not be able to provide enough care for my younger children while I took classes and worked in the college infirmary."

Sid decided to tell Verna what they had done on her behalf in the week since the town learned who murdered John and the motive for his death. "Miss Hays, at Dr. Frost's request, contacted the Director of Nursing at City Hospital in Louisville. They have the best three-year training program for nurses in Kentucky. They are willing to interview you based on Dr. Frost's and Dr. Clark's recommendations, but you will have to live in the nursing residence."

"How can I live in Louisville? What kind of nursing residence is there for mothers and children?" Verna saw the two men look at each other.

"The Masons will provide a place for your family in Louisville at the Widows and Children's Home. We will pay also the small amount you need to apply for the nursing program and your living expenses until you begin to receive payment." He smiled as if he had given her a sunbeam to catch and ride to paradise.

"That's very generous of you, but I need to be sure I understand." Verna remembered her grandfather's caution to: 'Look at rest of the deck, Verna. Not all the cards are on the table yet.' To illustrate he would hide a penny. When she thought it was in one hand, it would turn up in another.

"The Berea Mason's Lodge will pay for us to live at the Widows and Orphans home in Louisville while I go to nursing school and even help me with my expenses until I started getting paid." Verna looked Sid straight in the eye and watched the film cover his irises before he looked over to Reverend Simmons to see if the good man would finish the tale.

The Reverend remained silent forcing Sid to tell Verna the implications of their offer. "Not exactly, Verna. You have to live at the hospital for three years while you are in training. The children will live at the Widows and Orphans Home."

"You mean it's an orphanage." Verna let out her breath. "My children will live in an orphanage. How can I do that? You are making me choose between giving my children to an orphanage and watching them go hungry."

Reverend Simmons reached down, picked up a black Bible from the tea table, and opened it. "Perhaps the Bible will help you, Verna. I frequently look to my Bible for a message from the Lord. Open the good book, Verna."

Verna stared at the leather-covered Bible in Reverend Simmons hands. At times she had looked for comfort in her Bible. She tentatively opened the book toward the back thinking that the New Testament might offer better advice to her than the Old.

"Is this the page you want, Verna?"

She tenuously answered. "Yes."

The Reverend's voice began deep and sonorous. "Here is the passage that appears before us, Verna. Chapter thirty-eight, Jeremiah, 'Thus saith the Lord, He that remaineth in this city shall die by the sword, by the famine and by the pestilence, but he that goeth forth to the Chaldeans shall live.' Sid Neiman seemed stunned by what was read and looked at Verna sympathetically as the minister put down the prophetic book.

"What does that mean, Reverend?" She knew of widows and children in the hills who starved to death or were so weak, illnesses became fatal. The biblical prophecy confirmed her increasing fears of danger for herself and her children.

"It seems, dear Verna, that you must leave Berea to spare yourself and your children."

# CHAPTER THIRTY-FIVE

## MORE THAN ONE WAY TO BE A WOMAN

As the women from the Berea Quilting Society gathered in Verna's parlor, busy hands darned, knitted, or held small infants. The 1916 June afternoon sun came in the west window but didn't reach the deep shadows where Verna sat with Hazel and Belula by her side.

Ready to share her decision about going to Louisville and nursing school, Verna had invited her friends over to her home. Her calm face belied the torment she experienced in reaching the decision. She vacillated between bad feelings of being just like her mother and abandoning her children and the excitement of wanting something better for herself and her children. Entrapped in indecision, as if two competing forces had placed elastic bands on her wrists and feet and pulled her back and forth, she thought she would split apart. The pain sent her to Dr. Clark, convinced she was dying.

The fear of more loss -- her sisters and friends, her church, the hills, John's grave -- pulled her to stay. The fear of poverty limiting her children's future and assaulting her pride pulled her to leave. Her panic increased as Ellen's breasts budded. Verna remembered Granny's words the day her blood started, "With your first blood, you're old enough to know the truth about your mother."

Knowing she was more selfish than most women, made the decision harder from Verna.

"Let me freshen your cup before I start." Verna got up and circled the room pouring more lemonade and iced tea, while Hazel passed around ginger cookies that didn't quite snap. But no one expected Hazel to be a good cook. She got distracted while she was baking, adding too much flour or too little baking powder. A younger woman moved her baby to the other breast and an older woman stretched out her arthritic knee.

After Verna sat down, she took Belula's hand in one hand and Hazel's in the other, and the words finally pushed out her mouth, "The truth is I'm scared to tell you this. But I have to, 'cause I need your help. I need your prayers. She paused, but only just long enough to catch her breath. "I've decided to go to nursing school in Louisville." One woman gasped. A baby started cooing and an older woman next to the mother asked if she might hold him. Knitting needles grew silent.

"It's more complicated than I knew when I first spoke with you. Berea College nurses don't meet the new criteria to become registered nurses. The Louisville City Hospital program does." Verna stopped, hanging her head. The women shifted their bodies. "They may not accept me. I have to go first for an interview."

Blanche spoke up. "Why that's just splendid. Splendid. That's just the right thing to do. Of course you should try and go to the best. No woman should do less than her God-given-talents meant for her to do." And she clapped her hands as if she were in Chicago at the Opera, seeing Carmen tell off the soldiers.

One of the women with a small infant at her breast looked up from her sucking child and smiled, "I always wanted to go to Louisville, but I never got any farther than Richmond. Back before I got married." Then she re-entered that half-trance of a new mother not yet separated from her newborn.

The mother, whose son was somewhere in France, sighed. "What about your children? How will you keep them while you're studying and working to be a nurse? My sister's husband's cousin was a nurse. She said it was the hardest work she ever did. She didn't think she'd ever get through a day, much less years."

"Berea's Masonic Lodge will sponsor us." Verna said this so silently that neither Belula nor Hazel sitting next to her even heard her words.

"Speak up, Verna dear, I couldn't hear you," said a friend with her hand cupped over her ear.

"The Masonic Lodge here in Berea has offered to sponsor us." Verna said only slightly louder than before.

"Sponsor you for what?" asked a younger woman.

Verna took a breath, looked out the window at the far end of the room so she wouldn't have to see anyone's eyes and announced, "Sponsor us for the Widows' and Children's Orphanage in Louisville. The Masons voted to support us. The children will be able to go to a good school and learn a trade." Verna felt her eyes tear up. She shook her head, not waiting to yield to doubt.

The oldest woman in the group began. "You need to stay right here. Take care of your children. It's God 's will." Another woman, known for her long silences, took her pipe out of her mouth, blew out the smoke and in a change-of-life dry voice advised, "Your days of dreaming of being something other than a mother are over."

Blanche Wellington Welch knew the moment was hers. She rose to her feet and looked every woman in the eye before coming to Verna. "There's no one way to be a woman any more. I don't care what he says during this Presidential campaign, President Wilson is going to take us to war. With the men gone woman will need to pick up the work. Verna has a calling. I bet if we were truthful, we all had a calling. We just didn't listen or we thought we could wait. If Verna needs to go to Louisville for an interview, then I'll go with her. We'll see this orphanage. There's no need to judge before we take a look"

Belula, who rarely attended these women events in town, got to her feet and looked Blanche back in the eye. "I don't know about all this 'women's calling' malarkey. But I know from poor. If Verna needs to go to Louisville to take care of herself and her children, then I'll try and understand. Hiram and I will give her the money to take the train."

The older woman with the Bible slowly rose to her swollen feet and smiled, "Only God is the true judge. Sometimes I forget that and think old age has given me wisdom. Instead it's just given me a big head, with thin hair."

A younger woman walked toward Verna as her teething baby's drool fell to Verna's parlor floor, "I hope that I never have to go through what you've gone through, Verna. Doesn't seem fair to have to give up your children for a time in order to take care of them later."

The women began to hum an old hymn and sway gently. They didn't hear the kitchen door open or the children's feet until Ellen, Darcine, Son, and Nanny Marie burst into the parlor.

"Clinton brought us home, Ma. He's putting Rex away and says he'll wait outside until the meeting is over." "We saw the cookies. Is it okay if we have some?" Son asked, as his puffed-out cheeks anticipated the answer. Nanny Marie crawled up on her aunt's lap and began sucking her thumb while twirling her listless hair with a bone-thin finger. The older girls politely made the rounds. "Hello, Aunt Hazel and Aunt Belula. Hello, Mrs. Welch," greeting each woman there and noticing everyone's tears.

One of the mothers, with children the age of Ellen and Darcine, noticed that their foreheads and noses were bright pink and thought, "Why those poor children, they haven't been out in the sun until today. Verna must keep them inside with her most times."

Ellen took the room in with one all-encompassing glance and irritably shrugged her shoulders while moving beyond the hugging women. The eleven-year old dragged her younger sister after her and muttered behind her hand in her most judgmental voice, "Darcine, look at Ma. Now she's got all her friends crying too. I'm sick of her tears. I'm sick of her feeling sorry for herself."

Darcine whispered back in her older sis's ear, "I don't think they're crying about Pa. They all looked at us when we came in." She paused and lowered her voice even more, "I think it's about us."

# PART II

## LOUISVILLE

# CHAPTER THIRTY-SIX

## THE TRAIN TO LOUISVILLE

After several telegrams and one impossibly expensive long-distance long telephone call, Verna confirmed an interview with the director of Nursing at Louisville City Hospital. Afraid to go alone, she asked Hazel to accompany her. When Blanche found out, she inserted herself into the trip and proceeded to make all the arrangements. Now less than a week later, Blanche Wellington Welch and Hazel Blackhard Gentry flanked the widow Collins as the L & N noon passenger train left Berea on its way to Louisville. Three new wide-brim hats knocked when their heads simultaneously turned to wave to the entourage of friends and family on the station's loading platform. Verna's heartbeat accelerated as at the start of a horse race.

Kicking the straw hamper of food under her feet, Verna waved one more time at her children, clustered around Beulah and Clinton. She felt a sharp ache in her stomach as Nanny Marie waved vigorously from her perch in Ellen's arms. A surge of melancholy hit her heart when she lost sight of Darcine's fine white-china face glistening from scattered tears. The wind whipped smoke in Verna's eyes as ash settled on her clothes. The train whistle blew.

"All aboard. Richmond, Lexington, and Louisville." The conductor's final warning faded into the constancy of the wheels' rhythmic clang whispering in Verna's ears: "You can do this. You can do this. You can do this." Relaxing her shoulders, she sat back. "Hazel and Blanche, I'm really doing it. I'm really going to Louisville."

Hazel and Blanche giggled with excitement. "Blanche, in my whole life this is only the second time I've left Berea for more than a family visit to Richmond." Verna hid her mixed feelings behind a gloved hand. Thinking her sister might judge harshly her beginning feelings of anticipation, Verna turned three more times to wave good-bye long after her children's faces disappeared in the train's smoke.

Clinton's tall head and waving hand stood out of the smoke a little longer. Yesterday, as he helped take Rex to the horse's new owner, he had asked permission to tell Verna his feelings about her. Verna remembered the feel of his rough hands on her wrists. She had pushed her sleeves up to her elbow to prevent Rex's salvia from straining her cuffs. Clinton unexpectedly touched her exposed wrists as if afraid she would run away. Verna remembered the feel of the sun on her arms and the heat of his hands.

She had tried to hush him, but his words bounced out as if the pressure of his feelings had shaken the lid off a box of hidden thoughts. "At fifteen you were the most beautiful girl I'd ever seen. You're still the most beautiful woman in Berea. I've watched you grown into a woman any man would be proud to call his wife."

"Verna, stop looking out the window. You can't possibly see anyone through all that smoke." Hazel, while smiling, pulled on Verna's arm to get her attention. "Verna, I swear you and Clinton are acting like you are sweethearts."

Verna turned back, her cheeks aflame. "Hazel!"

Blanche had kept as a secret from Verna the arrangements she had made for their stay in Louisville. She smiled as she recalled telling Beulah how they could be reached "in case of emergency." And Beulah, the pipe in her mouth barely moving, shot back, "What are any of you – going to do – about anything back here – when you're all the way in Louisville?" Then, taking her pipe out of her mouth, she spoke the plain truth, "Hiram and I will take as good care of these children as Verna, 'cause they know better than to act up with us."

Hazel turned her head toward Blanche and spoke softly so Verna couldn't hear. "Verna and I could never keep secrets from each other. I think you're very generous. But let's surprise Verna when we get to Louisville. Let her see for herself. It might help take her mind off the children for the next three days."

Then Hazel turned to Verna: "Verna, look, you can see the county road out this window." Hazel pointed in wonderment as the familiar landscape appeared. "I bet if we sat on the roof of this car we could see your home." Guilty over indulging herself by accompanying Verna to Louisville, Hazel had stayed up until two or three in the morning for three days prior to leaving, canning early spring beans. She even bought a new hat when Verna and Blanche insisted that she couldn't go looking like "country."

"Hazel, there was a time you'd do just that, climb up to the roof of this train." Verna remembered Hazel's daringness as a teen. Turning to Blanche, Verna told one of their secrets. "Hazel snuck out of her house one summer evening when I was fifteen. Right after I had moved to town to live with John's family. She climbed in my bedroom window at night. I slept on the first floor beside the kitchen. Somehow she never woke me up. I wouldn't have ever known except she wrote an 'H' in my open math book, right where I stopped before going to sleep."

Blanche tilted her head to look at Hazel, a slight smile on her face. "I bet you have other stories to tell."

Embarrassed and angry that Verna had revealed to Blanche one of their secrets, Hazel let her guard down, retaliating, "I don't see how you can leave those chillun behind. I'd give my right arm for just one as special as yours and you've got four." The minute the harsh words left her mouth she tried to suck them back in. "Verna, I'm sorry. I don't know why I say things like that. There's times I sound like my mother, who would never let a good thing stand straight without having to take her shotgun of a mouth to it."

"Hazel, I don't have a choice. The Louisville City Hospital nursing school and the Masonic Home remain my only hope to keep the children together and close to me." Verna took the hands of both her friends, repeating the litany she used to quiet her own guilt. "I've run out of everything. I have no flour, no sugar, no baking powder. I had no money to buy seeds for the garden. All's that left are a few sprouted potatoes from the cold storage. Hiram gave me some bean and pumpkin plants, but they'll be gone by Christmas. As soon as the town finds a new sheriff, we'll have to give up the house, too. They've delayed making a decision to give Clinton a chance to see if he's ready for the job. Oh, everyone means well, but, as Granny said, 'You move with life, or you die.'"

Words tumbled out of Hazel's mouth like hot food. "Verna, if you don't get in nursing school, your family will help take care of the children. I'll take Ellen. Grover and Nan offered to take Son and Nanny Marie to Oklahoma with them. Beulah and Hiram, although Lord knows they barely have enough for themselves, said Darcine was welcome to stay with them." Hazel didn't add that Hiram had taken all their savings to buy that fancy grave site for John.

Hazel lowered her voice: "Darcine would go to school in the hills. She couldn't go in town with Ellen. It's not a safe walk for a girl her age."

"Hazel, if they won't take me in the Louisville City Nursing School, even with the family's help, I don't know what we're going to do. There's just not enough money. I've gone over this and over this. For the next two years, until she's old enough to go to school, I would have to take Nanny Marie with me when I clean houses like I've been doing. What kind of life is it when a three-year-old has to be tied in a chair so she won't break anything in someone's fancy house?"

Verna felt the ache in her knees and saw herself back on the floor in other women's kitchens. She wanted to scream, right out there in the coach car, no matter who could hear. But she didn't. She just fell silent again as she thought of all she had lost.

"Hazel, some days I think we should have traded places. You would make a wonderful mother. You have a way with children. Lord knows, much as I love my own, now that John's gone, I just can't find the fun in it anymore." Verna, picking at the ribbon in her hat, wished she hadn't been so truthful.

"Verna, that's to be expected. It's been little over six months since John died. I don't see how you've managed. What with finding out he was...he was, well, you know."

"Sleeping with my next-door neighbor. The lovely Lillian Harrison, you mean. How dare she come into my house as he was dying! Good thing she left town. I would have popped her in the mouth if ever I saw her." Verna's hand flew to her mouth. She couldn't believe what she had just said.

Blanche started to laugh. Then just as if some elf was tickling the three friends' feet, they started laughing, soon bent over in their seats, holding their sides. Each shared her vision of gentle Verna pushing up her black widow's sleeves, making a fist, and slugging Mrs. Harrison so hard that she fell to the ground.

They passed through the flat tobacco land north of Berea and followed the phone lines toward Lexington. As they approached the Lexington station, Blanche pointed out the window. "That's when the old fort was." Hazel added, "Some of my schoolchildren don't even know we had one of the last big battles of the Revolutionary War right here. Sad, too. Why, Daniel Boone lost one of his sons in that fight not far from here – over in Blue Licks." Verna listened politely but her mind wasn't on past wars.

When the train stopped in Lexington, they whispered behind gloved hands comments about the passengers who boarded their coach car. One stopped to greet Blanche. "Why, hello, Mrs. Welch. Don't know if you remember me. Darlene Goodheart from Lexington. We met at a Daughters of the American Revolution meeting last fall." Blanche introduced Mrs. Goodheart to her friends, who realized quickly that Blanche did not remember her.

When asked the purpose of her trip, Blanche quickly responded, "My good friend Mrs. Collins lost her husband last winter. She's on her way to Louisville to seek educational opportunities."

"Oh, yes, Mrs. Collins, of course, we heard about your husband's death.

In fact my cousin, whom we just visited in Richmond, went to the trial. He said it was tragic, tragic -- those awful things about the sheriff and the murderer's wife. The court should be more merciful and not say such dreadful gossip in front of family. Dear, dear, Mrs. Collins. Wasn't it just terrible?" The intruder looked at Verna as if she were a roasting chicken being prepared for Sunday's dinner.

Blanche suddenly recalled this dreadful woman. She became protective of Verna's privacy, invaded by Mrs. Goodheart like a bear entering an occupied outhouse. Blanche's light, warm voice abruptly changed. "I do remember you. Don't let us keep you. Good day."

Blanche reached over and put her hand over Verna's while Hazel sat stunned. "Why, I never."

Verna's voice cracked, "Oh, she didn't mean to be rude."

"Verna Gentry Collins, you will never make a nurse if you let people walk all over you like that. Now let's just sit back and enjoy the scenery. Let's not let her spoil the day. You are a brave, dear woman. Your husband was a loving man with bad ways about him as most men have." Blanche attempted to comfort Verna, although her voice still held an edge of anger at Mrs. Goodheart's thinly veiled malice.

"Blanche, I know that. My granny taught me to hold my head high no matter the taunts. She was with me, by my side during the trial. She's with us on this train. I know my John loved me. I know people gossip. If bad words could stop me, I'd still be in a cabin in the hills. But I do appreciate your helping out. I was just feeling so good. She came out of nowhere and caught me with my undies around my ankles."

Hazel unclenched her fist and giggled. She remembered twelve-year-old Verna screaming as if kidnapped by night raiders. Verna had forgotten to lock the privy door during a church gathering. John flung it open and barged in thinking it empty. He used to say, "The first time I really noticed Verna, she showed her true nature." Hazel told Blanche all the details despite Verna's trying to shush her.

Verna tried to cover Hazel's mouth. "Stop that, Hazel. You promised never to tell that story." Soon the three friends held hands, laughing until tears leaked from their eyes, as each told story upon story.

# CHAPTER THIRTY-SEVEN

# THE BROWN HOTEL

As the train shot straight through the bluegrass country around Lexington, the women looked out the windows, watching herds of horses running through the grass restricted only by white fences that stretched farther than the eyes could see. Blanche couldn't resist showing off a little more. "You'd never know this beautiful land was formed by violence."

Hazel this time didn't keep quiet and added knowledge she had from teaching geography to her students. "Yes, that earthquake sure moved the earth around up in these parts."

Verna, lost in her own world, was oblivious to the sparring going on between her friends. "Now tell me, Blanche, I've waited long enough. Where are we staying?"

"You'll see, Verna. It's good to see your eyes sparkle. John must have told you a hundred times, you have the prettiest blue eyes. Now you just have to rein in that excitement. Why, if this train stopped now I think you'd fly out the window and run wild with those beautiful horses."

"Oh, Blanche, you read my mind. I felt their hoofs pounding the ground and the wind blowing in my face. I felt free. Hazel, you know how much I loved John. I tried to please him. To do what I thought he wanted me to do. I kept a part of me reined in, afraid I would run away like my mother. So, I became like good old Rex, taking the same roads every day, back and forth, back and forth. Now I see new possible paths."

Just as suddenly Verna's excitement collapsed into painful doubting as they passed through the hills between Lexington and Louisville. Her eyes started to sting. "Look, Louisville. It's so big and dirty. See the smoke." "Oh, my. My goodness. The sky is black." Hazel joined Verna's cry of dismay. They held their noses as scents from the coal furnaces, stockyard, and thousands of people living close together entered the train's open windows to taint the sweetness of the June evening.

Blanche wasn't about to let their country ways spoil the trip. "Oh, you two. It won't be like this where we're staying."

Hazel stumbled as she exited the passenger car. Verna caught her sister under the arm while Blanche took command. "Hold tight to your bags. This is the city. You can't trust anyone. Not anyone, you hear, until we get to the hotel." Verna looked around and noticed a strikingly beautiful woman. "Look, Blanche, look at her skirt. I can see her ankles, but the fabric is beautiful." Her ears drew her to the city's version of geese honks. "And look at all the cars. Why, I hardly see a horse and wagon anywhere. When John brought me here the streets were filled with horses pulling the grandest carriages."

Blanche hired a man in a red cap to hail them a hansom cab. Verna and Hazel insisted on sitting by the doors while Blanche squeezed in the middle. The driver had to tell them twice to put their heads back inside the hack as the women stretched far out the windows to gaze up at marble buildings taller than the Berea foothills. They marveled at the beautiful women with their parasols and the handsome men with their tall hats and canes. Hazel waved at some of the children who ran out in the street.

"Hazel, don't do that. Those children are beggars. They'll pester us all the way to the hotel." Blanche realized that Hazel, despite her teacher's air of knowing, was as naive as Verna about city ways.

To the Berea women, the hurrying people seemed to be racing to a special event. Verna asked their driver, "Is the circus in town?" Before the surprised driver could respond, Blanche just laughed, observing, "City folk always have somewhere important to go. They just never seem to get there."

After about twenty minutes their driver announced, "The finest address in Louisville, ladies – the Brown Hotel."

Verna exclaimed. "Blanche, we can't stay here. This is too expensive." John took me here to see the lobby. We laughed about how we'd come back some day and rent a room for the evening. But we both knew it would never happen."

"Verna, I always stay here. You are my guests. I told my husband, the least he could do for you is to pay for these two nights. If I didn't help him spend his money, he'd take it with him into the coffin. How much fun would that be?" Blanche laughed with pleasure.

Behind her bravado, Blanche worried about Verna. Blanche feared what the future might bring her friend. She saw Verna as a naïve hill woman, brighter than most, certainly more fun than most, but not far-seeing. Nurses' training demanded toughness. Many women failed to graduate. They came back home, sick, worn out, with spiritless eyes. Some never returned home. Infected with the diseases of their patients, they died. Blanche resolved Verna would have two of the most special days and evenings of her life.

Far from Blanche's practical concerns, grandiose daydreams flooded Verna's consciousness. "Someday I'll take my friends to a fine hotel like this. I'll pay for the rooms and the dinners." Verna didn't think ahead to the dangers of the next two years in Louisville and the profession that demanded so much. She thought of escaping poverty and daydreamed of saving lives.

After marrying John, she dreamed of owning a large home like her father's and fine clothes for herself and her children. In her daydreams she was generous, unlike her father, who never sent a dime once he left and remarried. Since John's death, the growing complexity of her thoughts and new desires – respect, becoming educated, and being able to support her family with dignity – pulled at her, challenging her previous life dedicated to family and home.

Hazel stared in awe at the gleaming stone exterior of the Brown Hotel. "Mighty kind of you, Blanche. Although we don't need anything so grand." Inwardly, Hazel sighed with relief. Now she could take off her corset and shoes and put her feet up. Not impressed with fancy hotels, she feared the cigar smoke would hurt her eyes. She planned to tell Blanche her head hurt so she could retire early and maybe read a little. Blanche and Verna could attend that new film, *Birth of a Nation*, by themselves. After all, she taught history. There's nothing a movie could tell her about the United States of America that she didn't know already.

# CHAPTER THIRTY-EIGHT

# THE INTERVIEW

Verna took more care dressing for her interview than for her wedding day. She arose early while Hazel still snored in their shared room. Hazel had squealed the night before when she saw the new silent SI-WEL-CLO toilet in the bathroom. Verna had teased her half-sister, "What say we ask Mr. Gentry" – as both of them called their shared father – "How come your flushing closet is so loud?"

Momentarily, Verna's thoughts went to last night's movie, how grand the orchestra sounded, but she and Blanche left in a huff when the picture showed the hooded Klan as admirable. Blanche loudly said, "Let's go. The Klan is a shame on our fine country."

Verna was about ready to add, "This hatred killed my husband," when. several men in the audience yelled at them to sit down. Verna felt the crowd getting ugly. Blanche leaned over to Verna and said in a soft voice, "These people aren't from Berea, honey, we better just hurry out of here."

Shaking the disturbing pictures from her head, Verna admonished herself to focus on her interview preparation. She washed the train's coal smell out of her hair. Afterward, she dried her hair with two thick towels the size of her body and threw them on the floor with a laugh. While brushing her hair, she practiced what she would say in the interview. She would start by emphasizing what a hard worker she was. Then she would show them her grades from the six months at Berea College to demonstrate she could learn. Her minister's recommendation lay tucked in a valise Blanche loaned her. Even Miss Hays wrote on her behalf: "You needn't worry about her age or the fact that she's a mother. I've never seen a woman more determined to be a nurse."

Verna looked in the bathroom mirror, repeating well-practiced lines. "Hello, my name is Verna Collins. I want to be a nurse. It's the most important work a woman can do. I will work hard. You will never be sorry you took me for a student."

Blanche added the next part. "Yes, I know I'm older than most women you accept, but I'm strong and determined." Hazel suggested she add, "I've never been sick a day in my life. I got out of bed two days after my last was born." She didn't have to tell them that she got up because John left with a posse to capture a gang that had robbed several banks in Madison County. Or that both her half-sisters were in Oklahoma visiting Nan and Grover because the baby came earlier than expected. Or that she had started hemorrhaging because she wouldn't stay in bed as Dr. Benson had ordered.

Verna's ears picked up various bird songs on this sunny June day. She wondered if they always sang in the city or if they'd come in for the day to cheer her on the way to her seven a.m. interview. Barely sleeping because of Hazel's snoring and her own apprehension, she eagerly slipped out of their hotel room at six-thirty. Instead of yesterday afternoon's leisurely men in bowlers and women in long dresses, workers filled the streets. Men swept up from the horses, delivered milk, and hawked the latest overnight news. Women sold fruit and vegetables and despite the early hour offered a variety of personal services. Verna blushed when she saw one woman lift her skirt to show her leg to a man.

Verna found the hospital without difficulty, as Louisville City Hospital occupied a full city square, four blocks from the Brown Hotel. The white limestone exterior gleamed as the hotel clerk said it would. Walking up the stone steps, her heart beat loudly. She stopped a moment to catch her breath at the sheer size of this brand new 500-bed million dollar hospital. Realizing she was gawking, she looked around to see if anyone noticed; she was reassured by the friendly smile and tipped hat of a handsome young man.

As she opened the door, noise ricocheted off the granite walls.

Unlike the quiet haven she had pictured, this large city hospital exploded with the sounds of carts bumping, dishes clanging, and shouts of "Nurse, over here," followed by the pounding of running feet. The hurrying nurses looked like students while several older women in uniforms stood by watching. No one paid her any mind, so Verna took the time to admire their crisp white-on-white uniforms with four-pointed hats.

Looking into a room the size of a tobacco-leaf drying warehouse, she saw row after row of beds with bodies in them. The low drone of patients' moans seeped into the hall. Steady footsteps echoed down the long hall in front of her, as two doctors walked bent over while whispering to each other. Recovering from the shock of so much noise and activity, she walked quickly down another long hall, following the signs to the director of nurses.

The door stood open, exposing a large oak desk filled with papers and open books that dominated the small room. As a church chime clanged the final seventh stroke, a large, imposing woman, dressed in white, covered by a white apron and topped with a starched white peaked hat, looked up from her desk.

"I trust you are Mrs. Collins. You are right on time. Come in. Sit here. Give me your records."

Remembering her manners, Verna commented, "Your hospital is grand."

The director looked up at this country woman and realized she had probably never seen such a large edifice. She couldn't help bragging a little. "Mrs. Collins, we are one of the finest hospitals in the country. This new hospital is less than two years old. Because of our size and the vast number of illnesses our patients present with, we are able to offer superior training to our physician residents and nursing students. The city of Louisville spared no expense, one million dollars..." Catching herself, Miss Johnson drew in a breath and silently reminded herself, this woman was from the hills, not the daughter of one of their benefactors. The next thirty minutes passed slowly like the first stages of labor, as Verna answered questions thrown at her by Miss Eliza Johnson.

"Why do you want to be a nurse?"

"I believe nursing is the most important profession a woman can have. I want to save people's lives and help their pain."

"You can't save all the lives. How will you react if a patient dies?"

"I will try the best I can. That's all I can do."

Miss Johnson never smiled as she continued her questions. "How long has it been since you've studied?"

"It's been ten years. But I read the Bible and stories to my children. I know I can do the work. Here are my grades from Berea College."

"Yes, yes. But that was long ago. You aren't young anymore." Miss Johnson skeptically looked her over as if she were an old mare trying to pass for a filly. "Nursing is hard work and learning to be a nurse is even harder. You will work twelve-hour days, then go to classes and then study. Your only vacation for three years will be two weeks' leave, after your second year."

"Yes, ma'am, I know. I'm prepared to do that. I was raised in the hills of Berea. I'm not lazy and I'm strong."

"Mrs. Collins, you are a thirty-year-old woman with four children who hasn't been to school in over ten years. How in the world do you expect to keep up with eighteen-year-olds? I'll be truthful with you. I've seen women like you. They lose their husbands and think, 'I'll just go to nursing school and find myself a swell doctor.' Well, Mrs. Collins, we do not cotton to the student nurses bothering the doctors. In fact, if we see you even flirting, you will be disciplined and the second time you will be removed from the training."

"I'm not here to get a husband. If I eventually wanted to marry again, I should have stayed in Berea." Verna pushed away the image of Clinton's face while her uneasiness grew. Verna felt intimidated by this educated big city woman who ran a whole hospital's nursing staff. Then she remembered Hazel's words, "Don't beg and remember you can do anything if you want to bad enough."

"Miss Johnson, you read what my minister said. I'm not that kind of woman. It isn't easy to think about not living with my children and seeing them only on Sundays. But I won't have them go hungry. And I won't see them in bad schools where they don't learn anything."

Miss Johnson raised her hand as if to stop Verna's words. But having her caution released by the director's challenging words, Verna carried on, unstoppable. "I want to be a nurse and I'm going to be a nurse. I want to train here at your hospital. If I can't be a nurse here, I'll find another program to train me."

"Now, Mrs. Collins, I merely spoke the truth. Your age is a problem. I find older students don't do well, and truthfully, they don't last. You have the fire but you have no idea how hard the work is. You will be getting up each morning at six o'clock, giving baths, making beds, and distributing medicine to all your patients before the doctors' rounds at nine a.m. Like it or not. You're not as strong as you used to be. It takes strength to move a patient in his bed. It takes young bodies and minds that aren't distracted with worry about other things – like children."

"I buried my husband a little over six months ago. I thought I would die with him. Nothing will ever be as hard as deciding to live after he died. I've been getting up and working each morning all my life. I can learn as well as anyone. I can do the work, Miss Johnson. I'm asking you to give me a chance."

"Well, the decision isn't all mine. I need to talk to Dr. Fowler, the superintendent of our hospital. Some of my other nursing staff and a doctor also requested to talk with me about you. Please wait out in the hall. There's a bench in front. I will call you when we've made our decision."

The wait wasn't the longest in her life, coming in second to the last thirty minutes of her firstborn's birth. She kept her head bowed and stared at her rough, reddened hands. Passing students gazed at her curiously, remembering the awkwardness of their initial interviews. She crossed her ankles to the right and then to the left. She sang songs in her head. She recited the Lord's Prayer twenty times until she just couldn't say it again.

She waited on the hard wooden bench as the clock struck eight forty-five, nine, and nine-fifteen. Several women entered the room, staring at her as they passed. Two tall men in white, looking like important doctors, opened Miss Johnson's door and disappeared. One of the doctors looked at Verna as he left. She felt someone watching and looked up to find an older man regarding her face. Verna thought his compassionate smile resembled her grandpa's before he slaughtered a beloved cow, too old to give milk anymore.

Eventually she heard her name and returned inside the room to sit down again on the hard wooden chair before Miss Johnson. The director of nursing wasted no time. "Mrs. Collins, we can't accept you here at Louisville City. We have all the students we can take this year. As I told you, we are concerned about your age."

Verna couldn't believe it. She sucked in air as if the earth's atmosphere had been punctured and she'd better breathe while she could. If they weren't going to take her, why didn't they just send a telegram? She started to cry despite her vow not to show her emotions. "I thought you told me that sometimes you took older women."

"Mrs. Collins, it's not just your age. You're also a mother. But let me finish. We can't take you here at this hospital, but we have an affiliate, Waverly Hills. I talked with Dr. Duffield. You might have seen him leaving. He accepted you into his hospital's nursing program. But you must start July 1ˢᵗ."

As Miss Johnson talked, Verna felt like a witch had dropped her off a mountaintop and, as she fell through space, an Olympic god reached out to save her from the rocks. "Oh, thank you, thank you. I can do this." Verna went on as if Miss Johnson still needed convincing.

"Show up here July 1ˢᵗ. You must buy your uniform and books before that. You'll receive a monthly allowance of five dollars. Cut your hair. It's too long. Attracts germs. Sleep as much as you can. You will be working twelve hours a day and then have classes. Obviously you won't get time off this summer. But if your grades stay up, you will get two weeks next summer. We are very strict here. Officially you will be a student of Waverly Hills, but you must still obey all our rules. You will be working at this hospital also."

"I'm not familiar with the Waverly Hills Hospital." Verna said tenuously.

"It's not Waverly Hills Hospital. It's Waverly Hills Sanatorium. They treat patients with tuberculosis." Miss Johnson waved her hand as if annoyed by Verna's inquiry. "Now I'm sure you have more questions. But, enough for today. Personally I'm not pleased about having you here. I don't believe in married women being nurses. Dr. Fowler, our superintendent, agrees with me. I only agreed because Dr. Duffield spoke for you."

Verna's face crunched up. "Why did he? I don't understand."

"He said he wanted to repay your husband for a favor, something to do with his younger brother. I have a feeling this is not the first or last time you will be rescued by a man."

"Oh," Verna murmured, while thinking, 'Another time John helped a family \and never shared it with me.' Although curious, Verna respected John's honoring others' secrets.

"Dr. Duffield supports the nurses here at this hospital. We need friendly doctors. Conditions have improved, but for a while some doctors challenged our independence as a profession." Miss Johnson looked out the window, remembering the years of fighting for nursing to be certified as a profession. "But enough of that. You will be accepted in training in July. Show up at seven a.m. sharp. Remember, we do not tolerate foolishness. Particularly foolishness with the doctors or male patients. Good day, Mrs. Collins."

Verna breathed deeply. "Thank you. You won't be sorry. You'll see what a hard worker I am. And I will learn." Verna couldn't stop talking even when Miss Johnson lowered her head to read some papers, as if Verna evaporated.

"I'll be leaving now." Verna backed two steps, spun around and skipped the last few steps to the door.

# CHAPTER THIRTY-NINE

## THE ORPHANAGE

Verna's heart pounded in her chest as she walked out the front door of the hospital to reenter Louisville's bustling streets. The sun still shone, having moved across the sky to beam down on her head. The birds still sang. The trolley bells still rang. The newsboys still called out the latest headline. Knowing the success of her interview with Miss Johnson had depended entirely on the intervention of others more powerful than her, Verna turned with apprehension toward the orphanage.

Located in the southwest section of Louisville, the Masonic Home for Orphans, like City Hospital, was a stone structure. The Home sturdily anchored a city block less than a mile from the hospital. The reality of her limited choices preoccupied her thoughts. Either the children would be separated from her and live with relatives in Berea and Oklahoma or she would sign papers to admit them to the orphanage and be able to see them weekly.

On the sidewalk in front of her Verna saw a stylish woman with a light blue parasol positioned aslant to keep the July sun off her evanescent skin. The woman pulled an obviously reluctant boy by his hand. As he yelled, "Stop! You're hurting me," the woman looked around furtively. Seeing only Verna, whom she dismissed with a quick glance at her country clothes, she admonished the child, "You behave now or your father will hear of this." Verna blushed from the dismissal and remembered her own feelings of being better than Mrs. Dorsey, another Masonic widow, whose children were at the orphanage. Sid had arranged for Verna to met Mrs. Dorsey and talk with her about the Home.

Verna knew from town gossip that Mrs. Dorsey depended entirely on the Masons. In addition to no money she had the shame of debt and no pension to help with her expenses. Mr. Dorsey had died suddenly when his heart stopped in the middle of the night, right after he had put all their money into a down payment for a tract of land.

For the meeting Verna wore her best Sunday dress with the crocheted roses, even through the previously fitted top now hung over her waist. In six months she had lost almost thirty pounds. Upon meeting Mrs. Dorsey, whose faded dressing gown was held together by two large pins in the front, Verna recognized the signs of prideful lying -- the head raised a little too high, the eyes hooded like an owl, gnarled hands gripping each other rather than resting easily. Resisting the urge to flee, Verna forced herself to look at a burlap dress made by the oldest Dorsey daughter and a hand-carved chair by her son, both made during their stay at the orphanage. As Verna prepared to leave, the older woman hugged Verna's reluctant body to her withered breast.

Returning from her reveries, Verna looked about the Louisville street and noticed a society matron getting into a cab. She began rehearsing her list of questions and concerns about conditions at the orphanage. "Ask about the food. Tell them the children are used to biscuits and gravy. And the lessons. And what Nanny Marie will do during the school day. Look for cleanliness. See if the children seem well behaved." Verna began a litany to soothe her increasing guilt. "We'll be in the same city. I can visit. I am not my mother. I'm not just up and going heaven knows where."

"This is not my fault. If John hadn't ..." Thoughts of his betrayal flashed like silent pictures in her brain and she doubled over with pain. As she raised her head, a breeze touched her face; she felt his breath upon her cheek and she cried aloud. "Oh, John, what should I do?"

A pair of doctors in white coats stopped to ask if she were all right. Afraid they might be City Hospital doctors, Verna flushed and regained her composure. "I'm fine. Thank you." The doctors quickly hurried on. Verna looked around and didn't recognize any landmarks.

She felt disoriented. Unable to trust herself, she approached a woman sitting on a wooden bench with her feet stretched out in front of her and a basket of wilting flowers beside her. "Pardon me, I'm new to Louisville and I'm looking for Lee Street?"

The woman looked at Verna, sizing her up as country, and not unpleasantly replied, "Right here, Miss. You're right on it."

"I'm looking for the Masonic Home for Widows and Orphans." Verna resolved not to let the flower seller silence her. In back of her well-practiced smile, Verna felt like telling the woman, "I am going to school to be a nurse. I'm not abandoning my children." She caught the words in the back of her throat and swallowed them.

The woman pointed with green-stained fingers. "Right down the block. See those large stone towers. That's it. Going to visit your children?" The woman's voice softened.

"No. But I'm thinking about having them live there." Verna then rushed to explain. "Their father died and I just got accepted to nursing school."

"Well, you won't be disappointed. My sister lost her husband. We couldn't keep her children, of course. So she put them in there. She tells us everything's lovely." Reaching down by her side, the flower seller handed Verna a long-stemmed daisy. "Here. Put this in your hat. It will look nice with your green eyes."

Feeling some comfort from the friendly exchange, Verna slipped into the small crowd of people waiting to cross the street. She casually stepped into the street as she might in Berea. She felt a gloved hand grab her wrist and pull her back. "Really, my dear, that horse almost ran over you. You must watch yourself in Louisville. This isn't your country town."

Turning red and wanting nothing more than to disappear, Verna looked both ways and stepped out again, throwing a "Thank you" over her shoulder as she half ran and half skipped across the cluttered street.

The orphanage sat atop an entire city block with twin tan-stone towers flanking the main building. Verna recognized the castle-like structure from Mr. Neiman's picture. While she walked to the main entrance, her eyes fixed on this massive edifice, she looked for children playing in front. In her mind they would be laughing and singing the way Ellen and Darcine did as they left for school. Or the younger ones would be running and chasing each other, as Nanny Marie and Son did in the orchard. Meant to hold hundreds, this cold stone building with windows for eyes stood alone. Not one child played outside.

As Verna slowly trod a long sidewalk to the entrance, she barely noticed another set of simulated ancient Greek pillars by the front door. Her muscles weakened from the months of lethargic mourning, she had to grasp the door with both hands and pull. Surprisingly she entered the building unchallenged. Children's small voices filled the hall. "ABC..." As she stood before a closed classroom door, uncertain which way to go, a woman with sad eyes passed by her.

"Hello. I'm Mrs. Collins, from Berea. I'm here to see Miss Ford."

"Of course, Mrs. Collins. We're expecting you. I'm Miss Davies, the school nurse. Please come this way. Did you have any trouble finding us?"

Verna lied. "No, I could see your building a block away."

"We are very proud of our children's home and the brotherhood's generosity."

Verna's shoulders relaxed slightly as she continued down the long hall with Miss Davies. "Mr. Sid Neiman, he's from my home town of Berea, told me about your Home. I'm here to talk with Miss Ford about my children."

Miss Davies touched her hand. "I am so sorry to hear of the death of your husband. We understand he was a good man."

Verna's eyes filled up. Would she never stop crying when someone mentioned John? "Yes, he was a good man." Verna fell naturally into humbly accepting this stranger's condolences. Only with her sisters and Blanche could she even hint at her anger with John for letting himself be killed, leaving her to care for the family.

The school nurse's eyes opened wide with a filmy stare, looking even sadder than when Verna first saw her. Miss Davies's thin lips were a colorless straight line above her chin. A pile of brown hair sat atop her small head with a roll in front tucked under so tightly not even a wisp dared to creep out. A single strand of black beads rested on her protruding breastbones. Despite her sad appearance, Miss Davies stepped with a spring to her walk and lightness in her voice as she called out the name of each child they passed. The children responded to her attention with a smile and a quick, "Good morning, Miss Davies."

The coolness of the building defied the humidity of June, seeping through the thick stone. Verna saw tidy rooms and clean, smiling children. Thinking Ellen might disapprove of the plain uniforms the older girls wore, Verna asked Miss Davies, "My oldest daughter, Ellen, is mighty particular about what she wears. Do some of the children wear their home clothes?"

Miss Davies looked at Verna with concern, recognizing her denial of the drastic changes the Collins children would have to accept. She smiled compassionately. "Don't you worry. Miss Ford will explain everything. "

Verna, feeling overwhelmed by the looming changes in her life, drew in a deep breath, pictured herself in a white nurse's uniform, smiled automatically at Miss Davies, and felt her body go numb. Walking down an endless corridor filled with more children than she had ever seen in one place, Verna swept her mind clean of unpleasant thoughts.

Miss Davies identified the infirmary, as another woman stepped out to join them. "Mrs. Collins, this is Mrs. Miller, my assistant."

Verna thought Mrs. Miller very attractive, with light brown hair that frizzed on the sides and a round open face with pleasant, smiling eyes that reminded Verna of her sister-in-law, Nanny. As if she couldn't resist the smooth feel on her fingers, Mrs. Miller's fingers played with a double strand of pearls that circled her neck. Verna wondered what brought Mrs. Miller so low she needed to work for a living.

She realized Mrs. Miller was speaking to her: "...call me Mary Jane. How good you are able to visit the Home first. Some mothers simply can't make the trip to Louisville. It's just too far. To not even be able to see where their children will be living, why, it must be unbearably painful." Mrs. Miller clucked her tongue on the roof of her mouth.

The woman's unexpected thoughtfulness broke through Verna's reserve. She blurted out. "It's not like that for us. I'll be right here in Louisville. I wouldn't let my children be away from me."

"Oh, my dear. But how can that be?"

Verna, usually reserved with strangers, found Mrs. Miller's compassion soothing. Like an opened jack-in-the-box, her secrets popped out. "I've just been accepted into nursing training, this very morning, at City Hospital, well, not City but Waverly, an affiliate. After I'm a nurse, I can provide for my children. But until then, I plan to see them 'most every day. I'm sure since I'm right here in Louisville exceptions to the rules can be made."

"But..." Mrs. Miller began to respond to Verna's revealing burst. But Miss Davies admonished, "Mrs. Collins, we mustn't keep Miss Ford waiting." Verna noticed Mrs. Miller bite her lower lip as if to seal her mouth. Saying quick good-byes and "Pleased to meet you," Miss Davies continued to address each child by name as they walked down the long stone corridor. But Verna began to notice that the children, although polite, didn't really look at Miss Davies.

Finally the two women reached a large closed light oak door off the hallway with a trim darker wood plaque painted "Principal." Miss Davies knocked and opened the door immediately upon hearing a forceful "Come in."

Miss Belle Ford, the Masonic Home's principal, came out from behind a large desk with her hand outstretched to Verna. Miss Ford's serious face reminded Verna of her minister's demeanor as he talked about the sins of mankind. For the next twenty minutes, seemingly without taking a breath, Miss Ford outlined the resources of the Home as if reading from Verna's list of questions. Verna began to feel reassured. While imagining Son as a member of the Boys Band, she smiled. Miss Ford showed her pictures of the older girls learning to be nurse's aides, and she could picture Ellen and Darcine in uniforms similar to those the nursing students wore at the hospital.

They toured the vast acreage of the school and home. She saw children making shoes, sewing, canning, caning chairs, gardening, all seemingly happy as elves. Verna sailed into denial as if the O in the Home's title wasn't Orphans but, instead, Opportunity.

Pangs of doubt returned as they quickly passed the children's dormitories where rows of beds, each with the same cover, stretched endlessly. At first Verna thought the dormitories looked cheery, until she looked for toys and found none, not even on the beds. She wondered what Son would do if he couldn't take his soldiers to bed with him. Or what about Nanny if she couldn't wrap her arms around her corn husk doll? Sweeping away these thoughts, she focused on Miss Ford's description of the Home as, "An opportunity for children to reach stations in life they might not otherwise attain."

Brushing away her doubts like bothersome flies on a cooling pie, Verna began an inner dialog. "John's death needn't make us poor again. I'm not being selfish. Why, as Nurse Davies said, Ellen and

Darcine could be nurses before they turned twenty. They won't have to be dependent on a man, not on anyone but themselves."

Returning to Miss Ford's office, more comfortable with herself, Verna moved around the principal's office, admiring the pictures of graduated children that papered the walls. Miss Ford sat behind her desk crowded with paper and books, and motioned for Verna to sit. "Mrs. Collins, we have conditions that a mother must agree to before her children are accepted into our Home." Verna, lost in her daydream of an expanded future for her girl children, half listened and pleasantly smiled as Miss Ford outlined the details of method of payment, rules of conduct, dietary restrictions, clothing, and school attendance. Verna noted that Miss Ford's tone changed as she introduced the topic of parental responsibilities and visitation. "And Mrs. Collins, we have expectations of our children's parents."

Eager to please, Verna quickly reassured Miss Ford. "Of course. Of course. I fully expect to be very involved with my children and help out as much as I can."

Miss Davies hesitantly interrupted. "Miss Ford, Mrs. Collins informed me she has just been accepted into nurses' training right here in Louisville. She mentioned visiting her children regularly at our Home. I don't think she appreciates how demanding nursing school will be." She paused to check Verna's reaction while trying to catch Miss Ford's eye to signal a problem. "Perhaps the Lodge in Berea didn't explain our rules on visiting. I thought it best to wait until you could speak with her."

Miss Ford picked up on Miss Davies' cue. From her years as director she knew the visitation rules devastated most mothers. Hardened to the mothers' pleas and firm in her beliefs, she relied on her staff to assist her in controlling the mothers' emotions. "Oh, oh yes. Nurses' training is very difficult indeed. You will be very busy and I'm sure you understand. For the children's sake, we ask mothers not to visit too often. The children's learning comes first. We don't want these innocents to be unhappy here or get homesick. When mothers visit once a month, the children don't miss them as much."

"Once a month! Why, I've never gone a day without seeing my children. Well, until I came to Louisville yesterday," Verna stammered.

"Well, see, you've started the changes already. It only seems difficult now. Believe me. I know what is best. Your children will look forward to your visits while they concentrate each day on their learning, their new friends, and appreciate all the opportunities they have here at the Home."

"I don't know. I just don't know." Verna rubbed her fingers through her hair. Her mouth felt dry. "May I have a glass of water?"

"Of course, my dear. What was I thinking? You must be parched on this hot day." Miss Davies jumped up, leaving the room, grateful for a reason to escape this painful scene.

"I'm with some friends here. I need to talk with them. Visiting once a month will be too hard, particularly for my young ones, Nanny Marie and Grover." Having expressed her doubts, Verna felt stronger. She resolved not to make Miss Ford angry, but she would not be pushed into a decision. Verna remembered when Ellen declared, "I hope I never see you again," and for a fleeting moment reconsidered Miss Ford's harsh rule. Then she remembered Nanny Marie's arms tightening around her mother's neck as Hazel tried to loosen her hold so Verna could board the train.

Verna spoke up, quietly but firmly: "I need time to think about this. I understand you must have rules that you believe are best for all the children. But I'm worried about my little ones. Nanny Marie is only two."

Miss Ford's compassion for reluctant mothers never shook her belief in the school's policies. "Mrs. Collins, this is for the best of all the children. You will see. We can keep a place for your children, but only for two weeks. I encourage you to sign the papers now because we need time to prepare for the children. If you change your mind, don't worry. We'll just tear up the papers. However, if you don't sign now, we won't be ready when you need to start your training. My dear, don't forget your children will all be together here. You said earlier that relatives offered to take the children but they wouldn't be together."

"My oldest girls have always taken care of the younger ones. I can't see Nanny Marie and Son without Ellen and Darcine. Perhaps I'm thinking too much of my missing them." Verna's selfishness returned to complicate her decision.

Verna quietly pleaded. "Do you ever ease the visiting rule?"

Miss Ford, impatient to return to her ever-growing pile of paperwork, dropped her voice to signal the end of the interview. "Mrs. Collins, all the children here abide by the same rules. You saw how busy and happy they are. Be grateful for the opportunities the Brethren have given all these fatherless and sometimes parentless children." Miss Ford reached for a paper on her desk.

Looking over the contract Verna decided to sign the paper. Verna told herself, "Once the children are here, Miss Ford will change her mind on the visiting." Verna lowered her eyes and donned her gloves before shaking the director's hand and thanked Miss Ford for her time.

Verna, leaving the director's room with her head lowered, bumped into Mrs. Miller, and felt cool water splash on her hand. "Here's the water you wanted. It is good to drink before you go out again into this heat." Mrs. Miller studiously avoided Verna's eyes, giving the younger woman time to regain her composure.

"Let me walk you to the door." Mrs. Miller's warm voice drew Verna's eyes up from the floor to the other's woman's open face. Verna saw compassion and knew her disagreement with Mrs. Ford had been overheard. Verna slowly sipped the water as she walked, giving herself time to regain composure.

As they neared the front door, Mrs. Miller looked around, and seeing no one near them, leaned close to Verna. "I shouldn't be telling you this. I didn't have children, but I know the aching hole when my husband died. The Home may be the right place for your children, but it isn't for every child. Some children don't adjust well. Having lost their fathers, they can't bear being separated from their mothers."

Mrs. Miller's voice soothed Verna after the emotionless Miss Ford. "I appreciate your honesty. If I do let the children come here, I hope you will watch out for them. Particularly my small ones – Nanny Marie's only two and Son's not even five, just babies." Verna felt like hugging Mrs. Miller but held back.

As the older woman opened the front door, the heat, smells, and street noises overwhelmed Verna's dwindling resources. Verna suddenly wanted to escape this impersonal city with its tall buildings and stuck-up strangers. She wasn't ready yet to face Hazel's questions and Blanche's good cheer. She remembered the beauty of the Ohio River when she came with John and impulsively asked, "How would I get to the river from here?"

"The streetcar on the corner right over there turns around at the river, but why would you want to go there?" Mrs. Miller thought Verna might have become disoriented by the stress of hearing the visitation rules.

"When I was in Louisville with my husband, he took me down to the river. I found it both peaceful and exciting. I wonder if you would do me a favor."

"If I can," Mrs. Miller agreed, somewhat warily.

"I would appreciate it if you would call my sister, Miss Hazel Gentry, and tell her I've taken the streetcar to the river. I need a quiet place to think. She's at the Brown Hotel. The nice man at the desk can slip a note under her door. Oh, and tell her I won't be late for the train. If she would be so kind as to bring my bag, I'll meet them at the station."

"Are you sure that's what you want to do?" Mrs. Miller wondered if she should try to stop this countrywoman from wandering to the docks, an area some thought not fit for a woman alone.

"I need to let my eyes stretch out so my mind can think. I'm used to hills and wide fields. Everywhere I look in Louisville a building blocks my sight." Verna tried to explain.

"All right. Miss Hazel Gentry, at the Brown Hotel." Mrs. Miller reluctantly agreed to call for Verna, not concurring with her choice but understanding her need.

The women said good-bye as Verna emerged into Louisville's summer heat. Looking over her shoulder as she headed north, she saw the twin towers of the Home. For a moment she thought she heard a child crying and shuddered.

# CHAPTER FORTY

## THINKING BY THE RIVER

Verna hurried as the trolley's whistle announced its arrival. After climbing aboard, she grabbed one of the hanging straps before asking the man standing next to her for directions. "Pardon me. I'm new in town. Does this trolley go by the river?"

"Yes, madam. Although you shouldn't go there by yourself. It's not safe for a lady like you. You're not from around here, are you?" He tipped his hat, looking very serious while cautioning her.

"I'm from Berea, but I will be living here after I start nurses' training in July. At home I go into the mountains when I need to do some serious thinking." Verna stopped. She noticed one of the seated women frowning at her. Verna thought, "She thinks I'm flirting." Her friendliness cooled by the woman's look of disdain, Verna mumbled, "Thank you for your help." She looked away from the obliging stranger. Another younger man tipped his straw hat and offered Verna his seat. She thanked him and gratefully sat on the wooden seat, as the motion of the car made her stomach queasy. She turned deep within her own thoughts, uninterested in the scenery as the streetcar moved jerkily through the center of Louisville and headed north to the river.

"End of the line. All out." The conductor's cry broke Verna's reverie, and she vanquished images of her young children hugging

her knees and begging her not to abandon them. Verna politely
thanked the conductor for the pleasant ride, and he tipped his hat
while cautioning her to be careful around the river. After carefully
debarking so as not to catch the heels of her shoes in the slotted
steps, Verna lifted her head and looked around. The calm river filled
her eyes in all directions, wider than she imagined possible. As she
descended a grassy hill, she glimpsed silver-gray water. Upon getting
closer the water's khaki green color emerged. Her eyes opened in
astonishment as she looked down the river, past the Indiana Bridge,
all the way to Ohio. She wondered if her mother ever stood by this
same river, longing for her lost daughter. She imagined confronting
her mother: "How could you leave us! Did you ever miss us? Why
didn't you write?"

Verna thought, "Now I'm about to do the same thing. Abandon
my children." A familiar inner voice taunted her, "Selfish Verna."
Shaking her head to stop the recriminations, she muttered, "It's not
the same." She looked around to be sure no one heard her. Allowing
the thoughts to flow again, she resumed her internal argument. "I'm
not disappearing forever. I'm trying to make something of myself.
I'm not abandoning my children. I'm bringing them here with me
to Louisville." Then, as often happened when confronted with
unpleasant choices, she moved into fantasy. "We'll have picnics once a
month. I will find a way to bake Son biscuits. And Ellen and Darcine
will be smart in school." Her granny's disapproving face floated out
of the river. Verna could hear her hill twang: "You mustn't leave your
chillun, child." Verna answered the ghost voice back in a way she
never dared while her grandmother lived. "How come you never told
me how I could find my mother? You had no right to keep that secret.
No right."' Her chin jutted out in a stubborn line. She put her hands
over her ears as she continued to scan the busy life along the water.

Boats of all sizes filled the Ohio River that June morning. Flat-
bottom johnboats moved in the current, creating a pocket to capture
the fish. Verna could hear the noise of the cowbells on long poles used
to chase the fish into the nets. Small boats overflowed with nets and
fish while men rowed to bring the catch to market. Large steamboats
brought coal from Pennsylvania to the midland factories and cotton
from up the Mississippi to the eastern mills. Aboard flat barges of
tobacco leaves, laboring men wore frayed straw hats that partially
kept out the hot sun. The barges' painted sides boasted slimmer men

in black top hats smoking fat black cigars whose white rings flowed up into the endless sky's cloud puffs.

Music blaring from a showboat paddling the river serenaded Verna. Hearing the music and seeing men and women promenade on polished wooden decks, Verna fantasized that the *River Queen* captain, upon seeing her, abruptly changed course, brought his boat to shore, and ordered his men to "dispatch the gangplank immediately so this beautiful lady might come aboard." Verna imagined herself in a flowing hoop gown, climbing the stairs to this majestic vessel. Sweeping her skirt to one side, as she entered the boat, the boatswains' heads turned in fascination. Standing on the deck, she waved good-bye to her admirers on the dock. Her eye caught the glance of a man in a white suit as he bowed.

Then hearing Hazel's sharp voice and feeling cold mud ooze into her shoes, Verna returned shore-side from her reverie. "Verna, there you are. Who were you waving at? We've been looking all over the waterfront for you since Mrs. Miller called. She said she tried to stop you. This isn't Berea. You can't wander off by yourself. Good thing some nice people told us where the streetcar stopped."

"Oh, Hazel, there's so much to tell you. I've been accepted into a nursing program, but I can't visit the children except once a month." The words tumbled out of Verna's mouth. She wanted to tell Hazel all the news quickly so she could get back to considering her decision. "I am afraid if I let myself be excited about the acceptance to nursing school, I won't make the right decision for my children. I need to think. So much has happened today. I thought if I could go to the river where I had been with John, he might find me here and tell me what to do. Look, isn't it beautiful?"

"Verna, it looks like a big pond to me. I'm ready to get back on that train where we can talk all the way to Berea. Why, I'm missing the hills already." Hazel had jumped out of the hack and ran ahead of Blanche, who slipped on a muddy patch. Both Hazel and Verna reached out to grab her arms.

Verna began her explanation all over again for Blanche. "I had to think. I thought if I came down here and looked all the way to Ohio, maybe I could figure out what I should do. If I only knew why my mother left, maybe I could figure out if I'm doing right."

Hazel burst in, clearly upset. "Verna, I never wanted to say this before. Everyone knows your mother was the most selfish woman ever lived. There's nobody that would say that about you. You're a good mother. Your mother stole my father, got herself pregnant – and lit out. How can you even think about comparing yourself to your mother!"

Verna flared up in anger. "Hazel, you've no right to say those things to me." Seeing the hurt in Hazel's eyes, Verna wanted to suck the angry words back into her mouth. "I reckon you're right about my mother. Granny used to say those things you just said, and they were about her own daughter. But sometimes I just wish I could talk to my mother. How could she leave me? How can I leave my children?" Verna's eyes filled with tears.

Hazel just put her arms around Verna. This time she simply listened to her sadness. "I'm confused again. Back and forth, knowing I must try to be a nurse. It's our only hope. And then thinking, 'I can't put the children in an orphanage and see them only once a month.'"

At that moment, with river mud seeping in her new shoes and fearing the multitude of birds overhead might do something even worse to her new hat, Blanche cleared her throat. "If we don't start walking up this bank right now to the hack, he might just skedaddle and take that money I gave him to wait. Then we'll miss the train to Berea. There's lots of time on the ride home to talk about this. Look at how those men are staring at us. They're beginning to think we are women with favors to give. Though flattering that any man might still find me interesting, running off with river rats is hardly my idea of an exciting adventure."

Verna started, "Blanche, I'm..." And then she saw her friend's face and knew she was guilty of missing the clues in Blanche's face when she teased. Verna felt daring and decided to go along as if this were a serious debate. "Well, I don't know as I agree with you. I think it might be really lovely to just fly off with those men on their barge and never see Kentucky again."

Tentative giggles turned to laughter as the three companions, with arms around each others' waists and shoes covered in river bank mud, slipped and slid their way up the hill to their waiting driver, who was pleased with the increased fare. As the three friends whisked off to the train station, racing to make the two o'clock Lexington/Berea train, Verna imagined she saw the twin towers of the Home out the hack's back window.

# CHAPTER FORTY-ONE

# HER DECISION

As the train left the Lexington station for the final leg to Berea, the three women supped on chicken legs, coleslaw, sliced tomatoes, small early carrots, boiled salted potatoes, and slices of a delicate flour white cake iced with half a thumb thick of rich, dark chocolate frosting. All packed in a straw hamper, complete with embossed linen napkins, at an unknown cost to Mr. Welch.

As the train sped to Berea, Verna wondered why returning home seemed quicker than the trip leaving home. She became uncomfortably aware that she was looking forward to seeing Clinton and glanced up to see if Hazel had somehow read her mind. Relieved to hear her sister and Blanche talking about a women's rally in Lexington planned for next weekend, she tried to divert herself by thinking about the children. Instead of comforting pictures of the children smiling and welcoming her home, an image of Ellen accusing her of abandoning her children just like her own mother dominated her thoughts. The strength of her images propelled her to interrupt Blanche and Hazel.

"Do you all mind if I join in?" Without waiting for a response Verna began, "I dread telling the children about the orphanage. You simply must help me find the words. Ellen is going to give me the Blue Devil." Like the locomotive pulling her passage car, Verna rushed on.

"You know I told them all that we must move if I'm accepted into the City Hospital Nursing School. Oh, you should have heard Ellen's questions. Now I must tell them I've made the decision to place them in the orphanage. I feel cornered, trapped by their helplessness, just waiting to be sprayed by Ellen's buckshot."

Hazel froze, visualizing Verna with small holes throughout her body. Blanche, seeing Hazel's immobility, reached across her to hold Verna's hands and noticed their icy coldness despite the sweltering railroad car. They had chosen to close their window rather than have coal smoke fill their eyes and coat their clothes with black soot.

Blanche observed, "Now, Ellen might have a sharp tongue, but she's only a small girl. Honey, I know you've been through a lot, but yesterday you stood up to the director of nursing at City Hospital. I think something more than Ellen's sharp tongue is bothering you. Your face looks like you've been sucking lemons."

Verna looked up. "I don't want to put the children in an orphanage. I can't tell them that they will be living at the Home. That there is no other choice just because I want to be a nurse. That's selfish. Just plain selfish." Verna's face flushed.

Never timid, Blanche decided to offer an idea that came to her before the show last night while they sat in the hotel lounge. "How about your father, Verna? He has a big house and his children are all grown now. Maybe he'll take in your children while you study and make up for being so neglectful of you and your brother."

Hazel guffawed. Turning to her, Blanche insincerely reassured, "Hazel, I don't mean to butt into family affairs."

It was all Hazel could do not to retort, "Since when!" But instead she bit down on the inside of her lips, forcing them to stay shut. As Blanche observed Hazel's mouth tightening, she softened her voice. "I know he's your father, too. But Verna told me what a rotter he was, abandoning Verna and her brother. Maybe his heart's warmer now. He seemed solicitous at the funeral. I remember you telling me, Verna, how since John became sheriff, he'd invited you to his 'bigggg' Richmond home every year for the holidays. And how you loved walking down his winding staircase, knowing people were asking, 'Who's that?'"

Hazel relaxed and Verna laughed, not a raucous down-and-out whooping laugh, but a you've-got-to-be-kidding laugh. Verna looked her friend in the eye. "I see my father once a year, maybe twice at most. It's not much, but it's something. I can't risk losing him entirely again. I just can't. But let's be honest. My father will give up his freedom to take care of my children the day your father gives up his bottle."

Blanche hooted, "Oh, that soon. Huh. Well, we better put that plan on ice."

Blanche usually let Hazel's feelings alone, knowing that Hazel shared her thoughts but never her feelings. After the closeness of the two days in Louisville and because of the seriousness of the decisions Verna had to make, Blanche decided to take a risk. "Hazel. I never understood how you could be friends with Verna. After all, your father walked out to marry her mother. Verna talks about her father's neglect of responsibility, but you never do." Blanche regretted her thoughtlessness as Hazel's face scrunched up as if forced to swallow castor oil.

"Blanche," Verna softly cautioned.

"No, it's all right." Hazel's face tightened. Her eyes flashed as bright as a railroad crossing warning, and words sprang out of her tight lips. "I hated Verna. I hated her brothers." Hazel's body relaxed as the poisonous words evaporated without consequences. Given the long strain since John's death's and knowing Verna would be leaving Berea, perhaps never to return, Hazel finally let go of a long-held secret. "Once I even led some friends in taunting her. Remember that, Verna, 'Hillbilly, hillbilly, ain't got no shoes.'"

"I remember, Hazel. But I never knew you took part. I just heard the voices." Verna's fist tightened in her lap before she breathed deeply and relaxed her fingers.

Her story unleashed, Hazel's words rushed forward like Lexington thoroughbreds. "When Mr. Gentry married a third time and had three more children, I began thinking I was hating the wrong person, but I still desperately wanted him to love me. I knew he would have nothing to do with Verna and her brothers, so when I'd see Verna at town gatherings, I'd snub her deliberately. I'd walk up to where she was standing and talk to the person next to her, acting as if she just didn't exist. Even when our father wasn't there, I acted in a way I thought would please him. But I stopped instigating others to ridicule her." Hazel sighed. Blanche realized that was a long speech for Hazel, but from the look on her face there was more to come.

Hazel took out a handkerchief and wiped her eyes. "I think some smoke blew in my face. As long as they lived in the hills and had their granny, people didn't think about them not havin' a mother or father. But when Verna's granny died, I was eighteen and just started teaching school. Tending my students opened up my heart. I started feeling protective of Verna. Everyone knew she and Grover had no family to take care of them. They were like orphans." Hazel sat back on the hard train cushions and looked out the window.

Verna muttered under her breath, "An orphan. I was an orphan. I never thought of myself that way."

Blanche, wanting to break the heavy mood, decided to risk Hazel's rejection and threw her arms around Hazel's shoulders, jarring her from her reverie. "Hazel, you rascal, I knew you couldn't be that good all the time. Guess all three of us had rotters for fathers." Blanche guffawed, evoking a small smile from Hazel's drawn lips.

Verna, stunned to learn it was Hazel who instigated the hurtful teasing, looked wistfully at Blanche. "I remember the first time we swapped stories about our fathers. I told you about my runaway parents and how being poor was the worst possible situation. You looked me straight in the eye and replied, 'The nicest homes hide the wickedest people. Money can be evil's mask.'"

Blanche straightened her shoulders and drew her head straight up. "Verna, when I walked out of my home and away from the back of my father's hand, he told me I'd regret it. I never did." Blanche's eyes wandered from Verna's face to the blurred landscape rushing past. "Sometimes we make the best decision possible in the moment. And never look back."

"Blanche, what if it's not the right decision?" asked Verna in an uncharacteristically whiny voice.

Hazel softly said to her sister, "What if it's the right one? And you don't make it because you fear being wrong?"

Feeling other passengers' stares, she lowered her voice. "Verna, dear Verna, I'm so sorry for the cruel things I said when you were so vulnerable. I've felt guilt every since."

The two sisters looked warily at each other, not sure what it would take to repair their relationship after Hazel's confession. "Hazel, it'll take me a bit. But Lordy, that was a long time ago."

Blanche, uncomfortable with the tension between her two friends, changed the subject. Dramatically raising her voice and oblivious to the stares of others around them, Blanche loudly announced, "Verna, your decision to go to nursing school is right in step with the times. Everything's changing. You feel it. I know you do. This is a time of change for women. England and France are at war with Germany just waiting for us to help out. Women are marching in Washington, determined to get the vote. Other women are marching in their hometowns to close down the taverns. This is a progressive time."

For once Hazel didn't roll her eyes at one of Blanche's speeches. Relieved that Blanche had once again changed the mood, she declared, "Verna, she's right. There's more and more women like me. Women who choose to work because they want to."

"OK," said Blanche. "Let's put all the plans on the fence and see which one is still standing when we get through shooting at them."

That's what they did, from Richmond to Berea, not noticing when the grass turned to tobacco fields and the hills moved into view. When the train reached the Berea station, only one plan survived. Verna would leave Berea. She would go to nursing school in July and she would put the children in the Home in Louisville.

Verna summed up her feelings as they gathered their luggage before debarking to be swept up again by the children, Beulah and Clinton. "Blanche and Hazel, maybe I'll never really know what is the right thing to do for my children. I know I can be a silly dreamer, like back there by the river. But I can't help feeling if I don't do what's right for me I might just..." Verna stopped herself, "No point thinking that."

# CHAPTER FORTY-TWO

## TRAINING TO BE A NURSE

On the first day of July 1916, Verna woke up at six o'clock on a hard cot. She reached for John and her arm met only empty space, dropping until her hand touched the wooden floor. She heard unfamiliar noises. Then she remembered. She was in the student nurses' dormitory at Hawthorne Tuberculosis Hospital. Rubbing crusts of sleep from her eyelashes, she looked around at a room full of rows of cots just like hers, stretching to the far windows where the July sun beamed as if it were high noon. She picked up her watch, a present from Blanche, from a small, white bedside table, bare now except for Verna's black family Bible. It was six-forty-five. Verna sucked in air. She was due in the director's office at seven o'clock.

Awakened by the fullness of her bladder, she couldn't remember where the night attendant indicated the students' bathroom was located. Much as she missed Berea, she didn't miss going outside in the dark to the outhouse. When she arrived at the hospital after ten o'clock last night, an orderly had let her in, gruffly informing her, "I ain't gonna tell on you this time but don't expect it regular."

She recognized his accent and said, "You're from Estes, aren't you?" Verna confided, "I had a hard time saying good-bye to my children because Nanny Marie, she's my youngest, kept pulling on my skirt." She thought being from the hills he might understand.

The shrug of his shoulders made it clear she could have told him a meteor fell on her and he would have displayed the same indifference. His coldness increased her feelings of aloneness and the thought of Clinton crept into her mind. She smiled and the attendant's voice came back to her.

"Go down this hall to the end, turn right, that's the student nurses' dorm. The bathroom's across the hall to the left. Just don't be wakin' anyone up. You hear?" He looked at her as if she were deaf.

"Yes. I thank you." Verna had put on her best smile and the crotchety night attendant eased up enough to offer a quick, "Good night, Miss."

Verna couldn't resist, "It's Mrs. Collins and a good night to you." When Verna quietly entered the dorm, the other students appeared asleep. The noise they made reminded her of sleeping with her grandmother. Granny's snoring had bothered her. She hadn't really thought about what it would be like to sleep with two dozen other women. Aching from the pain of leaving her sobbing younger children at the orphanage, Verna had groped her way to the nearest unoccupied bed, undressed under the covers, and fallen into a fretful sleep.

This morning her feet reached down to the floor to feel for her shoes. Quickly throwing on her robe and grabbing the uniform folded carefully atop her white wooden foot chest, she slipped on her shoes and ran to the door. A cleaning woman, down on her knees scrubbing the hall's floor, ignored Verna's "Good morning" and grudgingly pointed to the bathroom. Verna took the maid's chastising look to mean, "You're one of those lazy ones who'll never make it."

Seven minutes later Verna emerged, straightened her bonnet-style cap, pulled down her wide, white cuffs, and smoothed her striped apron. Holding up her long white skirt, she ran to catch up with a woman whose uniform identified her as another student. "May I walk with you? I'm Verna. I don't know my way yet."

"Hey. Mary Lou's my name. I saw you slip in last night. You sure are brave coming in late our first night."

"Did I miss anything?"

"Just a lecture by the superintendent of nurses." Puffing up her small bosom, Mary Lou mock-scowled at Verna: "'Girls, you are entering a profession to serve our fellow citizens in their time of need. Don't expect to be coddled. You must work hard. The secret of successful nursing is sympathetic attention to detail. Nothing is too small. And remember most of all..." Mary Lou pushed her head forward. "Germs are the enemy!"

Verna couldn't help grinning at her colleague's mimicry of Miss Johnson. Mary Lou enjoyed the attention too much to stop. "Oh, and above all. Don't be late, ever."

"Do you think she noticed I wasn't there? Did she call the roll? Did she say anything?"

"No, she didn't call the roll. I got the feeling she remembered us all from our interviews. Besides, of the new students only four of us are from Hawthorne. She didn't say anything, but from her talk on detail, I'd bet my horse she knew. You should have heard her scold one of the new student nurses for having a smudge of dirt on her shoes." Without stopping for a breath or changing her merry expression, Mary Lou rushed on, "I heard you have children and you lost your husband."

"People sure do talk. Thanks for the warning." Verna wasn't about to start talking to a perfect stranger about John's death no matter how friendly the person seemed. Verna's face assumed a seemingly welcoming smile that her friends knew meant someone had come too close.

Verna and Mary Lou entered a ward filled with patients, where the other Hawthorne Tuberculosis Hospital student nurses clustered tightly around a bed. In the center stood Miss Johnson, who, although smaller than most of the young women, seemed to take up more space than any two of them. Verna observed the unnatural silence of these young women and how no one even raised a hand to greet them.

Verna and Mary Lou joined the group without being acknowledged, just making it on time as Miss Johnson's decisive voice addressed the group. "Good morning, students. Now your work and learning begin. I won't repeat what I said last night to the entire class when you all gathered at City Hospital, only to add that next year a third of you will be gone and three years from now only half of you will graduate – out of the entire class of twenty-four, here at Hawthorne and at City, only twelve of you will make it. Nursing is not for the fainthearted or the light-minded. Today I leave you in the good hands of Miss Duggan, Hawthorne's supervising nurse. Your classes begin this evening. I expect you at City Hospital at seven p.m. sharp. Good day."

Verna noticed that Miss Johnson looked each student in the eye as she spoke. Verna thought she glared at her during her turn to be inspected. Throughout Miss Johnson's brief words, Verna anticipated a reprimand. Instead, Miss Johnson stopped at the back where Verna stood with Mary Lou, and said, as if to an acquaintance, "I hope your children settled in to your satisfaction."

Verna could feel the other students wanting to stare at her but afraid to turn their necks. "Yes, ma'am. Thank you for asking," was all she managed to reply.

After Miss Johnson left, Verna noticed another woman in a supervisor's outfit in the midst of the student nurses, previously rendered invisible by the magnetism of Miss Johnson's presence.

"Hello. Welcome. I'm Miss Duggan. I'm so glad you will be with us at Hawthorne. This is our first year of affiliation with Louisville City Hospital. We hope to show them, through you and your work, how valuable this affiliation is. Remember at all times you are to address the doctors with respect. If they ask you anything, you are to respond, "Yes, Doctor."

Miss Duggan smiled while her eyes seemed to catch the light from the window. "I remember my first days as a student. Please ask me questions. Don't be afraid. Our patients are most in need of loving care. Many of them may never get better. Today I will show you how to make a bed when the patient isn't well enough to get up, how to feed a patient, and how to scrub an area so that it is germ free. You will work in groups of three on our wards. Each one of you will have at least twenty patients. It will be hard work, but there are so many good souls in need of our care."

She then turned to the patient lying quietly in the bed where the student nurses clustered. "Good morning, Mr. Grimes. Thank you for helping me teach these young women." She set about gently raising his body on one side and then the other, slipping out the bottom sheet, putting on a new one. She asked them to look carefully while she tucked in the corners, all the time talking soothingly to Mr. Grimes. Touched by Miss Duggan's caring, Verna listened carefully, noting the importance her teacher placed on leaving no wrinkles in the sheets. She thought how carelessly she had tended the bed where for hours John lay dying. She wondered if the creases felt like razors.

# CHAPTER FORTY-THREE

## A MONTH PASSES

The first month passed in a blur. Verna's knees hurt from kneeling to scrub the large patient dormitory rooms. She resented that student nurses filled in for attendants at times. Her arms ached and even trembled from the exertion of lifting patients. During the first week she almost quit, twice. Once, when she realized she was required to wash floors, just as if she'd never left Berea, and the second time when a male patient grabbed her breast. As she screamed out, a smirking attendant cautioned her, "Don't seem as if you have anything he would want. Just don't tempt him by bending down so close."

Sometimes all that kept her going was the drive to secure Miss Johnson's approval. In mid-July, a new nurse came on duty at the Hawthorne Hospital. Younger than Verna by ten years, she proudly showed the new students her certificate of graduation. Verna pictured herself addressing a group of nurse students, showing her own certificate and lightheartedly boasting; "Older women with children can graduate, too."

Classes lasted for three hours each night. Verna and the other Hawthorne students would rush to Louisville City Hospital, frequently eating as they walked from tins of biscuits and cold, congealed meat of an indistinguishable texture and taste. One of the younger nurses said they were being fed rat meat since Louisville's huge rats scurried everywhere.

Verna fell asleep the first night during the anatomy class as the lecturer droned on until after ten o'clock. Mary Lou punched her back just before the doctor looked up from his recitation of every bone in the human foot.

As July ended, Verna began a rotation at Louisville City Hospital. The teaching atmosphere dramatically differed from the increasing support she had felt from Miss Duggan at Hawthorne Tuberculosis Hospital. No matter how simple the task, she couldn't do it right. The omnipresent Miss Johnson noted each wrinkle, each speck of dust, each water glass unfilled. Each offense received a sniff through the nose, a forward thrust of the head, and then an icy, "Again. That is not satisfactory." To her humiliation, Verna had to remake one bed three times while all the student nurses were summoned to observe what they should never do.

The other supervising nurses seemed to pick up their cue from Miss Johnson that Verna just wasn't "City Hospital" quality. When she thought she had learned how to make a proper "City Hospital" bed, she was put in her place.

"Mrs. Collins, you would think a woman of your age needn't be told how to make a bed proper. Tighter, tighter. Take that wrinkle out. Redo that corner." Making beds, pouring water, helping patients eat overcooked food so they wouldn't choke became tasks Verna learned to do precisely the same way each time. "Wrinkles in the bed cause bedsores. Do that again, Mrs. Collins." "Water mustn't stand around too long in this heat, Mrs. Collins. Fill that pitcher again." "Do you see this dirt on the window ledge, Mrs. Collins? Germs, germs, germs. Wipe it hard again. It's not a baby's face."

Early on, Verna noticed that some nurses steered clear of certain patients while pampering others. The patients in private rooms got the best care, except for the aldermen's mistresses, who were avoided because of disdain for their sexually acquired diseases. Patients in the poorest hospital wards waited the longest for their care. Verna began spending time with them after she noticed the servings of thinned broth without any meat from the bone. The neglect of those who had so little tarnished the shine of the profession to which she aspired. Ashamed that even in a hospital, patients with money received better treatment, she tried to offset the neglect by bringing leftovers from the kitchen, remembering the patients' names, asking about their families, and spending precious minutes gently cleansing a patient's bedsores.

Although none of the hospital supervisors praised her, Verna felt confident in her skills with patients and their families. Verna learned early in life how to make people comfortable. Now she prepared to comfort the sick. She remembered Miss Duggan's kindness. Her teacher's model and Verna's intense memory of her own loneliness and anxiety as John lay dying in her arms combined to bring Verna's best graces to the bedside. She knew when to smile and just how broadly. She knew when to talk and when to listen. She knew how to make flattery seem truth.

Whether at Hawthorne or Louisville City Hospital, Verna, like a well-trained hunting dog, ferreted out the sickest patients. She instinctively knew how to soothe family members. Toward the end of the first month of training, Miss Johnson took her to one of the wards for the dying. "This is your assignment for the day. Do what you can to make the patients comfortable and be available if the ward's supervising nurse needs you."

Across the room, somewhat obscured by a pillar, lay a man whose thin arms, lying outside the sheet, looked like birch bark. Without being told by the ward supervisor, Verna headed toward his bed just like Rex headed toward his stall.

She passed without stopping for several other patients who yelled out or whispered requests; "Drink, Nurse." "Turn me on my back. Please, Nurse."

When she arrived by his side, he struggled to tell her something, but his weak breath failed to push the words out. From the mother within her came the knowledge of what he needed. She cradled his frail body in her arms and gently raised his upper body to a sitting position. He coughed. Weakly at first, then more viciously. Then once more, freeing the blood-tinged mucus caught in his throat. "Thank you, Nurse. I couldn't breathe."

Although the man appeared old and frail, Verna, looking more closely, saw a man in his late thirties, aged by his long illness. His wife sat by his side, weeping silently, not knowing what to do or how to comfort him. The film covering his eyes signaled his imminent death. As she watched, she saw John's blood expelled from the man's mouth as her patient exhaled a final breath. She touched his wife gently on the shoulder, "He's at peace. You did everything you could." Attending only to the crying woman, she didn't notice Miss Johnson watching her from across the room.

# CHAPTER FORTY-FOUR

## THE FIRST VISIT

Verna woke, joyful her first month had finally ended. Why couldn't July be thirty days like June, not thirty-one? The picture in the drawer beside her bed was stained with fingerprints and salt from her tears. No longer so afraid to let her fellow student nurses know about her family and the loss of John, she proudly displayed the picture taken after his death. Nanny Marie standing so straight with her angel face and folded hands. Son looking as if he would jump off the page if Verna didn't have her hand on his shoulder. Her fellow students' comments swelled her head. "Oh, what handsome children." "fine-looking children." "Four. I come from eleven." But even kind words didn't ease her guilt.

Verna worried about this first visit with her children. Would they be mad at her? Had they been treated well? Did they get enough to eat? First she'd decide all was well. She'd imagine them happier than since John's death. After all, now Ellen didn't have to watch the other children. Son had other boys with whom to play. Then, the image changed. She saw the children alone, wistfully waiting for her and John to return to them.

Darcine's face melted until it looked like Verna's face, after Granny died, standing alone at her new school, not knowing anyone.

To silence her doubts, Verna nervously brushed her now shoulder-length hair vigorously, distracting herself with blows to her scalp.

She cut her hair the second day in training after Miss Johnson's lecture on germs, and also to save time each morning. Crying softly for the thick, dark hair crumpled on the floor, she heard John's pleas. "Grow your hair longer, Verna. I love to watch it fall down your back." Once she actually felt his touch again and imagined he had come over while she brushed. In her mind her hair hung long again. He touched her hair gently, caressing from the top of her head to her waist, bringing a handful to his lips and kissing a strand. Now he didn't have to hurry. He moved his arm around her waist, gently lifted her to the bed, laughingly interrupting her strokes. "There's no point in having to brush twice."

Visions of early morning lovemaking were intruding more frequently since she left their home, where the bloodstains on the barn floor and the bed presented constant reminders of his last hours. She admonished herself. "Stop it, Verna. Today you'll visit with the children. Shame on you."

She hummed "Safer My Lord in Thee," while quickly finishing dressing. Even though no longer dressing in hopes of eliciting comments like, "Ah, doesn't the sheriff's wife look nice tonight," she dressed thoughtfully, mindful of Director Johnson's judgmental eye. Verna opened her bedside-table drawer and withdrew a plain, cream-colored handkerchief, crumpled as if used. From a tied corner she removed four pennies to give each child a penny and a quarter for Ellen to buy extras throughout the month -- all the money left after paying installments on her debts. She spent less than ten cents a month on herself. The hospital provided nothing free to the students except one meal a day.

Verna felt pride in the twenty-nine cents saved from her one dollar, eighty-three cents, monthly student allowance. "See, Granny, I didn't forget all you've taught me. I just put it aside for a little bit." She laughed, noting, "Why, I'm talking to all kinds of folks this morning, first John, then the Lord, and now Granny."

Picking up the small packet of letters posted from her children, she untied a yellow ribbon meant to encourage privacy. Verna riffled through the well-worn pages one last time so she could be sure to let the children know how she appreciated the messages.

Verna smiled as each message revealed the small writer's

personality in words or pictures. Ellen's letters with their heavily underlined words trumpeting what her mother could do better were read quickly. "You should write Son more. He seems unhappy, Ma. Your daughter, Ellen." Darcine's much-read pages with hearts around the side were smeared from Verna's moist-lip kisses. "Ma, we had a good supper last night. Their biscuits aren't as good as yours. I got a one hundred in arithmetic today. The teacher said I was better than most boys. I love you, Ma."

Nanny Marie sent pencil scribbles on odd-sized scraps of paper. Verna, unsure what they represented, noted an adult had written "my mother" on the bottom of several. Sketches of guns filled Son's pages, except for one stark message on a crumpled page, "I want to come home." Verna felt the sadness return as she reread Son's letter, knowing he didn't understand they no longer had a home.

During the month Verna alternated between images of her children making new friends, going to school, and playing merrily with vivid mind pictures of Nanny Marie falling down tall marble stairs or Darcine choking and unable to breathe from something caught in her throat. Verna's screams at night from her vivid dreams of John awakened the small group of Hawthorne student nurses who wiped her sweating brow, held her trembling hands, and learned to catch her vomit in a bedpan before it spattered all over the floor. The nightmares had started shortly after John's death but the vomiting was new. Verna's stomach ached most days. She wondered if she was getting an ulcer from all her worrying. Gently wrapped and held in caring arms, she still told no one of the repeated nightmares of her husband's murder.

When the children's letters came, Verna knew that they, too, had not forgotten. She briefly allowed herself to feel their unhappiness before forcing herself to focus on her duties for the day. She reassured herself, "They'll be all right. They'll be all right. Someone would call if they weren't."

Looking at Son's letter, she recalled a last view of her children. While kissing each one good-bye outside Miss Johnson's office, Son suddenly grabbed her like a sucking leech. Verna couldn't peel him off her leg. A matron removed him, crying and flailing his arms and legs. Nanny Marie then stuck her smallest finger in her mouth while her eyes became robin-egg orbs. Darcine tried to reassure her mother they would be all right. Verna put her fingers in her ears when Ellen yelled, "'I won't stay. You can't do this.'"

Verna slipped on the inexpensive black dress that had become her Sunday outfit. Despite suffocating in the stifling August air, Verna determined she would wear mourning clothes every Sunday for one year. As she put on the dress, the garment slipped easily down her body rather than needing to be tugged.

With no mirror in the nurses' dorm, Verna had stopped looking at her body. She only surveyed her face in the bathroom mirror to position her cap correctly. But today the droop of her dress revealed lost voluptuousness. Following John's death the previously lush parts of her body had shed pounds like a dog shaking off creek water following a swim. Since coming to Hawthorne, hard muscles replaced her slackening flesh and hid the gauntness of her arms.

She nodded to several student nurses while leaving the dorm and signed out at the supervisor's office for her weekly half-day off. This Sunday was different than the previous three when she had no place to go and spent the time in church and then under a tree, fanning herself to stay cool as she studied her anatomy textbook. Today she would see her children. She wouldn't just walk by the orphanage as she did each chance she had, hoping to get a glance of them. Today she would hug each one so tight that she could feel their little bodies melt into her heart.

Well wishes followed her down the hall to the sunlight. "Good day." "Good morning." "Have a nice day off." "Kiss them for me" came from Mary Lou, who had squeezed every detail from Verna about John's death and the children. Verna decided that Mary Lou's curiosity reflected genuine caring rather than an attempt to shame Verna. Separated by twelve years and unfathomable depths of events, Verna and Mary Lou ran together like Licking Creek and the Kentucky River. The younger woman looked to Verna for the sturdiness of endurance and Verna reached out to Mary Lou for energy and carefree moments.

Verna's eyes squinted as she left the shade of the hospital and emerged into Louisville's glaring light. Traffic noises so overwhelming they hurt her ears on that first visit with Hazel and Blanche now seemed muffled by a woolen blanket, compared with the constant clang of bedpans, orderlies' yells, carts, and the parade of people in the hospital.

Excitement blended with caution as she navigated the streets, always heading toward the twin towers. Soon she heard the chimes of St. James announcing the end of the early morning church services. She was on Albany Street, just three blocks from the Home and her children. She began to skip, not caring if others looked. "Oh, John. The children mustn't see me cry. I mustn't cry. I mustn't."

The children waited for her in the hall. The girls dressed in the same tan cotton muslin material and identical white worn but freshly polished shoes. Son wore short dark blue pants and a white shirt with white socks slipping down into his shoes. With his short chopped-off hair, he looked like every other boy she passed. The four children stood as straight as pieces on a chessboard. Ellen resembled the white knight as her head stuck forward and her arms embraced Nanny Marie's pawn-shaped body. Darcine, solid as the white castle, attempted to contain the queen's prancing horse, with a tight grasp on Son's right hand.

Son broke from Darcine and ran into his mother's knees, almost knocking her to the floor. Tears glistened on his cheeks. Verna crouched down and hugged her young boy, comforting him with pats and kisses, "Now, now. I'm here, Son." Her eyes began to mist over. She felt relief, and then an overwhelming sense of what would be lost again too soon. She ran her fingers through his hair.

"Ma, they cut my hair. I cried. They said it would keep the bugs away." Son looked at his mother woefully.

"Son, you look just as handsome as ever." Verna gave him an extra-long hug.

"Ma, you're late." Ellen scowled.

"I'm not, Ellen. Now, don't you start on me." Verna bent down and kissed Nanny Marie who remained still by Ellen's side. "Ellen and Darcine, show me where your classes are. I didn't get to see them before." Three of the children competed to hold her hands. Verna reached down to pick up Nanny Marie in her right arm, took Son's hand with her left, and asked Darcine to grab her elbow and Ellen to show them the way.

Son, putting his hands on his mother's cheeks, looked at her through saltwater eyes. "Ma, I don't like it here. They won't let me see Darcine, Ma. I told them she always takes care of me. But they just keep saying I'm a boy and have to stay with the boys. Tell them, Ma. Tell them I need to be with Darcine. Please, Ma."

"Shush, Son. Now don't cry. I'll talk with them about letting you see your sisters more. I'll see what we can do. But for now, let's just have a good time. I want you to show me everything and let me meet your friends." Verna put on a smile and began to feel a little happiness.

"I don't have any friends."

"Of, course you do, Son." Unwilling to let go of her too-short good feelings, Verna took lightly her son's complaints.

"No, I don't."

Verna didn't know what to say. Her small boy, usually so confident, clung to her. In the past she expected to peel him off the branch of an apple tree, not her arms. To still her rapid heartbeat, she stopped to catch her breath. Verna feared Son would lose his exuberance. She stopped, putting him down so she could look into his eyes.

"Son, tell me what's the trouble, boy. This isn't like you. What would your pa think?"

Ellen smoothed Son's rumpled hair and answered her mother because Son's sobbing muffled his words. "Ma, he's so lonesome. He's used to being with us. The matrons won't even let him sit in the dining room with us. The big boys call him Crybaby. After Darcine and I talked to the boys, they stopped. But Ma, he is lost here."

Darcine noticed her mother's pinched mouth and chimed in with her sweet voice to head off an argument between Ellen and her mother. "Ma, you know Son wiggles a lot. You and Pa are always after him to get off the kitchen table, not to run about and just hold still. Here you don't even have to run. The matrons yell at children just for wiggling. They're nice to us. But, Ma, they want us to be a way Son just can't be."

Verna looked at her heartbroken son and thought how like her brother Grover he was. Always squirming or talking. She and John just got used to it, she reckoned. She'd have to speak with Miss Ford. The director must know that boys are different than girls and some boys even more so. She'd also speak with that nice Mrs. Miller. Verna remembered how during the interview the associate nurse, Mrs. Miller, seemed to understand what it felt like to be a mother.

"Now, Son, get down and walk. I'll talk to Miss Ford. You'll get to see your sisters more. Sooner than you think, you'll be feeling better and have lots and lots of friends." Verna's face lost its wrinkles. Her shield of denial slipped back in place. She decided the school's discipline would help Son learn to be a man since he didn't have a father to show him the way.

The family passed children of all sizes. A group of girls tossed "Hey's to Ellen and Darcine. Verna's daughters smiled and said "Hey" back. As in Berea, Verna took pleasure in her older girls' popularity. Two girls, Darcine's age, stopped and asked, "Is this your ma?" clearly angling for an introduction. Children touched Verna's hand or her skirt. They stood close to her, absorbing her motherly warmth. Verna couldn't resist hugging a small girl whose thin arms hung listlessly from pale stooping shoulders. Nanny Marie pushed the small girl with thin arms away, declaring, "My mother."

To break the awkwardness Verna decided to give her children their small gifts but wanted privacy. "Children, show me where you sleep. Girls first." Ellen piped up, "We're not allowed to go into the dormitories during the day, unless we're sick."

Verna resisted expressing annoyance at Ellen's bossy tone.

"Now, Ellen, I'm sure it'll be fine since I'm with you."

"If we get in trouble..." Ellen started.

"You won't get in trouble, but if anyone says something, I'll say it was my request." Verna bit the side of her mouth to stop her growing crossness with Ellen.

The Collins family walked down the hall, conscious of the stares of mother-hungry children, and slipped into the empty dormitory. Feeling thin horsehair mattresses, Verna bent over to smell if the beds were aired regularly. In Berea Verna had aired her children's beds monthly even in the winter and beat the dust from them twice a year as they hung on the backyard clothesline.

Verna brought the handkerchief from the depths of her dress side pocket and unwrapped the precious coins. Honoring Ellen's place as oldest, she gave her coins first. Ellen thanked her mother politely, then closed her fist around both her penny and the quarter, then watched carefully to see if Darcine's gift was better. Nanny Marie turned her penny over and over in her hand, feeling its cool smoothness. Verna went to each child's bed as they carefully tucked each penny into a hideaway nook. She noticed Ellen kept the quarter tightly grasped in her left hand.

As they left the girls' dormitory, Son ran ahead to the boys' sleeping area, eager for his prized coin. By the time they caught up with him, he had found a small hole in his mattress into which he slipped the precious coin. Squeezing his mother's neck as she bent over to see the hiding place, he whispered in her ear, "Thank you, Ma. It's my best present ever."

Stopping briefly to see the dining room with places for three hundred children, Verna commented on the noise made by clinking spoons and chatter. Darcine looked at her. "We're not allowed to talk in here, Ma. The dining room is for eating."

Ellen led them down the hall to a dressmaking room filled with mannequins and tables strewn with patterns, cut material, scissors, and multiple spools of colored thread. Closing the door quietly, Ellen brought her mother to a table that she identified as her workspace. "Ma, I like making my clothes. Here's a dress I'm making for Nanny Marie." She held up the half-sewn garment for her mother's inspection.

"Ellen, what perfectly straight stitches. Why, if I didn't know better, I'd swear this dress is straight from the fine goods' section of Welch's department store." Verna beamed sincerely in her praise of her daughter's accomplishment. Before they left the room, Ellen, using sturdy, black thread, sewed the quarter into the hem of her dress.

Son walked so close to his mother that Verna kept bumping into his small figure as the family walked down the long corridor. A boy, about Son's age, came over and asked him to play ball. Son grabbed his mother's hand and loudly answered, "No thank you, my ma is visiting today."

Verna turned to him, "Son, that's perfectly all right. You won't hurt my feelings if you go and play with your friend."

"He's not my friend. And I don't want to play." Verna momentarily felt pleased that her son preferred her company to a ball toss game. Her thought quickly vanished, replaced by regret. "How sad, my boy who loved nothing more than to play all day. How shall we survive this separation?'" To push away her sadness Verna thoughtlessly asked the ball-tossing boy, "Where is your mother today?"

"She's home, ma'am." Then he ran down the hall as if caught by an unexpected windstorm.

One of the attendants came up to Verna. "I hope he wasn't bothering you."

"No, not at all. I'm Verna Collins."

"Yes, I know. I recognized you. Your daughter, Darcine, is the spitting image of you as a young girl. I'm Miss Sweetwater from over Webster way. I knew your father, Mr. Gentry. Used to work in his store occasionally when he needed extra help until I lost my husband. You must be proud of your children. Fine looking they are, and your girls are so well behaved. Never had children myself, but my husband was a Mason and they helped me secure this position. Can't much say I like Louisville. Bet you are missin' the hills, too."

Verna sighed. "I'm missing a lot I loved." The women let their hands touch each others' arms in a brief embrace before self-consciously moving away. Looking around, Verna saw only a few women with children clustered around them. "Where are the children's parents?"

"Most of their mothers live too far away. It takes a right lot of money to come to Louisville."

Verna agreed, and uncharacteristically confided in this stranger, "My children could have stayed with relatives, but I wouldn't have been able to see them except once a year. But it's so sad. How do the children stand not seeing their mothers?"

"Most get used to it. Some even have it better here than they ever did at home. They get chances they never might 'a got. Wish I'd had these chances. Maybe I'd have made more of myself." The attendant looked wistful as she continued folding the countless sheets in a pile before her, fresh with the smell of drying in the air.

"Who is that girl?" Verna indicated a young girl, probably ten years old, standing apart from the others. An ill-fitting dress hung on her small body while thick waves of brown hair surrounded her porcelain face. Motionless except for round green eyes, the child scrutinized each adult woman who passed her place of vigilance. Verna recognized in the girl's cocked head and restless eyes her own lifelong search for her mother. Remembering how her hearing sharpened as she strained to hear her mother's footsteps, she knew the wishful longing of this orphan girl. "Maybe today she'll come."

The visit passed so quickly, Verna started when the tower bell announced four o'clock as if each chime rang a word: "Time-To-Leave-Now." Verna stopped in Miss Ford's office as she promised the children. Seeing the principal's empty desk, Verna asked a passing matron about Miss Ford's whereabouts and was informed she would be back shortly. As the front door slammed repeatedly, signaling the departure of visiting mothers, Verna thought she heard a hum like cicadas before the fullness of their night's cry. She recognized the sounds as children's sniffles.

Miss Ford turned the corner, saw Verna standing by her office door, and hurried to her. "Mrs. Collins, did you have a nice visit?" She hurried on, wanting to reassure Verna with good news. "I'm getting excellent reports about your girls, particularly from Darcine's teacher."

"Hello, Miss Ford. Yes, it was a lovely visit, but too short. Too short." Verna sighed. "The girls seem to be doing fine. I appreciate you putting Nanny Marie close to Ellen in the dormitory. She's so little and her big sis means so much to her." Verna paused as her tone changed from pleasant to serious. "I need to talk with you about Son. He's unhappy..."

Miss Ford abruptly interrupted Verna as if she were a runaway horse needing a firm jerk on the bit. "Mrs. Collins, your boy has no discipline. I don't know how you managed him. He must learn to sit still and do what he's told."

Despite her previous struggles with Son's behavior, Verna pounced to the defense of her male cub. "Son is a good boy. He misses his father and he's lonesome for me. But you must realize he's never been separated from his sisters. They are all used to sleeping together. Darcine was like a second mother to him."

"That's not how we do it here. Girls are with girls. Boys are with boys. After all we don't want any...in-ci-dents." Miss Ford dragged out the word so long Verna thought she'd turn purple from breathlessness. "It works better this way" spilled out of her mouth like bitter sulfur water.

"It doesn't work better for Son." When it came to her children, Verna could fight like the last dog in the ring. Then remembering her granny's admonishment that you get more bees with honey, Verna lowered her voice: "You know a lot about children. Of course, I respect your rules, but I'm hoping you will find a way to let Son spend more time with his sisters, particularly Darcine. He'll be a better boy for it and save your staff some troubles." Lowering her voice to show the proper respect, Verna added, "I would appreciate it."

"Mrs. Collins, you know we have three hundred children here. I can't believe the tragedies that are befalling families. Thank heavens for the generosity of the Brotherhood. You have to trust we know best.

I personally think your boy needs discipline, not coddling." Miss Ford raised her hand and pointed her finger at Verna.

Verna tightened her jaw. "But you will try. You will try to let him have more time with Darcine? He's such a small boy. He always did what his father said. There never was any trouble when John was around. Darcine is so loving. Son calms right down 'round her. All I ask is that you try to let him be with his sisters more." Verna looked at Miss Ford's jaw and then her eyes. It reminded Verna of the time she tried to lead an old mule up the final slope of a hill. After repeated failures, she stopped tugging his rope and tied him to a tree, sat herself on the ground, and waited until he started braying from hunger. Then she untied him and let him lead her the rest of the way.

Verna didn't have time to continue arguing with Miss Ford; she must return to the hospital. She quietly thanked Miss Ford for listening, adding in her sweetest voice, "Mr. Neiman – you remember, he's the master of the Berea Lodge – asked me to write him about the children's first month in the Home. He'll be so pleased to hear how well the girls are doing. I will tell him we spoke about Son." Verna paused and looked the older woman square in the eyes. "Son was always his favorite." Verna paused again, hoping Miss Ford would indicate a softening of her position. The ensuing silence left Verna with the same apprehension that follows the thunderous clap of a sudden summer storm.

Looking down, Verna muttered, "I must go now." Biting the inside of her lip so she wouldn't yell at this childless woman, she turned slowly, counting each step to calm herself as she walked the long hallway to the front door. She managed only a quick good-bye to Mrs. Miller, afraid her mounting anger would run away with her manners.

Before stepping outside, Verna rejected the impulse to turn back, sweep her children up in her arms, and run. Turning around, she saw Miss Ford still standing outside her office. Further down the hall Darcine, Son, and Nanny Marie stood side by side, waving slowly. Beside them Ellen remained motionless, arms at her side. Verna trembled as her oldest child's anger radiated the silent message, "Can't you do anything right!"

This time Verna agreed with Ellen. She had failed to protect them – again.

# CHAPTER FORTY-FIVE

## ANNIVERSARY

On November 8th, 1916, in the early morning, the first anniversary of John's death, Verna slipped out of the hospital, intent upon seeing her children regardless of the Orphanage's rules on visitation. She needed to hold them. An unmerciful wind off the Ohio River whipped down the street, sending orange and brown leaves in a tumble. Verna wrapped a black shawl around her head. The cold made her eyes water. At the curb she shook her head, as if disagreeing with an unseen companion. Crossing the street she cried out, alarming an elderly man who asked if she were all right. She merely nodded and continued walking.

Verna arrived at the front door of the Orphanage. Finding it locked, she realized, "Oh, of course. It's not Sunday." She headed for the trade entrance. Passing a window, she heard children's voices from the dining room and smelled warm food. She envisioned her own kitchen with the children around the oak table, making biscuit-dough shapes. Suddenly the image changed. The dough began to shed drops of blood. Images of John bleeding on the kitchen table morphed into a slow-motion vision of her husband, slumped over Rex's mane, blood running down his back. She blinked and the image vanished. But then it returned and kept fading and returning. Each image the same.

The vision of John's blood-soaked back had been occurring less and fading quicker since she boarded the train to Louisville for her nursing interview. And the memory flashes seemed less vivid. Now, the horrific scenes of his death unfolded in her mind and wouldn't stop. John's blood spreading became her reality, more present than the cars and buggies starting to fill the morning streets.

She began talking to him. "Where are you? Show me a sign. Let me know you are here with me. I miss you so." The pain of his betrayal had settled into a dull ache; her anger dissipated. The loss of his tender attention remained unbearable as she longed for his caress. The void in her life before nursing school returned. "Why am I feeling helpless again? I can't go through that pain again." Crying and confused, she ran, paying no attention to what direction she fled.

The bells of St. James's church began to ring, reminiscent of her first visit to the Orphanage. Today she heard the chimes calling to her. She slowed down, walking deliberately toward the tolling sounds as light snow fell around her. Her visibility diminished, lost in swirling white flakes, she followed her ears, not trusting her blinded eyes.

The bells pealed louder as she stumbled up the church steps, lightly covered with the ashen gray of city snow. The heavy door yielded easily to her newly acquired physical strength. Lowering her head to bow to the cross, she slipped into a pew in the next to last row and looked up to find an altar ablaze with candles. For a moment she wondered about the church's denomination before deciding she didn't care. A black-frocked priest swung a golden ball that emitted a pungent smell. She knelt and asked God to stop the repetitive scenes of John's death.

At first nothing changed, despite her repeated, "Please, God, make the pictures stop." The soundless replay of John, slowly bending over Rex with blood pooled on his back and crimson drops the size of grapes falling to the ground, continued. She saw Ellen's mouth open in a scream: "Pa!" Then blood seeped into John's shirt and fell on Nanny Marie's feet, over and over.

"Forgive us our sins, as we forgive..." Voices from the congregation entered Verna's consciousness, causing her to open a prayer book and vainly search for the passage. The words blurred. The pictures in her head continued until a gentle touch on her shoulder caused her to start.

"You cried out."

"Oh, I'm so sorry."

"Please, come with me."

"No, I can't. I won't be a bother."

"You're not a bother. I'm not doing the service this morning. God brought you here for a reason. Please come."

Verna didn't protest. Her dissociated legs stood up and followed a different priest than the one remaining at the altar. They silently moved down a side aisle through a smaller chapel, past the choirs' changing room, into an arched hallway, until they finally reached the rectory.

"I'm Father Vernon, the assistant minister. Please come into my office. We can talk there. I believe you are new to our congregation. Let the Lord comfort you."

For the next hour Verna told Father Vernon about John's death, her children, and the visions. She shared the alarming details that made her fear madness – the pool of blood on John's back that seemed alive, her thoughts while holding him in her arms, and the mucus leaving his mouth as he lay dying. She even shared losing the baby and John's unfaithfulness. Father Vernon listened carefully without interruption or judgment.

"Mrs. Collins, may I tell you of others who suffered like you?"

Verna nodded her consent.

The minister began in a soft, soothing voice, careful not to get too close to the widow lest he startle her. "A widow, much like yourself, a good woman who loved her husband, saw him fall from their barn roof to his death. She came to me for comfort from her visions. Like you, she saw his fall – over and over. The Lord took her pain and helped ease her suffering. I have met with soldiers from the camp whose memories of their fallen comrades' deaths repeat over and over. You are not crazy, my dear. You have seen something so terrible your mind refuses to accept the truth. The image repeats over and over, trying to find a way to undo what it cannot accept. You did nothing to cause his death, nor could you have prevented it. Only time and the Lord will heal you." After concluding, he blessed her.

"The pictures have stopped for now. Thank heavens," Verna quietly told the priest. Looking about her, Verna noticed she was in a small office warmed by a coal fire and encircled with books. When Father Vernon offered a cup of tea, she held the warm cup in her hands for comfort before sipping.

"Thank you for your kindness." Verna put her head down, trying to hide her tears. If the minister noticed, he didn't say anything. Relieved he didn't touch her, Verna allowed more tears to flow. As she finished and wiped her eyes, a weight, heavy as wet laundry, shifted in her chest, allowing her normal breathing to return.

For the next hour they talked: Verna, about nursing school and her children; the young Episcopal minister about his family still living in the hills. They even talked about politics. Verna found herself telling the kind minister about her disappointment that the Kentucky House defeated women's suffrage by only one vote, 45 to 46. And was surprised when he responded, "That's why we need women to vote. So we can get rid of the fools."

As her mood lightened, Verna shared with him some of Blanche's antics as a suffragette and they both laughed. He told Verna about the appointment of Justice Brandeis to the U.S. Supreme Court and how maybe it would mean fairness for all regardless of their color or religion. He walked her to the door of the church and cautioned, "Watch your step." The light snow over, a weak November sun filtered through the coal smoke of the city.

"Come back and see us. Let God comfort you here." The minister smiled pleasantly.

Verna turned and waved, holding her skirt up to avoid the dusting of snow. "I will. You've been so kind." She politely returned the minister's smile, knowing she would never return to a place where a stranger knew her secrets.

Back at the hospital Verna went straight to Miss Johnson's office, expecting to receive punishment for missing the day. As she entered Miss Johnson's office, the older woman looked up. "Miss Johnson," Verna started.

Keeping her eyes down on the paperwork in front of her, Miss Johnson spoke in the voice she used to soothe patients. "Verna, it's all right. You need not say anything. Father Vernon called. I don't know what you told Father Vernon, but he said you would be an excellent nurse. He recommended I not punish you for today. I trust his judgment." Then Miss Johnson looked up directly into Verna's eyes: "We shall speak no more of this. If you are up to it, Mary Lou could use some relief. She's in the maternity ward." Miss Johnson looked down again and continued her work..

"Yes, ma'am." Verna turned and left. Surprised by the compassion in Miss Johnson's eyes and relieved she wasn't to be punished, she hurried to the ward. Verna noticed that for once the voices in her head were silent.

# CHAPTER FORTY-SIX

## PAIN

Five months later Verna woke with a pain in her left side. Rubbing the aching spot, she dismissed the continuing discomfort. She decided she must have lain on her arm at some point during the night. From midnight on, she barely slept, unable to find a comfortable spot on her small cot. Her body felt feverish and achy. After taking her temperature around 4:00 and finding it normal, she gave up trying to sleep and lay quietly waiting for dawn.

She'd actually been contented the past three months since Christmas, having settled into a routine: Patients and ward care each day from 7:00 to 7:00, with twenty minutes for lunch: then classes – practical nursing, anatomy and physiology, hygiene and bacteriology, and nursing ethics from 7:00 to 9:00 at night or sometimes 10:00; followed by blessed sleep until the attendants came into the trainees' room, ringing the morning bell.

By March 1917, she had survived eight months of nursing school, almost the time it took to grow a baby. She found her thoughts turning more to Clinton. They had agreed to keep in touch by writing "every once in a while." But she missed his morning visits. When Clinton's face came to her mind, she tried to replace it with John's but found it harder and harder to remember what John looked like. She wished that she had brought John's picture to Louisville, but at the time she packed she was afraid his image would be too painful.

To divert herself from her stomachache, she indulged in mentally listing her growing skills. "I can change bandages, sterilize gauze, move patients comfortably and safely, follow doctors' orders, and assist in some procedures. Even Miss Johnson commented on how I can soothe patients without feeling the pain myself. I've attended more deaths than ever in my life before and I'm strong enough now to no longer cry with each passing." Verna stopped as she thought of the young child who died yesterday morning. "Except I still feel the pain of each mother who loses a child."

Verna smiled as she remembered how even the nurses at City Hospital treated her with increased respect. She felt embarrassed for her colleague when a teaching nurse, or heaven forbid, a doctor, disciplined one of her fellow student nurses. She shed tears with her colleagues who didn't last their first year as they shamefully packed small bags and attempted to slip out without proper good-byes.

At the end of the first semester, Miss Johnson publicly dismissed five trainees; the first for "poor study habits," the next "for flirting with a doctor," although everyone knew the doctor initiated the contact, and the other three for "poor nursing." Verna secretly agreed with Miss Johnson about two of the nurses. They complained constantly about the work. One patient of a nurse dismissed for poor nursing got such bad bedsores that Verna and some of the other student nurses had started taking care of her patients as well as their own. The negligent student nurse pretended she didn't care, flippantly telling Verna, "Why anyone would want to be a nurse is beyond me." One student disappeared the night before, clothes and all her possessions gone, as if anticipating the dismissal.

Miss Johnson said a tart good-bye to the remaining four, seemingly untouched by either the tears or the smiles of bravado. Looking at the remaining students, the somber director admonished them, "Don't think it couldn't happen to you. More will leave before the year is over." Verna thought Miss Johnson looked straight at her when she issued the warning. She looked to see if anyone else heard the sound of her beating heart.

This March morning Verna tried to distract herself from the discomfort in her left side. She decided to focus on a pleasant memory – how Mary Lou celebrated the semester's end.

"Verna, I passed. All B's. Oh, my pa will be so proud. And my brother Billie, I can hardly wait to wave these grades in his face. I can still hear him yelling at me the day I left to come up here to Louisville." Mary Lou, ever the mimic, crunched her face into a stern look, lowering her voice to sound like a man with mush in his mouth: "You'll never make it through the winter at that school. You can't even finish milking an old cow without complaining her tits are too hard."

Verna had smiled and hugged her friend, envying her youth, her close family, and her way of taking life as it came rather than fretting over what might happen.

"Let's celebrate," Mary Lou exclaimed, jumping up and down. "Let's go to the Brown Hotel."

Verna, more cautious than her young friend, admonished, "Oh, I can't, Mary Lou. I mustn't spend the money."

"It won't cost you a penny. We'll have our dinners paid for and tons of fun to boot." Mary Lou, in a conspirator's tone, relayed the plan to Verna. "We'll wear our best dresses."

Verna interrupted her. "What do you mean, 'It won't cost a penny'? And I don't have a best dress."

"We'll borrow one of Susanna's. She's just your size."

"Mary Lou, I can't borrow someone's dress. It's not proper." Verna looked appalled but secretly hoped that Mary Lou would talk her into it. She'd envied Susanna's new blue-green dress that flared around her ankles. Verna thought the color would accent her eyes.

"Nonsense, Verna. You hush your worries, now. As to the money, we'll sit in the lounge. Drink tea in iced glasses. That way it looks like bourbon. Talk and laugh like we're having fun. Some men will ask us..." Mary Lou lowered her voice to imitate a middle-aged man... "Would you young ladies like to join us for dinner and maybe some fun afterward?"

Shocked to hear Mary Lou's scheme, Verna hid her disapproval. "Mary Lou, no man would ask me to dinner. I'm too old and not pretty like you." Two student nurses due to graduate in July overheard them.

"Mary Lou and Verna, we do that all the time. We're going to do it tonight. It's great fun. At the end of the dinner tell the men you have to powder your nose. They'll be flattered, thinking you want to pretty up for them. Then slip out the back door through the kitchen.

Oh, Verna, you should see your face." They walked off, giggling at the prudish widow.

Mary Lou threw her arms around Verna. "That's all right, Verna. Even though you don't talk about him, we all know you've got Clinton, who's sweet on you. Stay up and I'll tell you what fun we had. Hey, wait for me."

Mary Lou ran off after the other students, leaving Verna amused and relieved. Returning from her daydream, Verna smiled again, remembering that Mary Lou with the two other students did indeed have a dinner once at the Brown Hotel, courtesy of three unsuspecting Cincinnati businessmen.

The hospital clock chimed 3:00, dispelling Verna's reverie. The pain in her side returned. Verna remembered Ellen's complaint about a pain in her left side last Sunday during Verna's visit. Verna began to get annoyed again as she recalled the difficulty she had getting one of the matrons to promise to watch out and tell the nurse if Ellen's pain didn't stop or got worse. Verna even stressed to the uninterested woman how Ellen never complained about physical pain. To herself, Verna added, "Unlike my daughter's loud complaints about my mothering."

The matron, perhaps overwhelmed by the needs of so many children, dismissed Verna's concerns. "Your daughter probably ate something not right." As Son began to cry again, Verna focused on her son's unhappiness. Ellen's discomfort pushed out of her mind.

Unable to get back to sleep, Verna continued thinking about her children. Ellen and Darcine had found their place as Verna thought they would, even learning advanced sewing skills. Their reading and writing improved. Not that they liked it at the Home. Of course, Ellen listed their complaints each time Verna visited. Nanny Marie clung to her older sisters and would follow them everywhere the staff let her. When Nanny Marie ceased to ask about her pa, Verna, like her own grandmother, decided to not initiate talk about their father and only respond minimally if the children wanted to talk about him. Granny believed talking about hurts only made the pain worse.

Verna recalled her relief when Miss Ford relented and let Son spend more time with his sisters. She didn't even mind too much when the principal put a condition on his visits to Darcine. "He must act like a big boy." Verna's heart ached each time she saw her boy. Although now almost six years old, he still resisted staying at the Home. His whole body shook with racking tears as he tried to explain to her why she must let him live with her. Ellen admonished her mother with cutting words about Son's unhappiness and how he cried each time he saw Darcine.

Verna could hear Darcine's concern: "Ma, he slips out of his bed each night, trying to come into our dormitory. He always gets caught and punished, but he won't stop." As Darcine's words repeated in Verna's mind, she could see Ellen standing beside her sister bursting to tell her side of the story. As Ellen's jaw clenched and unclenched and her tight eyes became slits, Verna had invited her oldest daughter's thoughts. "Ellen, you look like something's about ready to pop out of your mouth."

"Ma, I get so mad. They punish him by not letting him go outside. That doesn't make sense at all."

Verna agreed with her oldest but wanted to be careful not to give Ellen permission to be disrespectful to her elders. "Ellen, I think Miss Ford just doesn't understand that boys don't behave like girls. We have to give her a little more time. Look how nice Mrs. Miller is to Son and Nanny Marie, too."

Secretly, Verna grew jealous of the special relationship developing between Mrs. Miller and Nanny Marie. Almost four years old, Verna's youngest child responded by perking up like a watered flower on a hot day whenever she saw Mrs. Miller. She would run down the hall and throw her arms around her knees.

Seeming like hours, thoughts of her children raced through her head. She dozed a little until she felt a hand touch her shoulder gently. "Mrs. Collins, wake up. The Orphanage has called. One of your children is sick. They want you to come."

Verna sat up, threw the light cover aside, and sprang to her feet before the attendant had fully moved back from the bed, causing her to lose her balance. "What! Who?"

"I don't know. They didn't say. They just said you should hurry to City Hospital where they are taking your child."

Terrified but mobilized, like a wolverine with threatened cubs, Verna dressed quickly, reaching into her drawer for the handkerchief with money in a corner, and put on her shoes as she tied her belt. Not stopping to brush her hair, she fled out the dorm door while the attendant still shuffled down the long row of beds.

Miss Duggan waited outside her door for Verna. "Verna, darling, there is something wrong with your oldest daughter. They didn't tell me what, only that the ambulance came during the night and took her to City Hospital. Come, I'll go with you." Putting her arm around Verna's waist, Miss Duggan steered her to the front door and a waiting hack.

Verna's soft tears moistened her cheeks. "What is wrong? Ellen never gets sick. It can't be Ellen. There must be a mistake."

"I don't know, dear. They didn't say. Only that you should come quickly."

The taxi barely stopped before Verna jumped out the door and ran up the long walkway to the hospital entrance. A senior nurse whom Verna recognized but whose name she couldn't recall quietly instructed, "Verna, follow me. She's in surgery."

"Oh, no! Not surgery! What is wrong?" Verna knew that many patients died in surgery and many more died in the weeks following. The nurses and doctors tirelessly fought germs, but infection remained the biggest killer of hospital patients. Frequently, sick patients refused to go to the hospital, saying they stood a better chance in their own homes.

The nurse didn't answer, as all three ran down the hall toward the surgery unit. Outside the door, Miss Johnson stood sentry. "Verna, you can't go in. The doctor is operating. They started about ten minutes ago, as soon as she arrived. I waited out here to tell you myself. My dear, you must believe in the Lord's mercy." Miss Johnson touched Verna's hand tenderly while firmly stating, "I need to be in surgery now. You stay here."

Verna tried to interrupt but Miss Johnson, as usual, wouldn't be stopped. Miss Duggan finally caught up with Verna and turned to the nurse at a medicine cabinet outside the surgery room. "This is the mother. She needs to know her daughter's diagnosis and preoperative condition."

"I don't really know. I heard someone say appendix." She looked at Verna and saw her face turn white. Verna knew that a burst appendix could kill a small child. "But I'm sure it will be all right. Dr. Duffield is operating. You know he's our best surgeon. I heard him say, 'I knew her father.'"

Verna remembered the kindness Dr. Duffield showed during her interview and his influence with Miss Johnson. She'd seen him a few times in the hospital and thanked him. He seemed to want to talk with her, but her station as a student made her uncomfortable. She would make an excuse before quickly moving away. After the first few encounters, she felt her cheeks redden as if he might think she was flirting with him.

Verna sat down. The pictures of John's death began again in her mind. She muttered, "Oh, God. Not again." She stood up and shook her head, sat down, and stood up again as John appeared before her with his ashen face and chest dripping blood. She moaned. Miss Duggan, not knowing about Verna's visions, tried to reassure her about her daughter's condition. "Verna, sit down. It's a good sign that the doctor hasn't come out yet. You must believe, Verna." Verna let Miss Duggan hold her sweating hands. As she was gradually comforted by the older nurse's voice and reason, the bloody vision receded and Verna returned to the present.

Verna began chattering nervously. "I wish you knew Ellen. She's so smart. She takes good care of her sisters and brother. She was John's favorite. They were inseparable until he... "Verna cleared her throat and began again. "Ellen would wait for her father to come home out by the road." Verna found it comforting to talk about her daughter.

"She sounds like a wonderful girl, Verna. You must be very proud of her." Miss Duggan hoped Verna hadn't seen Miss Johnson shake her head once from side to side to signal that the child wasn't doing well. She knew the risks of this operation. Few lived once the appendix burst inside the body. Her thoughts slid to wondering how to comfort Verna if her daughter died.

Verna began saying the Lord's Prayer. Miss Duggan joined her as they sat on the hard wooden bench. Other nurses would walk by and squeeze Verna's hand before returning to their duties. All the students and most of the senior staff appreciated the emotional tugs Verna experienced by working so close to her children yet being unable to see them. She had gained their respect with her hard work and dedication to studying. Verna asked a favor: "Please, God, don't let her die. Don't take another from me so soon."

The sun lightened the waiting room as the routine hospital noises began. Miss Duggan had encouraged Verna to stretch out on a bench and nap while she waited, but Verna kept a vigil as if prepared to wrestle death to the ground if he attempted to enter this operating room. Ellen had been in surgery for two hours when Dr. Duffield emerged from the operating room, taking off his white surgical mask to speak. "Mrs. Collins, we won't know for a few days, but I believe your daughter will make it."

"Oh, praise the Lord." Then registering the hesitancy in his voice, Verna pled, "Tell me the full truth. I simply must know everything. What happened? I haven't been told anything. She told me she had a pain. I got distracted by my son's problem. Oh, Lord."

"Her appendix burst while she was sleeping. I don't see how she stood the pain. The poison had spread through much of her insides before they got her in here. That's why the surgery took so long. I needed to be especially careful cleaning her up." Dr. Duffield attempted to soothe Verna with a well-meaning lie. "I don't think the pain she told you about earlier had anything to do with this."

Verna gasped as she envisioned her small child's innards invaded by green thick mucus death exploding from an organ within her abdomen. She was comforted by his words, took a deep breath, pulled back her shoulders, and raised up her head, attempting to increase her small stature before this intimidating doctor who had saved her daughter's life.

"Thank you, Dr. Duffield. I don't know when I'll be able to pay you. But I do thank you. May I see her?" Verna requested in a bold tone.

"Not now. She needs to sleep. We must be careful of infection."

"She needs her mother. I'm a nurse. Well, I will be a nurse. I'll be careful of germs. I know to wash my hands." Verna pleaded, experiencing the heat from Miss Johnson's eyes boring into her back as she did the unthinkable: She argued with a doctor. "Please."

"All right. But just for a minute. You know the rules." Dr. Duffield was secretly pleased that this diminutive woman fought so hard to see her child. He'd seen too many faint or be too in awe of the "mighty doctor" to fight for their maternal rights. He'd argued before the hospital board for increased parent rights, but he'd been thoroughly rebuked by the older doctors who controlled the hospital governance.

Verna scrubbed her hands, put on surgical garb, and entered the surgery unit. She almost fainted from the sight of her daughter's blood on the surgical dressings and drapes. The discarded nurses' gloves with pink fingers lay beside bloody swabs. Looking into one of the nurses' eyes, Verna saw pity, before the woman looked away. Ellen lay unconscious, on the large table surrounded by an orderly and two nurses. Verna held Ellen's hand while they rolled the cart to the recovery room.

After five minutes, Dr. Duffield touched Verna's arm. "You must leave now. We will let you know when she may have visitors." Gently taking her arm, he led her outside the room.

Verna vowed if Ellen recovered she'd never be cross with her again and announced to no one in particular, "I won't lose her. I won't."

The doctor and attending nurses watched Ellen fight for life. Her immunization compromised, poison seeped into her internal organs and raged unchecked. Ellen's face paled until it vanished in the white pillowcase covering. The nurses whispered behind Verna's back, unable to truthfully relate the extent of Ellen's danger.

Miss Johnson offered her phone so Verna could call family in Berea to tell them about the course of Ellen's illness. Verna followed the nursing supervisor down the hall, letting Miss Ford place the call to Clinton at the jail, since neither of Verna's sisters could afford a phone. Miss Johnson directed the Louisville operator to place a call to the sheriff's office in Berea, Kentucky, and impatiently waited for the wire to be clear before handing the phone to Verna.

Verna's voice blared out into Miss Johnson's office. "Hello, Clinton, can you hear me?"

"Yes, you don't have to shout, darling." To his alarm this daydream endearment slipped out; never before had he risked such boldness. Clinton knew only a serious crisis warranted the cost of a ten cent phone call, rather than a nickel telegraph. Clinton feared Verna had been expelled from nursing school given that the call was placed by the director of nursing. His mind began jumping from thought to thought.

Since coming to Louisville their relationship had ripened with the safety of distance and their increasingly revealing letters. Verna wrote her feelings about John's death and his unfaithfulness with a boldness she hadn't dared in person. Clinton returned the intimate sharing with his increasing admiration of her braveness and strength. The more he praised her endurance and praised her for passing her courses, the more Verna showed him another side of her previously kept hidden -- her intelligence and love of reading. Clinton began tenuously signing his letters, "With affection, Clinton." In her latest letter, after much deliberation and asking Mary Lou if the closing was too bold, Verna had risked, "Thinking of you, Verna."

Too numb to hear, much less respond to his endearment, Verna tried to control her crying enough to talk. "Clinton," her voice cracked, "Ellen is very sick." She began crying.

Clinton's anxiety caused him to become autocratic like his father. "Stop crying, Verna, and tell me what's wrong with Ellen."

Taking a deep breath and trying to speak between fits of crying, Verna managed to eke out, "Appendix. Her appendix burst. Oh, Clinton, she's so sick. Tell Hazel and Beulah, please." Verna couldn't talk anymore as her night of stressful waiting had exhausted her usual control.

Miss Johnson took the phone from Verna's hand and proceeded to tell Clinton the gravity of Ellen's condition. She gave the phone back to Verna with a stern, "Please say good-bye. Calls are expensive."

"Bye, Clinton. I'll write."

"Bye, Verna. Ellen's a fighter. She'll come through. I'll let Hazel and Beulah know. I love you, Verna," Clinton whispered as if Miss Johnson could hear.

"I know, Clinton," Verna whispered back.

Subdued for days, Ellen slowly threw off the effects of the anesthesia while her body fought to recover from the surgery. Each time Verna went by Ellen's bed, she smoothed out her bottom sheet and retucked the corners. "Ma, how are Darcine and Nanny Marie? Did you check on Son? I'm afraid some of the bigger boys will start picking on him again."

A week after surgery Verna became alarmed at Ellen's muffled cries. "Ellen, what's wrong, child?"

Lying on her right side, with her head hidden under the pillow, Ellen's small sobs escaped from the white linen. "Ma, my side still hurts. I'm scared, Ma. I'm so scared."

Verna knew Ellen's life depended on getting her out of the hospital. Ten patients died the night before and six the day before that. Despite the nursing staff's efforts, the germs in City Hospital ravaged the wards, killing the weakest of the patients, particularly young children. Feeling helpless to stop the danger to her daughter's vulnerable body, Verna and Mary Lou concocted impossible schemes such as securing a private hospital room for Ellen to get her out of the life-threatening ward. Verna's concern became alarm when two senior nurses insisted Verna find a safer place for her child to recover.

Verna confided in Mary Lou, "I must take her to Berea. She'll die if left here, and the Orphanage is no place to recover." Unwilling to use Miss Johnson's phone for fear of being overheard and knowing she was jeopardizing her scholarship, Verna took a precious nickel from her bedside cache and called the sheriff's office in Berea from a phone in the telegraph office across the street.

After a brief "Hello," Verna spilled out her fears. "Ellen's doing poorly. I'm going to bring her to Hazel's."

"You do that, Verna." Clinton voice lowered. "Is she getting worse, Verna? Is the doctor afraid she'll die?"

"She's not dying, Clinton. Don't even say that. She needs family and to be out of the hospital. Hazel will take her in, I know. Just ask Beulah to come into town and take care of Ellen while Hazel's teaching. I know she'll come, if you'd be kind enough to send someone to fetch her. The operator is going to disconnect us soon, Clinton."

"When will you all come to Berea, Verna?"

"I'm going to bring her on the train tomorrow. Please ask Hazel to wire me some money so Ellen can lie down in the sleeper car. But, Clinton, oh, Clinton, she will die if I don't get her out of this hospital."

"How long will you stay, Verna?" Alerted by the operator of only a minute left, Clinton yelled as if that would hurry his words. "You just get her here and we'll take care of the rest. I love you, Verna."

"I know, Clinton." The line went dead.

Verna and Clinton, apart for nine months, found their affection for each other increasing with the separation. With only one day a week off from the sheriff's office and lacking money for travel or lodging, Clinton poured his feelings into increasingly intimate letters. Verna released her pique at Miss Ford and the senior nursing staff in the safety of her letters to him. Her fondness for him grew as he shared his emotions. Pressed inside each letter, Verna found a flower or colored leaf. Both began daydreaming. Clinton's dreams included marriage, Verna's romance.

After the phone call, Verna went to Ellen's room and held her daughter's small white hand where veins showed through thinned skin. "Ellen, we're going to Hazel's. She and Beulah will take care of you until you're better."

"I would like that, Ma." Ellen barely raised her head off the pillow to look at her mother's face as she spoke.

After searching the hospital corridors for Dr. Duffield, Verna found him outside the back door smoking a cigarette. "Dr. Duffield, I'm taking Ellen home." Before he could interrupt her, Verna rushed on. "I would have left sooner but I can't afford her medication. I just have to hope she's had enough to fight the infection. Dr. Clark, our town doctor, will help out if he can. I know he will."

Dr. Duffield snuffed out the butt of his cigarette with the toe of his shoe still covered with white cloth protection. His eyes moved up and down the body of this woman standing beside him. He couldn't help being attracted to feisty females. "Dr. Clark's small pharmacy might not have this particular drug that's working on Ellen's infection. Verna," he took both her hands in his long-fingered, fine-boned surgeon's hands and rubbed the top of her pointer fingers with his thumbs, "Let's just borrow enough of that medicine to get your daughter well."

They walked to the hospital pharmacy and as Dr. Duffield wrapped up the pills and antiseptic salve for Ellen's scar tissue, he touched Verna's elbow. She tensed as his fingers lingered on her arm.

"Verna, you'll get in trouble if you stay in Berea. I'll write a doctor's order saying it's necessary for you to be with Ellen for three days but you have to make it back at the end of that time." The heat from his fingers pressed down on her arm.

"I will." Looking at his eyes, which she usually avoided for fear of blushing, she noticed a fleck in the white of his right eye. His dark blue eyes with thick brown lashes that curled upward demanded she return his gaze. Verna, not trusting her emotions, muttered a soft, "Thank you. How can I ever really thank you? She is so sick, but I think she wouldn't have made it without you."

"Verna, she is really sick, but I do think she'll live. Your little girl is a fighter. I think she got that from you." Dr. Duffield's voice was kind as he averted his gaze, allowing Verna to look away. "Verna, some doctors hide information from their patients. I don't. Miss Johnson thinks we should leave well enough alone and let you be thankful that your girl's alive. But a mother has a right to know." He paused to check Verna's face. If she looked faint, he would stop. Her gaze remained steady. "Some girls, when the infection from the burst appendix is as bad as Ellen's, aren't able to have children of their own. Now I'm not saying that about Ellen. We have to leave that up to God."

Verna wrinkled her mouth with as much disbelief as if he had announced the German emperor would arrive in Louisville by the Ohio River. "I don't think

Ellen will have that trouble, Dr. Duffield. You're a fine surgeon. If this hospital doesn't kill her, my girl will be fine."

Dr. Duffield's experience with parents' reactions to terrible news prepared him for Verna's denial. For now, he let her be. "You're right, Mrs. Collins, we don't know the future. Your girl's strong. She has a fine mother to help her. Let me know when you're back. I'll try to find a way to help Miss Johnson understand a mother's need to be with her child at a time like this."

Verna looked at him, surprised at his offer to help with Miss Johnson. She wanted to start planning how to get Ellen out of the hospital without Miss Johnson seeing her, but anger with the doctor for imposing needless worries of Ellen's potential childlessness intruded. "Why did he have to say Ellen might not be able to have children?" she asked herself. "A woman isn't a woman if she can't have children." Shifting rapidly into her soothing mode, Verna settled her worries with the thought that Ellen simply needed longer to fully heal.

Verna hid her thoughts and smiled at Dr. Duffield. "Good-bye, I must hurry if we're to make the afternoon train to Berea."

"Wait, Mrs. Collins, I'll drive you and Ellen to the train; you can't take her on the streetcar." As Verna ran down the hospital corridor to find Mary Lou to help her with Ellen, she repeated under her breath, "Ellen will be fine if I get her to Hazel's. Just fine."

# CHAPTER FORTY-SEVEN

## HEALING AT HOME

As Verna neared Berea after the frantic rush to the Louisville train station, the green shoots on the trees and color-dripped crocuses soothed her. She soaked in the pleasure of coming home with Ellen nestling in her arms as if five years old again. "Berrrrea," the conductor announced as he solicitously helped Verna with her small valise. As they debarked, Verna exclaimed to her weak daughter, "Everyone came to meet you, your aunts, Mr. Blake, even Dr. Benson."

Watching Ellen limp painfully off the train, the doctor encouraged everyone to hurry. "We have to get this little girl to bed right away. She's as pale as moonlight." Dr. Benson carried the weightless child in his arms to his new sedan. Everyone squeezed into the large black car except Clinton, who, after hugging Verna and patting Ellen's head, mounted his horse to meet them at Hazel's.

Hazel's white pillared porch overlooked the Berea hills. As adolescents, Verna and John had sat on this porch for hours watching the sun-changed patterns on the hills and planning their future. Now, Verna didn't even stop for a quick glance at the hills but quickly followed Dr. Benson into the small back bedroom. She assisted as he placed Ellen in a feather bed that absorbed her frail body. Beulah, who, like a portrait, never changed expression, gasped when she saw her niece's emaciated body. "Oh my, Verna, you certainly did right bringing this child home. There's chicken broth simmering. We're gonna put some meat on her." Beulah swiftly left the room, returning with the soup while the last of her words still lingered and before Verna finished shaking out the pillow.

Beulah blew on the steaming soup, testing a sip, and then carefully spooned the warm liquid into Ellen's mouth. Verna smoothed the sheets, drawing the corners tight, and then went back and re-created her motions. Dr. Benson somehow managed to do his medical examination while the two women fussed over the child. He started to shoo them away and stopped himself. Soon Ellen slept. Hazel offered to stay with her niece as Verna rested on the porch.

Clinton, reclining with his feet propped on the railing, brightened when Verna joined him. He patted the swing. As she leaned back he put his arm around her shoulders. Verna stiffened, wondering what her sisters might think.

"Verna, Doc told me Ellen's a mighty sick little girl. He hardly recognized her. You did right to bring her home." Clinton let his mouth push against Verna's hair as he took in her smell. Hearing an undisguised tenderness in his voice and looking at his worried eyes, Verna relished the comfort of this man's caring.

"Oh, Clinton. She's been through so much. You know Ellen. She keeps all the hurt inside and only lets her anger out. She must have experienced excruciating pain but never let anybody know until it was too late."

"How could she do that, Verna? Those appendixes hurt bad. When my uncle's burst, my aunt said you never heard a newborn baby cry as loud."

"Ellen told me she thought the pain would go away. She feared the matrons would laugh at her like they did when she complained about Son's treatment. Clinton, she's been taking care of all them, Darcine, Son, and Nanny Marie. I think the people at the Home stopped listening to her complaints."

Verna looked down at Hazel's porch floor, too ashamed to look at Clinton. She noticed a tall, straggly field daisy sticking out between two wooden boards and snapped off its head.

"If I hadn't been selfish, wanting something better for myself, she wouldn't be so sick." Overwhelmed by guilt and shame, Verna confided, "I only worried about Son. I took Ellen for granted." Clinton tightened his arm around her shoulders and pulled Verna close until she rested her head on his shoulder.

"Verna, you did right. You know that. You couldn't keep the children together if you'd stayed in Berea. Who knows what would have happened to the younger ones with you off cleaning people's homes? You tried that, Verna. Now, hush. Be worried about Ellen if you must. But don't be blaming yourself."

Verna relaxed into the back of the swing and let her body rest against Clinton's body. She felt warmth radiating from his cotton shirt. His smell triggered the memory of John awakening her that last morning to make love. She moved away from Clinton's body and quickly looked over her shoulder to see if Hazel had noticed.

The urge to confide in someone overcame her unease with their growing intimacy. "Clinton, I grew up expecting someone to always take care of me. First Granny, then John. I never made decisions on my own. Now I've tried, but I've failed."

"No, Verna. You've not failed." Clinton held her face between his hands, making her look at him rather than lower her head in shame.

Buoyed by his acceptance, Verna rushed to reveal more of her hidden thoughts. "Clinton, I've been thinking about sending Son to live with Grover. His Aunt Nan and Uncle Grover have begged me to let Nanny Marie and Son live with them. Nan's letter said the farm was too big for the two of them but just the right size for a family with children."

Clinton continued to look into her eyes while his hand tightened on her shoulder. "Verna, I want to take care of you and the children." More confident now, Clinton raised his voice. "I've wanted to tell you for a time. Now that John's been dead more than a year, I hope you don't think I'm being too forward." His fingers itched to hold a cigarette and he patted his shirt pocket before remembering he had vowed not to smoke in front of Verna.

"Clinton, I'm still learning how to care for myself for the first time." Verna looked into his eyes and found acceptance. "With Ellen so sick, I'm unsure I can take care of anyone. It seems no matter how hard I try something bad happens to those I love and they leave me."

"Verna, I won't leave you." Clinton leaned forward as if to kiss Verna. She moved toward his lips but caught herself upon hearing Beulah's voice. "Verna, are you out on the porch? Ellen is moaning in her sleep."

"I need to go to my little girl, Clinton."

"I'll wait until you're ready, Verna. And from now on, I'm coming regular to Louisville to visit with you, Verna." Clinton's firm voice left little doubt he meant what he said.

Verna decided not to argue. She'd see if he actually made the trip even once and then decide if she'd see him again. Relaxing her shoulders and tilting her head to the side, Verna decided to share a small part of her growing feelings. "I've missed you, Clinton. I still ache for John. It's too early to know what my feelings really mean. But I would be pleased if you came to Louisville on the Sundays I can't visit the children.

Clinton took her face between his hands. "Verna, I'd like to see the children too. For right now, I'll wait for you to let me know when it's right."

# CHAPTER FORTY-EIGHT

# Second-Year Nurse's Training, 1917

"This August heat is unbearable. The air feels like the hospital was built on top of a hot spring. Verna, come swimming with us. Don't say no again," urged Mary Lou. "Miss Johnson is giving that same old lecture to the new student nurses. She gets so much pleasure watching them squirm, she'll never miss us. The day staff is tending our patients. It's too hot to move about. Come celebrate with us. All you do is work, write letters, see your children, and wait for Clinton's next visit. Come along."

Since his declaration of love in Berea during Ellen's illness, Clinton had visited Louisville two Sundays each month, sleeping sitting up on the train to save money. Occasionally he did some business in Louisville and then the town of Berea paid his train fare. He wrote twice a week, telling her about the town doings and signing the letters, "Yours, Clinton."

After the awkwardness of the first Sunday, Verna had begun to look forward to his visits. They would walk in the Louisville parks and down the city sidewalks listening to the music drifting out of the hotels and salons. The threat of Prohibition was in the air, and from the crowded bars it seemed as if everyone wanted to get that last drink in.

Neither had enough money to go out to dinner, so Verna would cajole the kitchen help at the hospital into slipping Clinton an extra patient's meal. His visit last week had brought them closer. She had let him hold her hand as they walked and put his hands on her waist to help her down from the streetcar.

The city's heat surrounded Verna's body, sucking the moisture from her skin, drying the oil from her formally luscious hair, and causing her eyes to burn. She lay in bed listlessly, trapped by the heavy air. She longed for the Berea breezes rolling down from the hills carrying moisture upon their backs like desert camels. Mary Lou's offer stirred memories of slipping off with John to hidden pools in the hills.

"What if we get caught? I've already got two days discipline on my record from when I went to Berea with Ellen."

"We'll be back in time to prepare our patients for supper. Look, they're all asleep. It's too hot to even breathe in the hospital today. The spring's water will be so cooling. You won't believe it."

"I don't have a bathing suit."

"I knew you'd say that. Joyce left hers here when she went home to take care of her mother. She won't mind. In fact, you know, Joyce thinks you are an old stick in the mud. She'd want you to come. She said to me just before she went, 'Doesn't that Mrs. Collins do anything but work, work, work?'"

"Mary Lou, you know that's not true. I can't just wear her suit. That's not right."

"Verna, if you don't go, I'm going to tell Miss Johnson you go to the Brown Hotel and pick up men."

"You won't."

"Yes, I would," said Mary Lou with a fake pout.

"No, you won't." Verna was beginning to weaken.

"No, I won't. But Verna, you really should come. It's a celebration. Twelve months down, only twenty-four more. We even survived the cut when the program stopped the affiliation with Hawthorne Hospital. You and me, the only two from Hawthorne that made it. So you have to go. Anna Belle is driving. Hurry! Go put Joyce's suit on under your uniform. It's in the trunk at the bottom of her bed. She hides the key with a ribbon on the second coil from the top of her bedsprings."

"Mary Lou!"

"Go, Verna. You know there's a devil in you the same as in all of us. Let him play today."

Verna, breaking loose of self-imposed restrictions, started to grin as she fast-walked to Joyce's bed, giving a little hop to her step, like a young girl – not a mother, not a widow.

A chorus of voices invaded her mind. Miss Johnson's dry critical tenor voice began the medley: "Mrs. Collins, you're so irresponsible. You'll never make a proper nurse." Then the squeaky soprano old women of the Quilting Society: "Verna, you should be with your children." Then Beulah's stern alto, "Verna, it wasn't right to leave Berea. Your children could have been taken care of by family." Than the most familiar voice of all, her own, like a bass drum, "Verna, you are so selfish."

"Hush, you all. I'm not going to listen to you today." Verna revoked the chorus of voices in her head, shifting her internal eye around to look each in the face. "Hazel, I long for the spring's water cooling my skin, running down my back, pushing my hair against my head. Beulah, I desire the deliciousness of wetness, not just the bottom of me with my knees sticking up, like in the barrel. Nan, I long for the kiss of the water, like letting a cool drink slowly slip down my throat. John, I can't see the children today. It's not a visiting day and Ellen's back now, good as new, almost. Besides, we don't get any time off this summer." Verna's forehead lost its worry lines.

She found the skeleton key. Upon opening the painted chest, she discovered Joyce's bathing suit in a corner, hidden under a shawl. Holding up the revealing garment, she wondered if she dare wear the outfit with its short, full skirt, slightly scooped top, striped bloomers, and no sleeves. Seeing no one in the dormitory, Verna tried on the bathing cap. "Oh, my. Oh, my. What would Clinton think?" She giggled and looked around again. The glare from the sun blasted in the window, causing her to squint. Her skin tingled with excitement as she rushed to join the younger women.

# CHAPTER FORTY-NINE

## SON'S HURT

The week after the swim, Verna felt a new acceptance by the younger nurses. She let go of some of her reserve and even shared a little about John's death. They knew about her husband's murder but hadn't known she had seen him shot. The afternoon reminded Verna of how much she missed Blanche and their afternoons of carefree fun.

"Verna, come help me with this patient. He's impossible," one of the students called out to Verna.

"Mr. Hickens, you are looking very handsome this morning. I see your wife wrote you another letter."

"Mrs. Collins, I want to go home. I'm fine. Just fine. Tell that new nurse to leave me alone."

"Mr. Hickens, she's not a new nurse. You know she's a student like I am. You don't want to get her in trouble, do you? We just need to put you on your side for a little bit to clean you up."

"But her hands are rough."

"How 'bout I help? But next time, don't you be giving her a hard time."

Mr. Hickens smiled as Verna firmly touched his back and gently rolled him on his side.

She told her colleague about the importance of creaming her hands between washings and at night to reduce the roughness caused by the water and the antiseptics. Because of her second year status and age, the new students sought Verna for advice and maternal comfort. The student wanted to talk, but Verna kept walking rapidly to the hospital door. "I need to see my children now. But I'll stop by when I get back."

The maples in the front yard of the hospital displayed bright red leaves while the oak trees held on to their summer green. Verna began planning how she could save a little of her dollar and thirty-seven cents allowance from the hospital to buy each child a Christmas present. Shortly, Verna arrived in front of the orphanage. Last week the children begged that on her next visit, they could go and play in a nearby park.

Verna opened the large door, hurried down the hall, and quickly headed for the older girls' section. Verna first needed to see her oldest. Ellen, since her return from Berea, had granted her mother amnesty. During the last visit, Ellen took her mother aside and confided, "I know you try your best, Ma."

When Verna reached the dorm room, Darcine and Ellen ran to her. "Ma, Ma, we thought you'd never come."

"One of the new student nurses needed me to help her this morning. We'll still have time for our outing."

"Ma, it's Son. We tried to call you," Ellen declared in her old angry voice. Darcine, choking with emotion, stammered, "He's hurt bad."

"What's wrong? Is he... did he...?" Verna couldn't finish the sentence.

"He got beat up, Ma. Blood poured out his ear."

"Where is he?"

"He's in the infirmary. They caught us sneaking in and made us leave."

"Ellen, get Nanny Marie. Darcine, come with me. I have to see him."

The two raced to the infirmary located in another building. Verna slowed down as they neared the door. "Wait here, Darcine. I'll see if they'll let you in with me."

Verna assumed an "I know what I'm doing" attitude and swung open the door to the infirmary.

"You can't come in here," yelled an attendant from across the room. "Oh, it's you, Mrs. Collins. He's over here. He looks worse than he is. It was just a little fight between some boys."

Son whimpered "Ma" as he heard the attendant call her name. He looked so helpless, just a small lump in a single white bed with metal posts. He sat up, but the effort caused him to lie back down. Relieved to see his body move, she worried about the extent of his facial injuries and any injury to his internal organs.

Upon reaching his bedside, she inspected his facial lacerations. "Son, don't move now. Let Ma check you out. You tell me where it hurts." His face, swollen red with blue patches of skin, looked like a smashed berry pie with band-aids for the crust. His swollen eye sockets required him to turn slightly to see his mother.

"Ma, it hurts all over."

She raised his arms, relieved to find they weren't broken. He yelled when she tried to raise his right leg. Pushed out though swollen lips he whimpered, "Ma, that hurts. Curtis kicked me." When Verna touched his stomach, Son cried out so loud the attendant warned her to be careful. Verna lifted his shirt and found the imprint of a hand the size of her own on his stomach.

"Who did this to you, Son?"

"I don't know, Ma. They just came out of nowhere and jumped on me. I didn't see a thing."

"Son, I know better than that."

"Ma, I don't know, really."

"Son, if you don't tell me who did it, how can I protect you?"

"Ma, you can't protect me here."

He sounded old, though only seven this month.

"Ma, I don't want to stay here anymore."

"No, of course not, Son. Darcine's outside. She wants to see you. I'm going to ask that nice attendant to let her come in."

One by one, Verna was able to take her children in to see their injured brother. Darcine gasped when she saw him. Ellen swore she'd find out who did this and get back at them. Nanny Marie seemed confused and tried to kiss her brother. Verna held her so she wouldn't get too close to his battered body.

At the end of her visit, rigid with anger, Verna walked into Principal Ford's office. "You know what happened to my son. I demand that someone keep watch over him while he remains in the infirmary. He is not to be left alone."

"Mrs. Collins, I know the boys who injured your son. They will be expelled. I've placed calls to their aunt. We won't tolerate this behavior. I am so sorry." Verna's anger was mitigated somewhat by Miss Ford's indignation that anyone under her care would be assaulted.

Refusing to repeat her hesitancy with Ellen's illness, Verna instantly decided, "Son is going to his uncle's in Oklahoma, as soon as I can make the arrangements. I should have listened to Ellen. This isn't the right place for him."

"Mrs. Collins, I'm so sorry. The boys that hurt your boy are new. It doesn't help, I know, but I thought Grover's adjustment had improved." (Miss Ford never used the name Son; she insisted on called each child by his Christian name.) "Let me call the Berea chapter," she continued. "When a child leaves under special conditions, sometimes the chapter will help with the living expenses. And of course, you may use my telephone to send a wire to your brother."

Having won the battle with Miss Ford, fear and sadness consumed Verna. First John, then Ellen, now Son. Who was next? She didn't know if she could bear the pain.

# CHAPTER FIFTY

# APRIL, 1918 WAR

Eager to read the latest letter from Nan, Verna hounded the postman at the hospital boxes until he searched through the letters to see if any were for her. He was used to her greeting him if she could be excused from the floor. "Here it is, Mrs. Collins. Why, I could tell the days of the week from this Oklahoma letter, comes as regular on a Tuesday as my wife doing the ironing." Verna laughed and quickly opened the letter, eager to hear of Son's latest antics. Although Nan always reassured Verna that Son missed her and his sisters, Verna could tell he was thriving from the special attention he got from Nan and Grover. His school reports suggested he was a quick learner. As Verna read the letter from Nan and chuckled at Son's antics, tears leaked from her eyes.

"Verna, come look at this. Congress has declared war against Germany." One of her fellow second-year student nurses yelled to Verna over the heads of doctors and nurses crowded around the hospital's telegraph machine. "What does it mean?" "It means we're going over to France." Arguments broke out. "It's about time," was countered by "This isn't our war. Wilson promised to keep us out. That's why I voted for him." And back. "If Roosevelt had been elected, we'd have been there three years ago, when this European war started." "We've shown the Kaiser. He can't block our shipping."

Tempers flared among a few, as news of the war spread like whooping cough. But most felt excitement, confident the war would be over quickly.

Dr. Fowler, the hospital's superintendent, and Miss Johnson shushed the staff so as not to upset the patients. Dr. Duffield said, so quietly that only those next to him heard, "Thank heavens." One of his fellow doctors touched his arm: "Don't worry, Don, your brother will be home in no time. Now that Wilson's finally sending in the troops, we'll whip those Krauts."

"I don't know what made him sign up like that, worrying his mother. He's only seventeen -- my youngest brother – lied about his age. Maybe because our father never gave him much attention except to tell him he was no good. My wife believes he went to prove he is as good a man as his older brother."

The medical staff ignored Miss Johnson's and Dr. Fowler's demand they return to their duties. Irrational buoyancy filled the main hall when they gathered to read the papers and talk that April morning in 1918. Two doctors and three of the nurses left to enlist for duty in France. An orderly, caught up in the moment, yelled, "Let's have a party before you go."

Verna tried not to think about the war in Europe. Pictures of nurses in the battlefield now provoked flashes of John's death. Verna whispered to Mary Lou, "You'd think doctors would know the pain that's going to happen. I don't understand why everyone is so gay."

Mary Lou, whose closest contact with death was a cousin who died from a bull's kick, exuberantly declared, "Verna, if I were a nurse now, I'd enlist. The Germans can't beat us. I'd love to be in Paris to celebrate. Don't be a stick in the mud, Verna."

# CHAPTER FIFTY-ONE

## CLINTON GOES TO WAR

The first of June, Verna tenuously opened a telegram from Clinton, believing that such urgent messages carried bad news. Upon reading the brief large-type message, her eyes filled with tears. She repeatedly read the telegram until she believed its message. "Signed up for draft. Be at Camp Taylor June 16th. Love, Clinton." Tears ran down her cheeks. One landed on the pasted message, causing the ink to run. She brought the small, crumpled paper to her bosom and pressed it close to blot the salt water before the words ran together.

Unable to return to her duties, she ran down the hall looking for Mary Lou. A month ago Clinton wrote he couldn't be drafted because he was acting sheriff until the governor could confirm his appointment. He assured Verna he would not enlist. She still could hear his voice over the crackly phone: "I couldn't do that to my ma. I'm the only son she has left."

Verna thought he must have signed up for the Kentucky regiment the newspapers recently announced. Each paper tried to outdo its rivals with pictures of the Louisville campsite and boasts of how Kentucky men would join the war effort alongside men from Indiana and Illinois. Verna's stomach cramped. Bile came up her esophagus, causing her to choke.

"Why? Oh, why me? Ellen just back and complaining about the

orphanage again. Nan pressuring me to send Nanny to her. I can't take it. I can't. Not Clinton, Oh, dear God. Not Clinton." Lost in her thoughts Verna didn't notice how far she had gone down the long main corridor. Walking by the superintendent of nurses' office, Verna overheard Dr. Duffield arguing with Miss Johnson. "I want three second-year students from my surgery class to accompany me each week to Camp Taylor. They'll get experience that will prepare them for after they graduate."

Miss Johnson's distinctively cool voice answered him tartly. "No, Dr. Duffield. We can't spare any more nursing students at this time. We released Lula Caldwell to serve at the camp. That's all the students we can spare."

Dr. Duffield had lost his first wife and baby in childbirth ten years before. At first sensitive to his loss, Miss Johnson felt protective toward him. However, as the years went by and he never remarried, Miss Johnson became protective of her younger nurses, stepping in when he appeared too attentive. Hospital gossips speculated that Miss Johnson was herself sweet on Dr. Duffield.

"Miss Johnson, I prefer not reporting to the hospital's board that you are unpatriotic," Dr. Duffield answered, with a teasing lilt to his voice.

"Dr. Duffield, you know I am no such thing. Why, my grandfather fought with the Union in the States War against his own brothers. And my father was with Roosevelt in Cuba. How dare you even imply I don't love my country!" Miss Johnson countered.

Verna almost blinked from the flash she imagined in her supervisor's eyes. Verna recalled an early incident when an orderly, while attempting to roll a very fat, older patient on his side to ease the discomfort from his bedsores, abruptly let go of the man, who then painfully fell back on the hard bed. Miss Johnson fired him on the spot. She soothed the patient, ignoring the orderly's pleas. Compelled to listen further, Verna stayed to see which bulldog would win this fight.

"Miss Johnson, young draftees for the National Guard Divisions are coming to the camp from the hills with diseases and complaints the Army doctors have never seen. We'll go for the day and be back each night. Military doctors are used to battle wounds and the diseases they saw in their fancy teaching hospitals out East. Now, Myrtle." Verna had never heard Miss Johnson called by her first name. "You wouldn't want your nephews treated by those dandy doctors, would you? They'll learn, but they need me to teach them. And our boys. You know they don't cotton to someone who doesn't speak their language."

Verna held her breath during the long pause that followed Dr. Duffield's calculated argument. "All right, Dr. Duffield. Just don't let me hear about... Just mind yourself. These young girls aren't used to being around healthy young men."

"Miss Johnson, I promise to return them in body the same as I found them. It's only their nursing skills that will have changed."

Unlike trains, Verna believed certain opportunities only passed once; you either got on and rode to the end or you missed the ride. At age fifteen, when John asked her to marry him, she said yes despite Hazel's advice to wait until she was eighteen. Verna saw Dr. Duffield's proposal as an opportunity she didn't want to miss. As the doctor left Miss Johnson's office, Verna approached him.

"Dr. Duffield, may I speak with you for a moment?"

"Mrs. Collins, did you hear that?"

Verna wanted to lie. In fact, she didn't really mind lying if it were for something good, like saving someone from hurt feelings, but her thoughts froze. Caught eavesdropping, she'd remembered Granny's advice, "When you're caught, fess up."

"Yes, I heard you talking to Miss Johnson. I want to go with you to the base. You know I'm strong and I've got a way with patients. Besides, those boys from the hills, I know them."

"I'm taking younger nurses. These boys will be away from home a long time. This could be their last chance to see a pretty face."

Stunned and hurt, Verna recoiled. Dr. Duffield regretted his hasty words. He considered Miss Johnson's reaction if Verna told her supervisor what he said about a pretty face. And besides, even though she was a mother and a widow, Verna was still comely. "I'm sorry, that was thoughtless." He seemed to hesitate.

Verna saw her chance. "Dr. Duffield, I saw my husband die. I can take care of any of these men as good or better than any of the other nurses."

Dr. Duffield looked into Verna's eyes and saw her determination. "Of course, you can go. You will be a big help. The patients trust you. These soldier boys will be looking for women like their big sisters, also."

Verna, still wounded, soothed her pride by focusing on the opportunity to see Clinton. She couldn't let him go overseas without seeing him. She scrutinized Dr. Duffield's face. His eyes looked sad without their usual gleam. "Thank you. I won't say anything to the other nurses." Impulsively she looked up at him and flirtatiously quipped, "Sometimes aged cheese is the best."

# CHAPTER FIFTY-TWO

## CAMP TAYLOR

Three weeks later, at 7:00 in the morning, Verna, Mary Lou, and two other young, pretty nurses waited for Dr. Duffield outside the hospital's front door. A one-day signed leave from their director and a pass into Fort Taylor protruded from their uniforms' pockets. The conversation kept returning to the gentlemanly but shy university professor whose brilliant lecture last evening expounded on the growing importance of chemistry for the discovery of new medicines in the future. Mary Lou looked to Verna:, "That Dr. Derby's just right for you, Verna. And if you don't want him, I do." The others giggled, knowing how Mary Lou liked to tease Verna. This time Verna decided to tease her friend back: "Why, how did you know, Mary Lou? I thought it was a secret." And then all of them had to hold their sides for laughing. Mary Lou thought, "I wonder why Verna's in such a good mood today?"

Hearing a honk, Mary Lou yelled "Whee" to Dr. Duffield who waved from a shiny black Ford automobile with a rumble seat. The four women ran down the long sidewalk in front of the hospital, giggling as if eight years old, stopping only to admire, and then touch, his chugging steed. "What has got you all laughing so?" Dr. Duffield enjoyed the eruptions of the young nurses.

One of the more forward nurses spoke up. "Dr. Duffield, we

were talking about your friend's, uh, Dr. Derby's, lecture last night." She started giggling again and put her hand to her mouth in a vain attempt to stop the words that slipped between her lips. "We thought you might introduce him to Verna."

"Hush, you all." Verna blushed first and then got sterner. "Hush."

Dr. Duffield, enjoying teasing the younger women, turned around and playfully said, "Mary Lou, I bet you wanted him for yourself, but girls, he's married. And happily so."

The smell of June roses blooming in front of the hospital permeated the air, adding sensuousness to the excursion. The festive atmosphere was heightened by the beds of blooming flowers planted the previous month to please the city's Kentucky Derby visitors. Dr. Duffield motioned Verna up front beside him as the three younger nurses squeezed into the back, talking continuously. Their songs and constant chatter became background noise, like forgotten teapots boiling on the stove, as Verna retreated to her own thoughts.

When they arrived at the fort, criss-crossed wooden posts blocked the road. Mary Lou exclaimed as she patted her hair back in place under her nurse's cap. "Verna, look at all the tents. I can't see the end of them."

Behind barbed wire that stretched farther than a rifle could shoot, marching soldiers, with long rifles, some Springfields, or sticks upon their shoulders, mingled with horses, wagons, and dogs – all awash in mud. Hastily built, the grassless campgrounds resembled a flooded riverbank. The medical party stopped at the gate, challenged by an armed soldier. He leaned into the car and looked so intently at them Verna wondered if he mistook them for spies. Dr. Duffield showed their passes and explained the purpose of their visit while the young soldier relaxed his surveillance and simply ogled each young nurse in the rumble seat.

After they passed through the gate, drops of water spattered on Verna's forehead. Then a sudden torrent of rain poured down like tumbled tubs of wash water dumped by Louisville maids. The Ford's wheels spun uselessly in the thickening mud. After putting the top up, Dr. Duffield suggested they leave the car and walk to the surgery unit.

The student nurses tried to jump over the enlarging pools of water, but Mary Lou slipped and lost one of her white shoes in the sucking goo. When she leaned over to pick it up, the women heard a big whistle and then a chorus of whistles and hoots. Verna noticed Mary Lou remained bent over longer than necessary to pick up her shoe.

With the others distracted by the warm greetings of the soldiers, Verna quickly said to Dr. Duffield, "There's a soldier here from my hometown. After our work is done, I'm wondering if I might try to find him before we go home."

Dr. Duffield quizzically looked at Verna. "Verna, what aren't you telling me?"

John had befriended Dr. Duffield before Clinton became a Berea deputy, so the two men had never met. Verna struggled to explain her request without telling Dr. Duffield about her growing relationship with Clinton. "He's the new acting sheriff from Berea. He found the man who killed John. I owe him at least a hello, if that's all right with you, of course." Verna made an effort to put on her most proper face, hiding her secret behind social propriety.

He smiled slightly, the sides of his lips barely rising. "If that's all it is, Verna. I guess we'll have a few extra minutes. We must leave at 5:00. When I can spare you this afternoon, I'll let you know."

The day went by quickly. The medical unit contained men with diarrhea, fever, sore throat, lacerations, and a few broken bones and untreatable diseases like syphilis, asthma, and heart murmur. Grown men cried for their mothers after Dr. Duffield removed their infected tonsils. Having only morphine for the men's pain, Dr. Duffield carefully asked about their previous history with the drug, concerned that some might become addicted. He took a careful history, looking for signs of malingering. He sternly explained to a soldier who refused to let him lance a boil, "If that boil isn't incised and drained, the infection could kill you." He then ended with an almost casual, "It's your choice." The soldier relented and watched a large amount of pus drain into the pan Dr. Duffield placed under the wound.

Becoming pale, the soldier looked up. "Thanks, Doc. Guess that weren't too bad after all."

Around 11:00, Dr. Duffield brought a man over to where Verna and two other nurses were changing the bandages on a group of soldiers. "Nurses, this is Mayor George Wessinger Smith." Verna saw a rather stout-looking man probably in his late forties attended by two younger men, who kept glancing around the hospital tent. After greeting the mayor politely, the nurses began to return to their work.

"Dr. Duffield, tell me about these brave men's wounds," the mayor demanded as he blew smoke from a large cigar.

"Well, Your Honor, we see all kinds of medical problems. Since the 84th Division began training by the Watterson Expressway, we've had a few men with concussions or trampling wounds. They're used to riding alone, not with such a large group of men and soldiers. That's to be expected. But the worst are the wounds from gun-related accidents. Some of these new weapons have exploded in our young recruits' faces." Verna was glad Dr. Duffield spoke up to the mayor.

The mayor turned to one of the men in his entourage and said gruffly, "Look into that, Blackwell. Can't have our brave young men getting anything but the best."

Dr. Duffield continued, although Verna thought he looked a little skeptical. "A fair number of the new recruits come from cities like Louisville and are unfamiliar with the Springfield rifle. This young man here with the shoulder wound was hit when a soldier missed a practice target and hit him instead."

Around 1:00, when Dr. Duffield gave the student nurses a break to eat their hospital-packed lunch of fried chicken, hard biscuits, and apples, Verna approached a group of soldiers whose clean uniforms identified them as new recruits.

"I'm looking for a Private Clinton Blake, a Berea man. Heard he recently enlisted. His family asked me to check on him." Comfortable with her small fib, Verna looked at each man in turn.

A man with a falsetto voice, eager to please, piped up, "Yes, ma'am. He's in my section. We came in three days ago. I'm from Estes. Sam's the name."

"Why, Sam, I'm pleased to meet you. I'm Verna, Verna Collins. I had family from Estes. Hear tell my great-grandfather was from your parts." Sam looked to be around sixteen years old. Verna wondered if he lied about his age when enlisting. Earlier, when she questioned the age of a young-looking man, a hospital duty sergeant snappily replied, "Ma'am, the army stopped asking for birth records. If a man says he's eighteen, then he is eighteen."

"Ma'am, you wouldn't be Sheriff Collins' widow, now would you, ma'am?" Sam asked.

"Yes, I am." Verna said modestly.

"He was a fine man, the sheriff. He helped my daddy one time when some loggers started cutting our land. The man wasn't afraid of anyone. I'm sorry for your loss, ma'am." Sam shuffled his feet.

"Thank you, Private." Even though almost three years had passed since his death, Verna felt a twinge of guilt inquiring about Clinton to a man who knew John. She shook her head slightly to keep thoughts of John at bay and plunged on, "Where might I find Deputy Blake? He was close to my husband. I'd like to see if he needs anything."

"You'll have to go through a lot of mud to find him, Mrs. Collins. Why don't I go right now and tell him you're here at the hospital? I'm sure he'll come as soon as he can. Just depends if he's on free time or not."

"That would be mighty nice of you." Verna smiled a wistful smile as if she had been hiding it under a pillow just for Sam. "Have him tell the desk sergeant in the hospital tent to let me know when he's here. I have to get permission from our doctor before I can leave even for a few minutes."

Verna went to find Mary Lou and pulled her aside. "Mary Lou, you must promise not to tell."

"Oh, Verna, a secret. You know I love secrets. Cross my heart." Mary Lou's pleasure radiated from a slight jumping on her toes to tapping two fingers on the left side of her chest.

"Clinton's here in the camp. Will you cover for me? Dr. Duffield knows but I don't want the other nurses to know. When Dr. Duffield gives me permission to leave to see Clinton, I'm going to pretend I just got my period."

"Of course I will. Bet he's smooth looking in a uniform."

"Mary Lou! I bet he is." Verna thought how Clinton's dark brown eyes would look under a private's hat.

"Why, Verna, you're blushing." Verna turned away from Mary Lou, hiding her reddening checks. Since the time she and Clinton sat on Hazel's porch during Ellen's illness, Verna's images of John's bloody back occurred less frequently, but she remained reluctant to fully acknowledge how the awakening of her sexual feelings by Clinton had helped her healing. Mary Lou's curiosity about Clinton had built all during the winter, as Verna always arranged to meet Clinton away from the hospital to avoid having to introduce him to her friends and other hospital personnel who might ask embarrassing questions.

Holding hands and giggling, Verna and Mary Lou returned to the hospital tent. They passed Dr. Duffield leaning against a pole, smoking a cigarette. Pulling a pack of cigarettes from his white uniform pocket, he offered, "Want a Camel?"

Verna quickly refused with an abrupt "No, thank you," and couldn't help turning up her nose. Mary Lou without hesitation took one from the offered pack. Dr. Duffield lit a match with his fingernail. Mary Lou cupped her hand to cut the breeze from blowing out the flame. She drew in the smoke and held it in her lungs before exhaling with obvious pleasure. Surprised to find her friend an experienced smoker, Verna heard her granny's voice, "Everyone has secrets. Why your mother left is her secret. And that's all there is to it."

While cleaning a soldier's wound, she noticed he was staring at her. "Miss?"

"Yes," Verna answered him politely. "You look like someone I knew," he said.

Verna looked at the soldier. He couldn't have been much over eighteen. "Do I now?" Verna answered sweetly.

"Yes, ma'am. At Angers where I was sent to the hospital there was a nurse who meant a lot to me. I loved her starchy neatness. It was as if something out of all that mud could stay clean."

Verna wiped his brows. "Well, soldier. We're gonna keep you nice and clean here and fix you up just fine." As she looked away, afraid the young man would see the doubt in her eyes, Verna noticed the desk sergeant looking around for her. She asked one of the other student nurses to take over the care of her patient. Then she walked over to Dr. Duffield.

"Dr. Duffield, Clinton's here now. May I take a few minutes to visit with him?" Verna was surprised by the urgency in her voice and felt her face flush.

"We can share you for a few minutes, Verna. But no more than fifteen. Otherwise you'll be missed and people will ask questions."

Verna nodded her head toward Mary Lou, who picked up her cue and motioned the other nurses to gather round her. As Verna slipped off, she heard Mary Lou saying, "Verna has woman troubles. She may even have to lie down a bit."

Dr. Duffield played along. "I've told Mrs. Collins to take care of herself and come back when she's, ahh, better."

"Dr. Duffield, I'll be right back. I just want to make sure Verna is all right." Mary Lou ran quickly away as if not hearing Dr. Duffield's, "There's no need for that, Mary Lou." Stifling a grin she quickly turned to catch up with Verna, curious to see her friend's mystery man. She got outside just as Verna slipped behind a large tent. All Mary Lou could see was Verna's arm tight around the back of a tall soldier as she ran to catch up with them.

"Verna." She whispered, not wanting to interrupt the embrace. Verna's arm dropped as the man turned around.

"Mary Lou, what are you doing?" Out of embarrassment, Verna scolded her friend as if she were one of the children.

"Dr. Duffield said to take your time. Not to hurry back until you were 'betttttter,'" stretching the last word to tease her friend. "Thought you'd want to know."

"You did not. You wanted to see what I was up to. Well, come on over here and meet Clinton." Verna made the introductions, secretly pleased at how handsome Clinton looked in his uniform.

After Mary Lou left to go back inside, Verna and Clinton began walking away from the surgery unit, in case someone else decided to come out and see how she was. They walked swinging their arms so that they touched each other until Clinton held her hand and wouldn't let go.

"Clinton, since being in Berea with Ellen I've been thinking of you, a lot. Here I've known you all my life almost, and yet I never really noticed you." Verna stopped, embarrassed by what she'd said. "Oh, Clinton. That was rude. I didn't really mean that."

"Verna, I noticed you when I was fifteen. The first day John's mother took you in after your granny died, I was there. You looked so sad and so pretty, all at the same time."

"Clinton, I remember a little of that day. A bunch of boys playing ball in the front yard jumped all over the smallest one. I yelled at them to let him up."

"That was me. I was always hanging around with John's friends even though they were older." Clinton reached over and removed a strand of Verna's hair that had blown in her face. He let his fingers linger on her cheek.

"Verna, I've got special feelings for you now. At first I thought it was just because you were John's wife and I felt responsible for his dying. I should have known something bad was going to happen to him. If I had been with him that coward wouldn't have dared shoot."

"Clinton, you know that's not true. If you'd been with John, you'd be dead, too. What would that prove! But I know what you're feeling. For a long time I blamed myself. 'If I had done this, or hadn't done that.' I don't know when it became different, but gradually I realized I just didn't want him dead, and blaming myself was a way to pretend he wouldn't have died."

"When the war is over, I want to come home to you."

"You will, Clinton, I'll be here."

"No, I mean, I want to come home and have us be together." Clinton felt uncomfortable explaining his feelings. He thought she should know what he wanted without him having to put it in words.

"My grandmother used to tell me what it was like while she waited for my grandfather to come home from the Civil War. It was his pension we lived on after he died. But Clinton, I don't understand why you enlisted in this war. So many have been killed. I couldn't stand it if anything happened to you." As Verna cried softly, Clinton put his arm around her shoulder, not caring if all the soldiers on the base began to heckle him.

"Hush, Verna, hush. Two Army men came to Berea to enlist men for the Kentucky unit. Most of us signed up, Luke, Evert, Judd's boy."

"I'm surprised Judd would let that boy out of his sight." Verna raised her voice in alarm.

"Since Wilson condemned the lynching of Negroes, Judd gave him permission to fight in Wilson's war. For me, fighting the Germans seemed the right thing to do. You know I'm a good shot and can take care of myself. Some of these city men haven't even held a rifle before. I'm not afraid to kill a man who needs killing."

"But Clinton, it's not just the shooting. It's the gas." Verna put her head down in her hands to catch the tears that fell faster than she could wipe them away.

"I'm more afraid the war will be over before we get there," Clinton declared, deciding their talk had turned serious enough. "Verna, I'll be back. Then we'll talk some more. Just remember I want to take care of you and those young'uns of yours. Look, we're back at the base hospital. We must have been walking in a circle. I'll call you before our unit leaves. Even that fussy Miss Johnson you keep talking about can't deny a departing soldier one last call to his sweetheart. I heard tell we're getting on the train tomorrow for the East." He leaned down and kissed the top of her head, smelling the scent of her hair and remembering how beautiful it used to be, flowing down her back.

"I'll write."

# CHAPTER FIFTY-THREE

# THE WAR IS OVER

After five agonizing months of following the war closely in the paper and asking Dr. Duffield for any news of the front, in November 1918, the Yanks were coming home. As flags flew everywhere, Verna stood with a crowd of "welcome homers." The men exiting the Army truck moved slowly. White bandages hid faces; crutches supported bodies. Attendants leapt up into the trucks, handing down paralyzed bodies to other attendants waiting with wheelchairs. Verna realized these vehicles held only wounded men. She was about to move to another disembarking spot when she saw Clinton climb down awkwardly from the back of the hospital truck. He was smoking a cigarette. She'd never seen him smoke before.

She waved and he nodded, acknowledging he'd seen her. Several men patted him on his back. She heard one say, "She's a looker all right." She stared at Clinton's empty left sleeve tucked into the belt of his army khakis. She became embarrassed and diverted her eyes to watch a family group embrace.

Clinton's last letter stated only the day and time he would arrive back at Camp Taylor in Louisville. He asked her to meet him and ended with a sentence she didn't understand until now: "I'm no longer the man you knew."

Verna moved toward Clinton through a crowd of crying women, punctuated by gruff men's voices inquiring, "How are you, son?" With despair and disbelief, families embraced their maimed youth. Moving slowly through stunned families, Verna finally reached Clinton. Using her nurse's training, she swallowed her own feelings and instead slipped her arms around his neck. "Oh, Clinton, I'm so glad you're home."

He stood still, not reaching out to hug her back. Although feeling foolish, she understood his embarrassment, having seen proud men rebuff solicitous wives and mothers. Clinton muttered, "I think this collar is too small. It's choking the air out of my lungs." He nodded at a few immobilized soldiers who also seemed indifferent to their visitors.

Verna stepped back and with exaggerated motions of her arms as if surprised said, "Look at that stripe on your arm, Corporal Blake. You received a promotion. Tell me how, when."

Clinton shriveled. "I'd rather not, Verna."

Verna dropped her arms by her side, waiting for Clinton to reveal how he wanted his injury acknowledged. Over the summer and early fall of 1918, she and the other student nurses made weekly visits to the camp. Their eager anticipation of a quick end to the war turned to disillusionment and then stoic grief as they nursed men yelling from the pain of phantom limbs and coughing up blood from gas-damaged lungs. They carefully tended to wire-mangled bodies and uncountable diseases while looking into blank eyes -- windows to muddled minds. They recognized the signs of morphine withdrawal and held shaking men.

Aware of the pride of injured soldiers, Verna put aside her feelings and treated Clinton like a patient rather than a loved one. Clinton ground another cigarette out on the trampled ground, gave a dry cough, and while continuing to look around him but not at her eyes, asked, "Tell me about Son and the girls."

Although she hadn't wanted to let him see how much she missed her boy child, Verna thought, "If I'm not honest with Clinton, how can I expect him to be honest with me?" "I miss him something awful, Clinton," she said. "I'll be going along and then his face will pop into my head or I'll hear his voice and look around. But then I tell myself how well he's doing with Nan and Grover. In my mind I see him running among the corn stalks." Using the sleeve of her dress, Verna wiped the tears that slipped from her eyes.

"I'm glad to hear that, Verna. Boy will do better when he can run free from time to time. Not all the time, mind you." Clinton smiled as he remembered the summer he kissed his first girl among the tall August corn. He lit up another cigarette as she told him about the girls. Ellen's grades had improved since she didn't need to worry about her brother so. Again Clinton tonelessly responded, "Ellen's a good girl. She'll find her way." He then said, "It's good to hear about family. Keep talking, tell me more, please."

Verna noticed Clinton avoided her eyes. He looked at his feet or out to the side, anywhere but her face. "Clinton, tell me what it was like. I read the papers, but some people said not to believe what was in them."

"I'd rather not, Verna."

Verna pushed on, remembering only how it helped her to tell the priest about her vivid memories of John's killing. "One of Mary Lou's brothers died over there. She said he was the best of the bunch."

"A lot of good men were killed. They were all the best of the bunch."

Verna noticed an edge to Clinton's voice. "You sound angry, Clinton."

"I'm not angry, Verna. It was just different than I expected. Our officers said we were paying our debt back to Lafayette. Maybe that's easy to say when you're on a horse rather than in the trenches. But I've never seen so much death. That's all I'm going to say. Don't ask me again."

To ease the tension, Verna suggested, "Clinton, let's go walking by the river." Then remembering his injury, Verna quickly added, "if you can."

"Verna, I lost my arm, not my legs." Clinton sounded exasperated.

Verna blushed, not able to look at him. One of the women beside her touched her shoulder, asking, "I'm sorry to bother you, but my boy's arm is starting to bleed. Would you help him?"

Verna realized the woman mistook her for an army nurse. She hadn't taken the time to change, and her student nurse's uniform looked official. "Ma'am, I'd like to but I don't have medicine or gauze with me. Over there by the trunk is an Army nurse. She will help you."

"Clinton, let's walk by the river. It's not far from here. When I was in Louisville for the nursing interview and to see the orphanage,

I came to the river and walked until my choices became clearer. The river's not the hills, but still, the water calmed me."

"Verna, I first have to check out with my sergeant. We're supposed to be here when Governor Stanley comes. Probably pin another medal on us. As if that..." Clinton's emotionless voice finally penetrated Verna's denial. "Of course, I'll wait over in that tent with other families until you're ready to go, Clinton."

After a few hours Clinton rejoined Verna. He seemed less distant and actually smiled at her. Verna decided not to ask questions, to just let him tell his story when he was ready. He lit another Lucky Strike as they started walking to the trolley line. Fearing Clinton might tire, Verna was relieved when she heard the familiar bell announce a streetcar arriving.

She pointed out the sights along the trolley ride down First Street as they avoided each other's eyes. Walking down by the docks, Clinton cupped his hand to shade his eyes, as he gazed first up the river toward Ohio and then looked to the dam. "It's not as big as I remember. When you're on the ocean..." Abruptly he stopped.

Verna held his hand as her toe dug in the earth before her. But Clinton's fingers slipped out of her grasp. "Tell me about the ocean."

"It's big. You can't see the other side like this here Ohio River. When we crossed heading to France, I felt so seasick; I stayed below with what seemed like a mile of men stretched out on our bunks, moaning. It smelled like vomit everywhere. Couldn't have eaten if I wanted. On the way back I was too doped up to remember much – sorry Verna, you don't need to know all this."

"I want to, Clinton." Verna thought of the misery of these Kentucky men unused to the sea. Getting caught up in his story and forgetting her resolution, Verna eagerly said, "What was it like in France?"

"Don't ask me, Verna. Ever. I made it through by thinking about you. I would imagine touching your hair, holding your waist and lifting you on Rex, and then riding into the hills." Clinton shifted; he looked away. "Verna, I'm not the man you knew."

"What do you mean? All that matters is that you're home." Verna tried to be cheery. She wiped the sweat from her palms on her nurse's apron. She wanted to soothe Clinton with the reassurances she had learned from the surgery nurses: "You'll be fine. The doctor will fix you, perhaps an artificial arm." To relieve the man's concerns about supporting his family, a senior nurse might say, "'You'll be able to work again. And your wife and children will love you just the same. " With Clinton the practiced words failed her. Instead personal thoughts intruded. "How will he hold me?" "What will he do?" "How can he be a lawman?"

"Verna, don't be playing the nice girl act with me. I know you've got more feelings than that." Clinton challenged her to be honest with him. "Verna, I've only got one arm. There's not much a man like me can do with just one arm. That possum playin' dead left me half a man. I don't even know if I can take care of myself, much less you and the children."

"I can take care of you." The words rushed on. She stammered, "Not now, next year after I graduate. I can do private duty nursing and..."

"Hush, Verna. I'm not asking you to take care of me." Clinton recalled his dreams as he recovered in an Allies medical tent: Verna, standing by his bed, dressed in her nurse's uniform, leaned over and whispered in his ear, "I will take care of you. Always."

After the mud of France, the horror of the slaughter of the machine guns, and the constant pounding of the big artillery, Clinton longed to lie under clean white sheets in a silent room while a caring woman brought him hot food. Lots of food – no hard tack or boiled potatoes. He imagined her slipping in bed with him, loving him, and the sex, lots of... Clinton stopped himself. He looked fully into Verna's face for the first time that day, but he stayed silent.

"Clinton, I needed you after John died. You became like family, dropping by each day. Bringing special treats for the children. I grew fond of you. Since you left for the war, I worried about you each day. The news was so dreadful. When your letters came with the censors' holes cut in them, I looked on a map trying to guess where you might be. I don't know much about France."

Clinton thought, "Fond of me. Fond of me. What the..." His anger built, and he wanted to shock her. "Verna, war changes a man. I saw awful things that won't get out of my mind." Clinton shook his head as if trying to shake out the memories.

"I know, Clinton. I know."

"You can't know. You weren't there"

"I can't know the pictures in your mind. But I know how something horrible you've seen can stay in your mind and keep coming back.

Clinton, I still see, not as much, but every once in a while, John's bloody back. Clinton, please talk to me. I know, darling, I know."

Clinton, soothed by Verna's endearment, scrutinized the woman before him. A few new lines etched the skin from the corners of her chin and eyes. Her eyes looked into his; her head stood firm on her shoulders. Her manner radiated confidence while retaining her graciousness.

"Verna, I can't go back to being acting sheriff, not even deputy, for that matter. Look at me. Did you ever see a one-armed law officer? I wouldn't last a week."

Verna wanted to reassure him but stifled the impulse, afraid of crying. She held her breath without knowing it. Her complex emotions spun from repulsion at the lost limb to the intense love she had felt when he bravely hopped off the back of the Army truck and came to her.

Clinton took her hand in his. "There's something else, Verna. I don't rightly know how to say this. Over there I decided if I make it home, I want my own child, as well as being a father to your children. Maybe that's selfish. Maybe you can't understand. Death was always something that happened to other men. Now, when I die, I want a part of me to go on. You know I'm all my ma has left. I don't know how you feel about having another child."

Verna paused; she hadn't expected this. "Clinton, when our first two babies were girls, John loved them, but he wanted a son. When the newborn boy died, John couldn't hold in his pain. I heard him cry, 'My son. My son.' I understand your wanting your own. I won't say no. For right now, could you just hold me?"

# CHAPTER FIFTY-FOUR

## GRADUATION, JULY 1919

Seven months later Verna straightened her white peaked cap, wiped perspiration from her brow, smoothed down the apron over her uniform, and then retied Mary Lou's crooked bow, loosened from the motions of her friend's squirming body. "I'm so nervous, Verna. I'll never make it across the stage. My knees won't let me."

The two women hugged each other, stirring a slight breeze as they jumped up on their toes into the still moist Louisville summer air and whispered, "We did it. We did it. We showed Miss Johnson." Verna flashed for a second on the self-doubts aroused during her first interview with Miss Johnson. Two young women joined the hug until they all looked like a mound of snow. A senior nurse shushed them and then smiled. For a moment the difference in ages faded as Verna blended into the pile of young giggling nurses-to-be. The laughter turned to near hysteria as Mary Lou elbowed Verna in the ribs and challenged, "Tell me the name of this bone, Mrs. Collins."

Verna envisioned her anatomy teacher's chart of bones. How hard it had been to study these last six months. Her relationship with Clinton continued to grow and she missed him in the time between visits. The returning soldiers, the expanded city of Louisville, the changes in the country all conspired to accelerate Louisville's growth. New diseases came into town with soldiers and their families. How many nights had she and Mary Lou stayed up late, burning forbidden candles? How foolish they were to risk a fire just to please an arrogant doctor who felt his subject was the most important of their entire three years. Finally Mary Lou taught Verna a jingle about bones. Verna couldn't remember a word of it now. It lasted in her head only long enough for the exam.

She wished John and her granny could see her. Half the starting class gone. But she remained. One of fourteen to pass, to be a nurse. "What are you thinking about, Verna? You look so serious," Mary Lou asked her friend.

"I was thinking about John. What he might say."

"'I'm mighty proud of you, old Verna Collins.'" Mary Lou couldn't help giggling as she imitated a man's voice, although she knew Verna still struggled with her loss.

"I don't know. I just don't know. For three years I've wondered if he would have approved of my doing this. I still don't know. He believed a woman belonged at home with her children." Turning away so her lips couldn't be read, she murmured, "Thank you, God, for giving me the strength to stay with the studying and with the work. Help me use these skills and talents you gave me in the way they should be. Amen."

Verna rejoined her eager classmates. Noises from the gathering crowd, talking and shuffling, echoed off the bare walls and wood floor. Miss Johnson always insisted that the nurses' graduation take place in the hospital lecture hall. All the graduating nurses had at least one family member present. Hill folk began arriving the night before and slept on the hospital grounds in their farm wagons. The medical teaching faculty sat on wooden chairs in the front row, the male doctors on the right and the women nurses on the left. Miss Foreman, the new director, who replaced Miss Johnson when she retired, stood in front beside an oak lectern.

Verna peeked from behind the curtain to look for her family. Ellen was in the front row with Nanny Marie on her lap, flanked by Hazel and Blanche. Son, of course, couldn't make it from Oklahoma. Grover and Nan's congratulatory telegram lay on top of her packed bags. Blanche held Darcine's hand, oblivious to how her wide brim black hat with red, blue, and purple foot-high feathers annoyed the woman behind her. With Hiram not feeling well, Beulah sent word she couldn't leave him alone. Verna looked for Clinton.

Mary Lou pulled her back from the curtain. "Did you see my family? Let me look. Oh, Verna, there's that handsome Dr. Derby sitting with Miss Foreman on the stage."

Verna didn't have another chance to find Clinton, as her fellow graduates crowded around to peek at the audience. One of the senior nurses reprimanded them. "Girls!" Verna cringed.

Miss Foreman announced the ceremony's beginning. The graduating student nurses entered to sturdy hand clapping and foot stomping reminiscent of country dances. Even the city families joined in the contagious rhythm. The nurses-to-be sat in two rows of wooden chairs on the small stage, hands folded, eyes straight, discipline broken only by eyes searching the audience for a loved one and a slight nod to acknowledge a relative's wave. Miss Foreman announced that her address would be brief, given the heat of the afternoon, proceeding then to go through each class taken over the three years and samples of the increased responsibilities in their hospital duties. Clearly proud of the graduates, she stressed how every graduate had recently passed the exam to register as licensed nurses, whereupon a congratulatory shout erupted from the audience. She talked about individual acts of dedication and skill. Toward the end, when the small children were squirming to get out of confining laps, she put her hands out, asking the audience to hold its applause for a minute.

"I want to give special congratulations today to one of our graduates. Each year the faculty votes an award for the student they believe most exemplifies the standards of nursing: dedication to the profession, unstinting services to patients, and personal sacrifice. Our honoree overcame major obstacles to successfully complete her degree. Older than most of our students, a mother of four and recent widow, raised in the hills of Berea, Verna Collins has been unanimously voted by the faculty to receive our 1919 Nursing Award of Honor."

Mary Lou pushed Verna forward. Stunned, Verna's mouth dropped open and her glasses slid down her moist nose. She knew each year the faculty gave an outstanding student award. She assumed the winner would be Bette Ann, who received straight As and always volunteered for extra duty on the weekends. She resisted the impulse to say, "Not me. You must be mistaken," and found the presence to graciously accept the award from Miss Foreman and then turn toward where the faculty sat and quietly say, "Thank you. Thank you so much for this honor." Miss Foreman spontaneously reached her arms around Verna, which startled both women, and they quickly drew apart. Dr. Duffield, with Dr. Derby beside him, made a special point of coming forward and shaking Verna's hand vigorously.

Verna looked at her family. Hazel clapped vigorously, even Ellen clapped. Verna smiled at each one, feeling their pride. Blanche lifted Darcine up to see her mother over the heads of the now standing, cheering adults, as all the audience seemed to rejoice in the accomplishment of this woman from the hills. The rest of the ceremony sped by with the announcement of the names and class rankings and the awarding of diplomas. Miss Foreman placed a nurse's pin in each of their starched collars, and then pandemonium broke out as caps flew into the air.

Afterward Verna hugged Ellen, who self-consciously wiggled out of her mother's embrace. Darcine, at twelve, still enjoyed her mother's hugs. "You were so beautiful, Ma," making Verna giggle and give her second oldest another tight squeeze.

"Ma, let me see your pin."

Verna bent down so Darcine could touch the blue and white enameled symbol of her new status.

"Maybe you'll be a nurse, too, Darcine. We need to think of yours and Ellen's future." She paused, and then shook her head. "But that can wait."

"Ma, I'd like to be a nurse like you. I'm so proud of you, Ma." Darcine gave her mother another hug and nestled her warm cheek against her mother's cheek and stroked her mother's hair. Verna squeezed her eyes shut as she hugged her daughter. When she opened them, she saw Clinton hugging Ellen with one arm. Verna had warned Ellen and Darcine not to stare at Clinton's arm. "Clinton, there you are. I thought you hadn't come."

"I saw you get your pin and heard Miss Foreman announce your award. Congratulations, Verna."

"Where were you earlier?" Verna's eyebrows scrunched together as she crossed her arms. She didn't want to be mad at him. Maybe he wasn't ready to let the children see his injury.

"One of the Republican Party organizers in Louisville asked to speak with me while I was in town. I met him for breakfast. You know me. I always think there's more time than there really is."

"What did he want that was more important...?" Verna almost added, "than my graduation?"

"It's something good, good for us." Clinton's head tilted and his scrunched mouth projected a "Don't stay mad at me" message.

She couldn't help smiling. He came, after all.

The family ambled outside where Hazel and Blanche spread out the picnic lunch packed by a local restaurant for the outrageous sum of 25 cents. Verna had warned them not to fix boiled potatoes. Since the war Clinton would leave a table if boiled potatoes were served.

Verna oohed and aahed over the loaves of baked bread, slabs of cured sugar ham, fried chicken, Hazel's special sweet pickles (Darcine's favorite), apples that survived the winter with just a few bruises, hush puppies, boiled cold cabbage, baked beans, cornbread, and two large strawberry pies so full of fruit that juices ran down the sides. Blanche added a small jug of "something special just for the grown-ups" and gave a congratulatory toast to Verna for her accomplishments. She then added, "And to Justice Brandeis, our own from Kentucky, who is fighting for the rights of all women."

Verna laughed. "Blanche, do you have to make every occasion into the fight for women's rights!"

When Clinton offered to go buy some lemonade for the children, Darcine went with him to help carry it back. She laughed with delight as Clinton commented on her new shoes, "Why, Miss Darcine, I think those are the prettiest pumps I've ever seen."

The hospital lawn, looking like an outdoor bazaar, vanished under gingham cloths upon which chattering families gathered. The graduates skipped around, hugging and kissing each other while introducing their mothers, fathers, sisters, brothers, grandparents, aunts, uncles, and even distant cousins. Hazel, thinking of Miss Foreman's remarks about Verna and looking at the other younger graduates, admired Verna even more for surviving a nursing program designed for women ten years younger than her half-sister.

The extended family ate and laughed. Clinton managed to eat with minimal awkwardness, refusing help with cutting his meat, instead laughingly spearing a chicken leg and eating the meat in circles around the fork. After an hour, Hazel nudged Blanche, reminding her they must hurry if they were to catch the early evening train to Berea. There was no money for a fancy hotel this time. Verna looked at Clinton as he rose.

He had been quiet during the picnic but almost everyone else, particularly Blanche, chattered so much only Verna noticed. Holding one of her hands and looking into her eyes, Clinton risked sharing his thoughts in front of the children. "Verna, I'm so proud of you. Seeing you in your uniform, hearing about your classes and the different types of diseases you all treated. I guess I never really realized how much you had to learn. But..." He started to grin, recalling the old Clinton, before the war. "Verna, it just came to me. You're a real smart woman, as well as being pretty."

"Clinton, I thought you were staying."

"Verna, I must go back tonight." He looked down at his feet and then into her eyes. "I've decided to run for state representative from Madison County."

Verna drew in a breath. "Why, Clinton. I never dreamed you were interested in politics."

"I wasn't, Verna. You know. I was more for being outside rather than stuck inside a building talking. But I can't do what I thought would be my life. And after what I saw in France and in our Army camps, I sure have some ideas about how I'd like to see things. But I gotta run, Verna. I really gotta. I'll write you on the train."

"Promise."

"I promise."

# CHAPTER FIFTY-FIVE

# ON HER OWN

It took almost four months after graduation for Verna to get the appropriate licenses and registrations and establish herself with several agencies. Then another several months passed before she could afford an individual phone number. Now a little over a year later, August 1920, Verna had settled comfortably into a routine of private nursing.

Verna passed the soda shop on the way back to her rented room. Louisville's August heat closed in, causing her nursing uniform to stick to her body. Although she wanted a cool drink, she decided to delay the pleasure and write Hazel first. How she longed to go to Berea and sit on Hazel's porch.

After graduation, through phone calls and letters and an occasional weekend visit, Verna and Clinton talked about their plans without directly acknowledging that both needed more time to heal their wounds and sort out their changing relationship. Verna would stay in Louisville the next year and a half to be close to her girls as they approached their high school graduation and see Nanny Marie often. They had adjusted as best could be expected to the orphanage. Verna was making enough money to support herself as a private duty nurse, but not enough yet to support all her children and their educational needs.

Clinton needed time to campaign for the fall election. He went from small town to small town, standing on stumps, making speeches about how America won the war and made the world safe from the Kaiser, sounding like Roosevelt for his new conservative party as he kissed babies and talked economics as did the Republican president, Taft. He flattered the women and met in back rooms with their businessmen husbands, who financed his campaign. He learned how to drink whiskey slowly without anyone noticing and stopped hiding his empty sleeve. His letters to Verna got shorter and shorter and his phone calls less frequent as he complained he didn't have the time -- sometimes several hours -- to wait until there was an open line and the operator could place the call.

Verna found she enjoyed the freedom of private duty nursing and being able to work directly with the doctor in caring for a patient. She went into her patients' homes six days a week to provide care. Sometimes, when intensive care was required, she accepted only one patient. Other times, she might have as many as five patients in one day or substitute for a sick nurse at the hospital. Every other penny she earned she put away toward the day she could have her children, all of them, including Son, live with her again.

An early riser, Verna left most mornings at 5:30 before the clamorous city noises began. Exhausted at night, she barely kept up with her washing, mending, letter writing, and studying nursing journals. Sundays she spent with the children, missing Son's laughter and chubby arms wrapped around her neck but secretly enjoying watching Darcine's body change from an awkward ten-year-old to a twelve-year-old with budding breasts. She and Ellen fought less, but at times, Verna still wanted to put her hands over her ears when her oldest began complaining. But she took comfort in holding Nanny Marie as if she were still a toddler instead of six years old.

Verna climbed the three stone steps to her ladies' boardinghouse where she and two colleagues roomed. Taking a handkerchief out of her sleeve, she mopped her brow. Her small room faced the front. She envied Lucy's large back room away from the street noises and Mildred's room on the second floor that looked out on the park.

After three years of living in the student dorms each woman had luxuriated in the privacy of separate space. Sometimes the three nurses, if their schedules permitted, ate dinner together or shared a cup of morning coffee and gossip. Noticing mailboxes overflowing with local business circulars, Verna was disappointed to be the first one home and unable to share her afternoon's adventure.

Verna imagined Mildred's measured response and Lucy's outrage at Verna's patient's behavior. Mildred approached nursing like a business. She taught Verna how to list her new address and phone number in the city directory. "Tell people what you do and where to reach you." When the phone book arrived, Verna proudly underlined her listing: Verna Collins – Private Duty Nurse. The three women shared one phone located in the front hall of the rooming house, but its long cord allowed each one to talk within the privacy of her room, if she were fortunate to have a first floor room.

Twenty-two-year-old Lucy saw nursing as a calling. Completely dedicated to healing others, she seemed unaware of her physical attractiveness. Five feet, six inches, she towered over Verna. Her bright red hair, light blue eyes, fair freckled face, and bouncy walk elicited stares and whistles that she ignored. As Lucy's nursing schedule filled up, she sent new requests to Verna.

Needing to tell someone but reluctant to spend money on a phone call, Verna decided to write Hazel about her experience with a new patient. Throwing her white gloves on the Berea Society memorial quilt, she lightly touched the figures of the children running and John's star, then drew out paper and pen from her bedside stand, and sat on the bed to write.

*Dear Hazel,*

(After writing about the children, the weather, and commenting on some gossip in Hazel's latest letter...) *I'm fine too. Well, now I'm fine. I'm learning it's not easy to be a woman living alone in Louisville. Hope you don't think I'm bragging, but I felt proud when the new Louisville telephone directory listed me as a Private Duty Nurse.*

*A woman with nine children, whose leg broke in so many places that the doctor told her to stay in bed, called me first. Her husband claimed he couldn't help. Her sister came for the children but was afraid to move her, so she was getting bad bedsores. After a few days of my showing her how, the sister was comfortable doing all the needed care. I left that position. Then an elderly woman asked for help but she moved in with her family and didn't need me anymore. I am enjoying private duty nursing. It pays better than doing shifts at the hospital. Also, the physical work isn't as hard.*

*This morning I got a call from a man on the other side of town. His voice sounded pleasant enough over the phone, although he had a hard time describing why he needed a nurse. I told him I'd come to his place – maybe he could tell me better in person. I rang the bell for his apartment. A man asked through the door, "Who's there?" Raising my voice, I answered politely, "Mrs. Collins, the private duty nurse you called." I heard him clearly say, "Come in. The door's unlocked."*

*Hazel, you won't believe this. I opened the door. There he stood – naked as a jaybird. Well, I lit out of there, practically falling down the steps. Hope you don't think I'm in any danger, because I'm fine. Did teach me a lesson. I'm only going to take patients referred by someone I know from now on. It wouldn't be as much money and it may take a little longer for all the children to live with me again. But, Hazel, there are some ugly-looking men in this town, and I don't care to see another one. Love, your sister, Verna*

# CHAPTER FIFTY-SIX

# A PARTY MAN

A month later, in mid-September, Verna got a letter from Clinton. As she ran her fingers over his name on the top left of the envelope, a longing to look out her kitchen window into the Berea hills returned. She recalled how in early fall the hills' red and yellow crowns refreshed a soul wearied by August humidity, unlike Louisville, whose summer heat wilted the city trees and burned the soles of her shoes. Reading Clinton's letter, Verna flushed, so excited about his political future she talked out loud to herself. "You are going to be elected. I just know it." She couldn't resist calling him on her new phone for details.

"Clinton, it's Verna."

"What are you doing calling me in the middle of the day?" Clinton's tone irritated her ear and she briefly pulled the phone away to rub the lobe.

"Didn't think you'd mind. I just got your letter. I was so excited I had to call." Verna knew Clinton's nervousness about spending money. But John indulged her whims, and she was used to getting her way with small expenses.

"Verna, you can say the same things tonight. It will cost less."

"I can't wait."

"Yes, you can. I'll call you after 6:00 before I leave the jail."

"I'll be here, Clinton."

"I love you, Verna."

"I know, Clinton."

"Verna," Clinton started, then stopped.

"Yes?"

"Never mind." The silence of his disappointment lingered until the final click.

At four minutes past six according to her new watch -- a graduation present from Blanche -- Verna's phone with three quick rings signaled a call for her on the party line. Upon hearing Clinton's 'Hello," Verna proclaimed, "This is a private call." Four hang-up clicks followed her announcement. She waited until hearing one more.

"Clinton, tell me everything."

"I don't know much more than I said in the letter. Some Berea businessmen, Mr. Welch being one, talked to the Republican Party bosses. They want me to be their man in the race for the state legislature next year. They say..." and his voice deepened, "there's a place in the party for men like you." '

"What does that mean?" Verna teased. "You know the amendment hasn't passed yet, so as a 'non-voting woman' I'm pretty ignorant about these things." He laughed. Under Blanche's tutoring, Verna's knowledge about politics rivaled most men's, but she continued to defer to men in conversation while maintaining her independence in actions.

"I don't know if I'll be elected. You understand better than anyone that a lawman makes enemies. I'm determined to campaign hard in support of restoring Roosevelt's progressive agenda. I want to make laws, not just enforce them. Starting here in Kentucky. Who knows, maybe someday..." His voice trailed off.

Verna became animated. "Clinton, you'd be a fine legislator. Heaven knows, we need men who appreciate the rights of all – women, Negroes, hill and poor folks."

"A few important men in Richmond will support my countywide campaign. Since I backed Governor Black against Morrow, some of his men have joined my campaign."

Verna exclaimed, "Why, that's wonderful, Clinton."

He paused wistfully. "With all that traveling I can't come to Louisville for a while."

Verna heard the phone click. "We're still talking. Thank you." Her polite but firm voice shamed the eavesdropper into hanging up.

"Clinton, one of us is always waiting. You waited for me to finish nursing school. I waited until you returned from the war. You waited while I established myself as a private duty nurse. Now I need to wait until your campaign is over. It's only fair, much as I wanted..." Verna stopped herself. "Hazel, Beulah, and Hiram will work for your election. Lord knows, if you say you're for women's voting rights, Blanche might even help fund your campaign."

Clinton laughed. "Verna, the attention from this campaign makes me feel like a man again. First time since I stepped on that mine in France."

"Clinton, you always are a man to me."

"I love you, Verna."

"I know, Clinton." Hearing Clinton's sigh, she felt his disappointment but was afraid. During her struggle after John's death, one of her granny's sayings kept coming to her. "Don't draw attention. Don't think you're better than others or be loved best."

The one she loved best died. Ellen's illness, Son's beating, Clinton's lost arm, all warnings, to be careful, careful not to draw attention to her loved ones, careful not to love --- too much.

# CHAPTER FIFTY-SEVEN

## ESCAPING INFLUENZA

The influenza epidemic of 1919 invaded Louisville, starting outside the city limits in Fort Taylor before moving into the tenements. Illness and death reached every part of town. Money no longer protected a family. Verna saw the blackened faces of the dying and decided to remove her children from the disease-plagued city. The orphanage planned on evacuating to the outer limits of Louisville to protect the children under their care, but Verna wanted them all out of Louisville immediately. She hurriedly packed two valises with clothes, one for herself and one for the children, and bought tickets for the first train west.

She had wired Clinton for money, promising to pay him back the first month after she returned. He wired back the money, reassuring her that with the government's new policy to give monthly disability payments to wounded soldiers, he had more money than he needed. In order not to frighten the children she simply said she'd decided they all needed a vacation and they were going to Oklahoma to visit Son.

The train ride went smoothly. They left in late afternoon. Nanny Marie slept most of the way and even Ellen and Darcine succumbed to sleep before the train reached the western boundaries of Kentucky. The next morning as Verna debarked from the train in Oklahoma, a flying missile of a ten-year-old boy wrapped himself around her body. "Ma, Ma, you came." He jumped off her quickly and prepared to launch himself on Darcine when Verna bent down and calmly said, "Give me a proper hug, Son."

For two weeks the family romped through the Oklahoma countryside around the Gentrys' place. "Ma, this looks like Berea." Ellen exclaimed on the second day. "It's got tall, green hills. The air smells sweet. Everyone's nice, just like at home."

Verna feasted her eyes on the expanse of land and sky. "I'm never going to stay away from the hills this long again," she vowed to her sister-in-law. Nan hugged Verna and let her eyes fill with the sight of Son romping with his sisters. "Verna, I've never been as happy as I am since Son came to be with us. Look at him, Verna. He's a happy boy again."

Sitting at the kitchen table enjoying the late-night quiet, Verna filled Nan in on Clinton's campaign. "Verna, how did he ever get the money for such a campaign?" Nan knew Clinton's family barely got by when he was growing up.

"The city of Berea gave him money for the years of service he gave before he got wounded, and the federal government has a new program to provide disability pay to wounded soldiers."

"Yeah, I heard of that. One of our neighbor's boys came back with his leg shot off. They say he gets enough to get by, barely. But still it's something. Never thought a Democrat would do good by us. But that Wilson's a better man than anyone figured. Does that mean that Clinton went off to the Democratic Party?"

"No. No. Heavens, no, Nan. A Republican merchant in Richmond became interested in financing him. The family lost a son, oldest child, in the war. Left only with a daughter. Mother died in childbirth is the way Clinton tells it. The father took to Clinton, said he reminds him of his boy. From his letters, Clinton admires Mr. Otis like a father, a sober, successful father. They've been campaigning together for six months now. I guess the campaign is going just fine. I haven't heard much from Clinton this past month. Except he responded real quick to my telegram asking for help in buying tickets. But I reckon he's too busy for idle chitchat."

"Does it worry you, Verna?"

Verna's eyes gazed off. "Nan, I'm a little surprised I haven't missed his letters more. My life's so full with my work and seeing the children weekly, now that the orphanage lets me visit regularly."

"I never did understand that old rule, Verna. Wasn't right."

"No, it wasn't. Now I dream of being all together again."

Verna saw Nan look down and pretend to stir her tea. She put her hand on Nan's. "I won't take Son from you soon. I still can't afford to have any of the children with me. First, Ellen and Darcine need to graduate with skills to support themselves."

Nan, reassured that Son would stay for at least one more year, freely gave Verna advice. "You know the girls'll just get married, Verna. Why bother?"

"Nan, look at me. You and I married poor men. Good men. Hardworking men who expected to take care of us. I want Darcine and Ellen to be nurses, so if they must, they can support themselves. After all, do you really want them to marry someone like my brother?"

The sisters-by-marriage laughed, breaking the serious mood. Verna knew that although Nan and Grover got their land in Oklahoma by homesteading, they worked all the daylight hours just to eat and pay the bills. Living in Louisville, socializing with the doctors and nurses, Verna glimpsed the possibility of a different life for her children than working the land in Berea or Oklahoma.

The days passed as the children played outside, riding the pony, following their uncle while he worked the fields, and avoiding the house lest they be asked to help with the inside work. Verna and Nan cooked, sewed, canned, sat on the porch, and took long walks when the day cooled. Verna sought out her children, playing with them separately or together. She conspired to help the youngest avoid all work except setting the table. Ellen and Darcine still had to set the table, wash all the children's clothes and do any mending needed, bathe their younger sister, and sweep the porch and kitchen. Ellen only complained once to her mother and then caught the look on her aunt's face and stopped.

The adults deferred talk of the future until the last night of the Collins' stay. A peek upstairs revealed the small sleeping children intertwined, while the older girls whispered, enjoying the luxury of privacy unavailable at the orphanage.

"Son looks so good, Nan. You and Grover returned my boy's spunk."

"Verna, you gave me what I always wanted, a child to raise. You've seen him with his Uncle Grover. Why, you know that man cusses with the best of them when he gets mad. Son just stands there

– not running off, until Grover picks him up and says, 'Never you mind me.' I think they're good for each other."

Nan paused, got up, and poured herself a cup of tepid tea. "Verna, Oklahoma's a good place to raise children. With lots of room to run. Why, some say that's why Jim Thorpe got so good." Nan smiled and then looked down and picked at a biscuit before continuing. "Verna, let Nanny Marie come live with us for a while. My heart pines for that child with her angel face."

"It's been real good for Son here, but Nanny Marie is doing fine at the Home." Verna's chin moved to the left as she bit her cheek. She wouldn't say "orphanage." "She'd miss her big sisses."

"Is that the only reason?" Nan looked into Verna's eyes trying to force the truth, knowing her sister-in-law's evasiveness.

Verna tried to avoid Nan's gaze. How had life so changed them? Nan was the one with a home now and a hardworking husband. Now she wanted Verna's children, too. Verna stopped herself from saying the cruel words that flooded her thoughts, saying instead, "I'll take some more tea, too. If you don't mind."

After the ritual pouring and sipping, Verna returned to Nan's question. "I'm not ready to have Nanny Marie so far away, if the truth be told. Not being able to see Son is like an ache in my stomach. I plan on making enough money to bring us together. Next March, Ellen will graduate. Then she can help out. I'm just not ready to let go of another child. I know Nanny Marie would be happy here, but... Let me think on it tonight."

"Verna, don't say anymore. You know I love you like my own sister. Whatever your decision is, Grover and I will provide a home for your children as long as I live. When you are ready."

They heard a thud from the loft. Verna went to the stairs and gently admonished, "Enough now. Go to sleep, all of you. We have a long trip tomorrow."

At the head of the stairs, Son stood, rubbing his eyes. The salty tears burned. "I woke up."

"There's nothing to be frightened about. Shush, you'll wake Nanny Marie."

"I'm awake too, Ma."

"All of you. Go back to sleep." Even Verna's sternest voice showed hesitancy, undermining her authority.

"Tell me a story."

"One story is all."

"Tell me a story of my pa." Son walked down the stairs, holding Nanny Marie's hand.

"Not that, Son."

"Please, Ma. I want to hear about Pa."

Verna looked at Nan, who shook her head yes in encouragement. Verna took her young boy upon her lap. "Son, John Collins, your pa, was the most beloved man in Berea. He was the sheriff..." As Verna rubbed her son's back and told the story of his father, her older children slipped down the steps, listening quietly in the dark. Verna noticed that Nanny Marie slipped her hand in her brother's and the two of them leaned closer together.

In the morning Verna had made her decision. Nanny Marie would stay in Oklahoma. During the night she had asked herself two questions, "Are you being selfish, Verna Gentry Collins?" And "Isn't it time to do what you know is right?" Ellen and Darcine hugged their mother when she told them and asked her not to cry. Verna wondered how they had grown up so quickly.

In the morning she went to town and called the director of nursing, asking permission to extend her visit for another week. Then she and Nan went to the general store for material for one Sunday dress and underwear. Verna had Nanny Marie try on a pair of shoes and stuffed paper in the toes so she would have room to grow. They purchased three cotton sacks and a nightgown.

During the week Grover cut down a large maple tree in the backyard where Nan had wanted to expand her kitchen garden. He cut the widest section of the trunk into a gigantic log, eight inches taller than Nanny Marie. He then spilt the log in half and carved out the soft insides. He spent hours sanding the inside until no splinters were left. He added a headboard and used brown barn paint to stop the flow of sap. It fit perfectly along the wall of Son's bedroom closest to Nan's bedroom. Nan added layers of blankets until Nanny Marie's new bed was more comfortable than the living room settee.

# CHAPTER FIFTY-EIGHT

## HONESTY HURTS

Dropping her valise inside the door of her rented room, Verna raced to open her letters. First, the one from Clinton. She sat in the sole chair in her room, positioned to look out a window onto a stunted city tree. The letter read like a telegram.

*Dear Verna,*

*I'm coming to Louisville. Need to talk to you. Be waiting for your call at the jail Sunday evening. Clinton*

Puzzled at first, Verna decided Clinton posted the letter so she would receive it when she arrived from Oklahoma on Sunday evening. She immediately placed a call to him.

Clinton picked up the phone so quickly, Verna envisioned him standing with his hand on the receiver. After brief hellos, Verna began talking about Oklahoma.

"Verna, I want to hear about the children, but wait, please, until I come to Louisville. When may I see you?" Clinton's voice sounded far away.

"I'm not off again until next Sunday. Oh, Clinton. Son has grown at least two inches."

"That's nice, Verna. I'll come Sunday afternoon. Bye. I have to go now."

"Bye, Clinton." She waited for his, "I love you." Even after the click.

"Ma'am, your party has hung up," the operator's pleasant voice informed her.

"He always likes to save money." Verna laughingly shared with the operator.

At week's end, a male patient from the eastern coal mines told Verna how tired she looked. Verna surveyed her face in a mirror, surprised to find dark circles under her eyes.

"I've been waking at night." Verna shared.

"Bad dreams? I get them since I got sick. I dream my lungs turn blacker and blacker until I die." The patient looked at Verna for sympathy.

Verna kept her face immobile, hiding from the patient her belief that dreams predicted the future. "You are fit as can be. Now don't you be worrying. You need your rest." Verna regretted sharing her sleeplessness. Since Clinton's call, Verna repetitively dreamed of being lost in the woods around Granny's cabin, calling for help. But no one came. She decided her dream meant she missed the children.

On Sunday afternoon clouds covered the sky but lifted briefly for a teasing peek at purple and pink streaks. Verna changed her dress twice, finally settling on a pale blue one, tight around her hips and shorter than most as the hem hit the top of her ankles. She didn't want to wear her comfortable brown dress, since Clinton told her he liked the new, lighter colors.

Clinton arrived at her boardinghouse slightly out of breath. He suggested a cup of coffee at the small café close by. He didn't comment on her dress. Verna thought she might as well have worn the brown and saved herself from having to iron the blue. While they sipped coffee and waited for the pie, Verna told Clinton about the children and Nan's offer to take Nanny Marie. Verna found herself staring at Clinton's face. She noticed he looked younger, more handsome. "Clinton, there's something different about the way you look."

He blushed. "I got a new haircut. It's supposed to make me look like a man of substance." As he smiled, Verna glimpsed his boyishness, absent since John's death.

The waitress unloaded their food onto the table, as if with a pitchfork. Clinton cleared his throat. "Is something wrong, Clinton?"

Verna tried to look into his eyes, but he persisted in gazing around the room.

"No, Verna, nothing's wrong. Well, yes, yes, there is." He fiddled with his empty sleeve; a habit started since his return from the war. "Verna, I... This is real hard."

"Clinton, does your arm hurt?"

Verna knew about phantom pain and had explained the phenomenon to Clinton. At first he didn't believe her that the pain existed in his imagination. He kept yelling, "I know it's got the green. Don't let them cut it off at the shoulder. Don't let them, please, Verna." Finally he accepted the doctors' reassurances that he would not lose his entire arm.

Verna persisted. "I can tell there's something you need to say. I used to say to John, 'Just open your mouth and it'll pop out.'" She took a deep breath to give her the courage to say what was on her mind: "John got that look when he was interested in another woman."

Clinton jumped as if startled by a turkey flying out of the bush. He lit a cigarette, drew in deeply, and patted the ash onto the floor. "Verna, I find myself thinking about Colonel Otis's daughter."

Verna's mind left the room for a moment. "The Colonel Otis who's been supporting your campaign?"

"Yeah. I think my feelings grew from being around her all the time. I didn't know at first, Verna. I thought I just enjoyed her company. I've cared about you for so long that I didn't really notice at first how my feelings for her were changing."

"Clinton, what are you trying to tell me?" Verna unclenched her fists, deliberately placing her hands in her lap. He kept avoiding her gaze. Her cheeks began to burn.

"Verna, nothing's happened. Miss Otis doesn't know how I feel. I wanted to tell you first. You are special to me, Verna. I'm not John. I couldn't start courting her while we were... Oh, you know I'm no good at talking about my feelings." Clinton stopped, angry at his stumbling, and lit another cigarette.

"Clinton, let me see if I understand. You're telling me you want to start courting her." As Verna looked at Clinton's slumped shoulders and averted face, her own feelings became clearer. "Clinton, I'm mad and more than a little hurt that you find another woman attractive. But Clinton, I feel a spot of warmth for you. It took courage to tell me that you have feelings for another woman. And to do it before you've started courting her. I wish John... Never mind."

Verna willed herself to stay in the present and not let her angry and hurt feelings about John's betrayal spew themselves on Clinton.

"Clinton, I don't know how I feel." She paused and looked now at her hands, roughened and reddened from the scrubbing of patients. "Alone, scared of losing you." Verna looked up and saw the fear in Clinton's face, fear that he had hurt her. Knowing he cared helped the heaviness of loss to lift from her heart. "You've been there since John died, but something died in me when John was killed. I loved him and only him for so long. Then suddenly one day, he wasn't there anymore." Verna reached out to enclose Clinton's perspiring hand.

Emboldened by Verna's confession, Clinton confided, "I watched the two of you and thought, 'I want a woman to love me like that someday.' My idea of love came from watching you and John, not my ma and pa who did more fighting than loving.

"Verna, I always figured you would grow to love me like you loved John. I felt you holding back. I'd tell you 'I love you.' You'd change the subject or say, 'I know.' Truth is that made me kind of mad. Miss Otis tells me, not in words but in looks, of her affections. I believe she can give me the love you felt for John." Clinton's hand relaxed by his side. If Verna had been his ma, plates would be flying all over the café.

"Clinton, the days after John died I stayed in bed until you started coming round. I needed you in my life. Right now I'm scared, thinking of being without you." Verna lowered her eyes and sipped from her water glass. "But you're right. I never told you I loved you. Something held me back. I felt tenderness. I felt like I did for my grandpa, the most important man in my life, until John. That kind of love."

"Verna, do you think we could be friends again, like before John died?" Clinton hesitated to ask the question. "I want you and your children in my life."

"Clinton, I don't know, but I'm willing to try. If you think your chaste Miss Otis wouldn't mind." Verna's anger eked out in uncharacteristic sarcasm. "I'm sorry, Clinton, that was uncalled for. You were there for me in the darkness and I grew to care for you." Verna looked away. She could feel tears gathering at the corners of her eyes and she didn't want Clinton to see them. After taking a deep breath, she continued. "I'm a little hurt now." She wiped her eyes and then sincerely said, "I hope you'll always want to be part of our life."

As Clinton escorted Verna back to her boardinghouse, he held her elbow. She let her body lean toward him as if to store his warmth for a long winter. Reaching the door, Clinton bent down and kissed her cheek. She touched his warm hand, running her fingers over his veins. Standing on her stoop, she watched him walk down the long block and wave as he turned the corner.

# CHAPTER FIFTY-NINE

# THE NEW PATIENT

In December of 1919, after missing several doctors' calls, Verna asked her landlady to take messages when she wasn't home. Hearing the ring, Mrs. Randolph let herself into Verna's apartment in order to respond privately.

"Hello, is this Mrs. Collins? This is Mr. Derby." The man's deep voice projected respectability.

In a prideful voice, Mrs. Randolph responded, "No. Mrs. Collins asked me to take calls about private duty nursing for her. If this is a personal call, please call back later."

"I need, rather, my wife needs, a private duty nurse, as soon as possible. Her health is failing." The voice cracked as the caller appeared to lose control of his emotions.

Mrs. Randolph's family lost their wealth following the Civil War. Never married, she retained genteel manners and responded compassionately to those people she thought 'were the right sort.' "Just a moment, sir. Let me get some paper to take your information." She quickly found the notebook Verna kept in her desk drawer for recording patients' calls. "I'm ready now."

"My wife has the influenza. She is very sick. Very sick. We've just let the nurse go. Her care was so, so..." Clearly unable to find the words, Mr. Derby stammered, "inadequate or worse. Her doctor says we must have someone immediately. I simply can't do it. We've not been able to get decent help. Everyone is afraid they will catch the influenza. She's not getting better. And the children... Do you think that's enough for Mrs. Collins to know? She must call me soon. Dr. Duffield recommended her highly. And I remember her from the nursing graduation."

"Mr. Derby, I will leave your message here for her. I will also personally let her know, the minute she comes home, that we spoke. I do wish your wife the best. It is hard these days with the illness in so many homes. You have children, also. I will certainly tell Mrs. Collins."

When Verna returned, she longed for a warm bath and to sit with her feet propped up. She deliberately avoided her phone message pad. Kicking off her shoes and easing her right foot into a slipper, she winced as Mrs. Randolph knocked on her door. "Verna, I thought I heard you."

"Come in," Verna reluctantly offered, as she slipped her other foot into a well-worn slipper and sat down on the single bed, leaving the chair for her landlady.

"Verna, did you see my note? He seemed like such a gentleman. Very concerned about his wife. Not like many of the men who call you, gruff and all, as if you've got nothing better to do but answer their calls. And he knows you. He said he remembered you from the graduation."

Verna picked up the note. "Is it Mr. Derby? I think that's the name you've written. Sometimes I have trouble with your handwriting when my eyes hurt at night."

"Yes, I remember, it was Derby, just like the race."

"Thank you again. He's Dr. Duffield's friend but I just don't know when I'll have a chance to meet with him. There are so many sick people these days. I'll call him in the morning."

"Verna, you should call him now. His wife is very sick. He was polite but worried. I thought he might cry."

Verna, remembering all Dr. Duffield had done for her, helping her get admitted and including her with the younger nurses in taking care of the soldiers at Camp Taylor, felt obligated to return the call of his friend. "All right, I'll call him now. Appreciate your taking my calls so carefully." Verna could tell her landlady didn't want to leave. "I'd best do this confidentially, don't you think?"

"Yes, yes, of course. " Mrs. Randolph reluctantly left Verna's room. With her own children grown and moved away, she depended on her roomers' lives for excitement.

Verna, picturing the quiet, distinguished man who lectured them on the growing importance of chemistry for nursing, called the number carefully printed on the sheet of paper next to the name, Derby. A man answered the phone. She quickly heard the desperation described by her landlady.

"Oh, Mrs.Collins, thank you for calling. Thank you. Dr. Duffield suggested I call you, and of course, I remember that you received an award on Graduation Day. We so need your help. My wife is sick, very sick. And..." Verna could hear him struggle to continue without showing his emotions. "We had to let the other nurse go." Verna waited patiently while Dr. Derby repeated word for word what Mrs. Randolph had already conveyed. Her landlady had a perfect memory for people's woes while forgetting to keep the porch swept in the summer or restock the coal in the winter.

"Dr. Derby, I am very sorry about your wife. Nurse Mildred Braun has just finished with her patient and would be quite good for your family. She graduated two years ago from the City Hospital nursing program and specialized in working with adults."

"Mrs. Collins, please help my wife. She is so sick. Our maid has quit also and the previous nurse before this one was dreadful. I heard your qualifications at the graduation and my children need the care of an older woman. I am a professor at the University of Louisville and must return to my laboratory. Besides, I simply don't know how to help her."

She gathered from his accent that Dr. Derby wasn't from Louisville. "Do you have family who might help?"

"No, they are still in the East."

Verna thought, but didn't say, that distance shouldn't keep family away.

Although she regretted his obvious distress and believed his wife to be in true need, her current patient required skilled care. "I can't possibly, Dr. Derby."

"Please, call me Mr. Derby."

"You said you were a professor at the university."

"Yes, I am. But the title isn't necessary. After all, I'm not a medical doctor.

We met at your graduation."

"Oh, yes." Verna appreciated his humility given his stature in the community. Verna and Mary Lou imitated the presumptuousness of two university professors who insisted on being referred to as "doctor" at a hospital benefit event.

"I simply can't, Dr., Mr. Derby, not at this time. It wouldn't be fair to leave my other patient. Their infant son is very ill and I don't know anyone available who might help them. Please let me contact my friend, Miss Braun. I'm so sorry, but I'm sure you understand."

"Mrs. Collins, I understand your commitment to your patients. Let me talk with Dr. Duffield again. Perhaps I will ask your friend. I'm very disappointed, but I appreciate your returning my call."

Verna hung up the phone reluctantly, sensing the heaviness of this man's burden as a husband and a father. Less than five minutes later as she readied her bath, the phone rang again. "Verna, it's Dr. Duffield."

"Hey, Dr. Duffield. I just spoke with Mr. Derby. He said you referred him. Appreciate your thinking..."

He interrupted her impatiently. "Verna, Mr. Derby must have help. His wife is quite ill. I think it's more than the influenza. She's not recovering. When he called, I thought of you immediately. They have children a little older than your Ellen. I don't know anyone better able to help his family. You must remember him; he gave a lecture during my class on the role of chemistry in discovering new medicines."

"Oh, I do. He seemed brilliant and very concerned about finding new medicines to help the sick, but I just can't, not at this time."

"Verna, Mr. Derby's modesty belies his importance as a scientist. I've gotten three calls from the university and two from businessmen asking us to help so he may return to his laboratory. I've seen his wife myself. Her care has been dreadful. Her skin, well, I can't describe how terrible it is. The family is helpless with the illness being so severe. Two nurses quit already, afraid of becoming ill themselves. They complained about the boy. Apparently, he won't behave."

"What's he doing?" Verna queried

"Why, he's just invented..."

"I don't mean Dr. Derby. I mean his son."

"He won't go to school. No matter how his father threatens him and the nurses cajole him, he refuses to leave the house."

"Why, Dr. Duffield, I understand that. The boy's afraid his mother's going to die if he leaves her."

"Verna, I think you're right. By gum. That makes good sense. Of course. See. I knew it. Ira said you were caring for an infant. I know a nurse, specializes in infant care, graduated before you entered at City. The Derby family needs you. Say you'll help them. For me. I never asked you for a favor before, but you owe me, Verna, and I'm asking now."

The very day the infant nurse took over for Verna and she felt it safe to leave her small patient, Verna, in her starched uniform with her nursing pin on the collar, arrived at the Derby home. Putting her cloth valise down and looking up before knocking on the large wooden door, she admired the red brick three-story home, which was the only house in the neighborhood without Christmas decorations.

Her acceptance of the position happened quickly. Dr. Duffield did find a skilled infant nurse for Verna's patient and assured Verna that the Derby household was released from quarantine by the City Health Department. Mrs. Derby, while still appearing seriously ill, was no longer contagious. Mr. Derby suggested that Verna's children spend Christmas Day in his home and visit on Sundays for as long as she worked for them. Verna thanked him for the offer and silently decided to wait until she herself felt the house medically safe for her children.

Mr. Derby met her at the door and took her valise. "Mrs. Collins, how good to see you. Thank you for making arrangements. We certainly do need your help. But come in, come." He appeared awkward and somewhat shy to Verna – different from his self-assured presence at school. "May I show you to your room?" His tall, lean stature reminded Verna of Abe Lincoln, except instead of a full beard, a trim mustache curved atop his light pink lips. His pale, long thin face, accented by darkened smudges under his eyes and held tenuously on a skin-slackened neck, resembled the starving patients Verna had seen admitted to the poverty wards of the hospital. Dressed in a rumpled suit soiled around the pockets, Mr. Derby looked more like a chimney sweep than the distinguished professor she remembered lecturing to her nursing class.

On the way to the third-floor servants' quarters, Verna noticed enviously that each member of the Derby family had a separate bedroom on the second floor. After shaking Mr. Derby's cool, veined hand, Verna refused his offer to unpack. "Not yet. I would like to meet your wife and begin now, if you don't mind."

She walked behind him up a large carpeted stairway with carved spindles, running her hand over the smooth wood and admiring the gas fixtures that had been converted to electricity. Mr. Derby opened his wife's bedroom door, announcing, "Darling, your new nurse, Mrs. Collins, is here."

Upon entering the room, Verna recognized the offensive odor. Putting on a smile, she approached the frail woman lying in a four-poster bed, partially hidden by a flowered panel screen.

"Hello, Mrs. Derby. I'm Verna Collins, your new nurse. Would you like a drink of water?" Verna asked Mr. Derby for a clean handkerchief. Then she moved over to the bed and raised the slack head gently while moistening her patient's lips with water from a bone china pitcher sitting on the marble-top table by the bed.

Mrs. Derby managed a weak hello and tried to raise her hand from the pillow for a proper handshake. Verna placed her own hand gently on the sick woman's shoulder. "Please, just stay comfortable. Is it all right if I freshen you up a bit?"

"Yes. I would like that." Mrs. Derby weakly sank back into her rumpled sheets, exhausted from the attempt to greet her new nurse.

Verna gently pulled back the arm of her patient's nightgown and saw the beginning of bedsores. She asked Mr. Derby for a clean hand cloth, a towel, and fresh water. She noted the formal manners between the husband and wife, who called each other "my dear." For the rest of the morning she bathed her patient, put on clean sleets – smoothed and pulled tight to eliminate any wrinkles that would irritate Mrs. Derby's skin. She made a note to have Mr. Derby purchase sterilized lotion for his wife's damaged skin.

"Mrs. Derby, did your previous nurse turn your body over in the bed frequently?"

"No, I don't remember her doing that except when I asked her. Then she would complain about how heavy I was. Do you remember her turning me, Ira? Perhaps, while I slept."

"No, Helen. I don't. She seemed to sit over in that chair a lot. She said it was important to watch your breathing. I hate to say it, but I caught her sleeping several times when I came in unexpectedly." Mr. Derby's mood turned from embarrassment over taking the nurse's word rather than trusting his instincts to anger as he began to realize the extent of the previous nurse's neglect of his wife.

"Mrs. Collins, should my wife be turned frequently?"

Verna decided not to explain to her patient and Mr. Derby that avoiding prolonged pressure on any one place on her body was extremely important. Angered by her patient's visible neglect, Verna vowed to find out more about the previous nurse's care and credentials, reporting her, if necessary, to the Nursing Board of Registration.

For now Verna decided to respond to his question with a simple statement. "Yes, Mr. Derby. But don't you worry. I know how to do the turning myself without hurting your wife. And I'm sure you'll help me, won't you, Mrs. Derby?"

Several weeks later, as Christmas approached, the household, relieved by Verna's tender professional care of Mrs. Derby, began to actually look forward to the holidays. Verna attended to her patient as she would a small child: feeding her liquids, soothing her skin, turning her, minimizing visitors, and calming the alarmed family members. Mrs. Derby's skin improved under Verna's care but her attempts to breathe did not.

Concerned with her patient's obvious respiratory difficulties, Verna suggested that Mr. Derby contact a specialist in pulmonary diseases rather than the general practitioner who had been treating his wife. The specialist agreed to come on Christmas Eve. After entering the room, he asked the family to leave while he examined the patient. Verna watched him expertly listen to his patient's lungs, and then, after asking her permission, examined Mrs. Derby's breasts. He looked at Verna with sad eyes as he reassured Mrs. Derby he would give her something to help her sleep better.

Verna stayed in the room talking quietly with her patient, as the doctor drew Mr. Derby into the hall and shut the door. They both heard Mr. Derby's "Oh, no! Oh, God, no!" Verna held Mrs. Derby's hand as her patient looked at Verna. "It's cancer, isn't it? I've known for a while. I felt it growing, but Ira didn't want to know. You will stay and help us, won't you? Please."

Verna, touched by the gentility of her patient and the helplessness of her caring husband, agreed to stay.

Later, as she comforted Mr. Derby, she reaffirmed her commitment to stay. "Your wife's a lovely woman. I've had training on working with patients with such serious illnesses. I believe I know how to make her comfortable. However, I can only stay until March; then you must find someone else."

"I appreciate that Mrs. Collins. I..." He couldn't go on. "Excuse me, I need to return to my wife."

"Of course."

# CHAPTER SIXTY

# A LAST FAVOR

In early January of 1920 the doctor gave Mrs. Derby only a few months to live. On the day she was to leave for college in the East, Elizabeth, the Derbys' daughter, refused to return to Bryn Mawr. She went into the parlor and played softly on the baby grand piano. Mr. Derby's words reached the kitchen where Verna was preparing supper. "Please, Elizabeth, at least talk with your mother. You need to be sure that your decision does not cause her distress."

The music stopped and Verna heard footsteps on the stairs. As Verna wrote later to Hazel, "I don't know what Mrs. Derby said to her daughter, but she came out of her mother's room, head down, and didn't speak to any of us. Went straight to her room, packed her bags, and Mr. Derby took her to the train. Personally, I believe she belongs with her mother, but these Easterners have their own ways."

Verna found the patience to work with Gordon, the Derbys' son, helping him catch up on his schoolwork for the private day school he attended in Louisville. After completing each night's assignment, Verna joined him on the floor playing with iron soldiers that he had never been allowed to touch and reading adventure stories, starting with his favorite, *Gulliver's Travels*.

Verna encouraged Mr. Derby to buy fresh flowers daily, which she arranged in vases throughout Mrs. Derby's sick room, filling the air with pleasant scents. The household settled into the routine of a home with a seriously ill family member.

Verna and Mr. Derby became friends. Not as employer and employee sometimes do, but as two people who, under distress, slowly remove the barriers that separate them. She was touched by the concern he showed his wife and his loving ways with his son. After Mrs. Derby went to sleep at night, they would talk. Tentatively at first, Mr. Derby spoke of his upbringing in New Hampshire. As he described skiing in deep snow though pine tree forests, Verna thought, "How similar we are in our love of hills and forests."

One night, after several attempts to light his pipe, he laughingly put it aside as his tone became serious. "Verna, Don Duffield told me you lost your husband. I'm deeply sorry. " He looked down as if to avoid the sadness in her eyes, but then looked up realizing he would soon share her loss of a spouse.

"I admire your courage coming to Louisville and starting a career. Not many women would be strong enough to do that. How did you find the will to go on?"

At first Verna thought about evading the question. She found it easy to distract men by turning their questions back to them. Most were more than happy to talk about themselves. He looked at her earnestly without guile, and she returned his gaze knowing he wasn't just asking about her, but also about himself.

"I don't consider myself strong. Many's the time I wanted to quit, go back to Berea. Do what was familiar. I had a granny who took care of me when my mother left..." Sipping her now-tepid tea, Verna talked about her past. She found Mr. Derby an unusually attentive listener, never interrupting, taking advantage of her pauses to ask questions that encouraged her to share more. She was surprised to hear the clock chime 9:00. "Excuse me, Mr. Derby, I want to check on Mrs. Derby before I retire for the evening. Goodnight."

"Thank you, Mrs. Collins. Your story gives me strength." His eyes looked sad as he tried again to light his pipe while she cleared away the tea service and shut the library door quietly as she left.

Mr. Derby came to his wife's sick room each afternoon when he returned from his laboratory. After greeting Verna, he sat quietly by the four-poster mahogany bed. Verna left them alone and supervised the cook's fixing of the dinner. When Verna first came, the disorderly house flaunted its neglect. Dust balls rolled out from under her patient's bed, the maid having fled, afraid that Mrs. Derby's illness was contagious. The Derbys, unfamiliar with Southern cooking, mistook their cook's dried, overcooked chicken for the "Kentucky way" and never complained.

Upon Verna's recommendation Mr. Derby fired the cook and asked Verna to supervise the new German cook and maid, who, because of discrimination since America entered the war, were having a hard time finding work in other homes. Verna, unaccustomed to being waited on, helped out in the kitchen when her patient slept. She marveled at the Kerneator garbage disposal that dispensed refuse through a little door. She occasionally made biscuits, soothing Mrs. Derby's increasingly finicky stomach with their honey-covered softness. Verna, having watched Mr. Derby put salt on his morning grapefruit, smiled at his attempt to tolerate the excessive sweetness – "These are tasty, Mrs. Collins."

Shortly after she arrived, Mr. Derby asked Verna to eat at the dining room table with his son while he took his meals with his wife. She sat at the daughter's place on the side of the table closest to the kitchen. Mr. Derby directed the cook to set places for both him and his wife, reminding Verna of the months she and the children dined with John's plate and cup as empty company.

During one of their evening conversations, Verna spoke to him about her children. "In a year or so I will be able to have my children with me again. Ellen can get work in one of the stores after school and help out. I feel as if I have been holding my breath. The older girls can live with me again. Whoever would think I would look forward to Ellen's tongue! Now I can hardly wait. Ellen's talking about getting a job in retail. Just as Blanche predicted, since the war more women are working outside their homes. And young women just a little older than Ellen are coming into Louisville to work in the stores. So many more opportunities than when I was young." Verna stopped abruptly, embarrassed at how she was going on.

"Verna, please continue. I like to hear you talk." Dr. Derby sat back and relit his pipe. Verna remained quiet. She had noticed on previous occasions that when he drew deeply on this pipe, it was better not to interrupt his thoughts. He put his pipe down and leaned forward.

"Your older children are welcome here now. They can stay on the third floor with you. There's an extra room since the new cook lives out. We can enroll them in the local public school. It's just around the block and has committed teachers and well-behaved children."

His voice became quieter. "I've become fond of your children during their Sunday visits. Although," he smiled, rare since his wife's condition was declared terminal, "your oldest daughter is certainly outspoken."

"They are comfortable here. You've been so kind, Mr. Derby. "

"Verna, please call me Ira. I would like that."

He looked so sincere, Verna agreed with no compunction. "Ira, if you think my Ellen is a handful, you should see Son." She laughed at the thought of Son in this grand home.

In March Ellen and Darcine moved in with their mother on the third floor of the Derby's home. The girls avoided Mrs. Derby's sick room but made friends with the Derby's son, Gordon, only a year older than Ellen. Ellen found work after school as a clerk at a soft goods store, selling dresses and undergarments to women. Darcine helped her mother and the cook in the kitchen. Both girls told Verna that the new school was "peaches" and she asked them not to use the new slang they were picking up.

One day, as Verna and Ellen folded the laundry; Ellen stopped and looked up at her mother. "Ma, I don't know how you could put us in an orphanage. You keep saying it was the right thing to do. Just once, I'd like to hear you say, 'Ellen, you're right. Children should not be raised in an orphanage. After all, look at Son....'"

Verna stopped listening when Ellen got to the words "look at Son." Instead she surveyed her oldest daughter's face. Usually she avoided looking at Ellen, afraid the rage would char her heart. But this time, instead of a monster with verbal flames streaming out her mouth, she saw an attractive young woman with hurt eyes, pleading for understanding.

Verna calmed, breathed deeply, letting the air out slowly before speaking. "I agree with you, honey. Being in an orphanage is hard for a child. Worse than having to be raised by a grandmother." Momentarily stunned, Ellen blinked, then, taking advantage of her mother's attention, she demanded, "You are never, ever to tell anyone, I mean anyone, that we lived in an orphanage."

"I'll try not to, Ellen." Verna wanted to respect her daughter's request but knew it would be hard as long as they lived in Louisville.

Afterward Verna attempted to listen attentively while trying not to be defensive, as Ellen and Darcine began telling their mother small details about their life in the orphanage and Ellen's experiences working in Louisville. Surprised to learn from her daughter how many young women lived away from their families in order to work in the big city, Verna began to realize the changes in younger women's attitudes. Mother and daughters talked about women's rights, how the war changed Clinton, the children in the orphanage who died of the influenza. Darcine announced she was a suffragette and expressed excitement at women being able to vote in the next presidential election.

A month after the children moved in, Mrs. Derby asked Verna to sit beside her on the bed so they might talk privately. "Mrs. Collins, I believe my time is near. I was raised in a family where we faced the truth head on," she continued. "I want my family to face my death, and I need your help. I am too weak to get out of bed. What good am I? The pain is too much for me. The doctor must increase the laudanum."

Verna admired Mrs. Derby's bravery in the face of pain and certain death. "I understand what you're saying, Mrs. Derby. I'll speak to him."

"Mrs. Collins, thank you. You restored my dignity and helped my family during...during our difficult time."

Verna called the doctor, who came over in the evening after his rounds at the hospital. He spoke privately with Mrs. Derby, then gathered her husband and son around her bedside to pray. He left instructions for the medication and promised to stop by each evening. He recommended the Derbys call their daughter home from college to be with her mother.

A week later Mrs. Derby died peacefully in her bed, surrounded by her family.

# CHAPTER SIXTY-ONE

# CLINTON'S REQUEST

In May, six weeks after Mrs. Derby passed, Verna continued to live on the Derby's third floor with her oldest daughters. Although he protested, Mr. Derby accepted a small monthly rent payment for the girls' room, respecting Verna's pride in being self-sufficient. Verna showed Mr. Derby a surprising letter she received from Clinton and asked if he would have any problems granting Clinton's request.

> "Dear Verna, I hope you don't find my request too bold, but I am coming to Louisville next week. Some of the party bosses there have arranged interviews with several Louisville papers that are read in Madison County. I'm wondering if I might bring Miss Otis, my fiancée, to meet you."

He wrote other news about the campaign and gossip of Berea, but Verna kept going back to the words "... my fiancée to meet you."

Mr. Derby gave his permission for Clinton to come to the house but recommended that a female friend might help her more on the "...cough, cough, cough ... other details of the visit." Verna smiled at how awkward men can be when it comes to love matters, particularly if they think a woman might become jealous.

Verna telephoned Blanche, ambivalent about Clinton's unusual request. "Blanche, you won't believe..." and proceeded to ask her friend's advice about Clinton's unusual request, ending with "...I can't believe he has the nerve to ask me to meet her."

Blanche suggested, "Let him come, Verna. I believe he has some unfinished business with you. Clinton knows you never loved him. But honey, you awoke his feelings. The man never loved a woman, besides his mother, before you. He probably doesn't even know why he wants the two of you to meet. Verna, I've seen her and believe me, she's no match for you. Wear that pretty new light green dress with the pink roses, polish your nails, and brush your hair until it shines. Show that man what he lost and his woman what she has to live up to." At that remark Blanche laughed so long and so hard, Verna held the phone out from her ear.

"Blanche, I've got to hang up. Can't imagine what this call is costing Ira.

By the way, Mr. Derby continues to insist that Ellen, Darcine, and I stay on the third floor. He says it's helpful to his son, who misses his mother so."

"I like your Mr. Derby. " Blanche rushed to add, having met the Derby family several times when she traveled to Louisville, "He's smart, but a quiet man. A man who arranges the best care for his wife and remains so loving to her during her illness is rare. Staying on could be helpful to both families. Verna, did I tell you..."

Verna interrupted her friend. "Blanche, I'll have to sell that green dress you want me to wear to pay for this call if we don't say goodbye soon. Bye, Blanche."

"Bye, Verna."

Verna, encouraged by Blanche, felt strong enough to write Clinton. "Of course, come by and bring Miss Otis."

Two weeks later Clinton stopped by the Derbys to introduce his fiancée. Before the visit, Verna shared with Ira her changing relationship with Clinton following John's death. He asked Verna if she'd like him to be present during Clinton's visit, and she quickly said, "Oh, yes. Would you?"

The afternoon came with a brief spring shower and then burst into bright sunlight that filtered through the sheer drapes in the parlor. Verna and Ira together had taken down the heavy winter drapes and had the new maid shake them out before putting them in the attic storage until the next season.

Mr. Derby had hired a gardener in April to prepare the vegetable garden and add a flower garden under his wife's bedroom window in the hope that the blossoms' fragrance would cheer her. Verna picked Oriental poppies from the garden and arranged them in a Chinese porcelain vase. She vowed that if she ever had enough time and money she would buy a half-dozen vases and fill her home with exotic flowers.

Verna supervised the kitchen help on making a light lunch that could be easily eaten off laps, hoping that would speed the visit more than a sit-down meal. Ira filled the crystal decanter with a fine burgundy, saved since Christmas when no one felt like celebrating. Verna and Ira sat on separate straight-back needlepoint chairs, which required Clinton and Miss Otis to sit on the small needlepoint sofa.

The conversation focused on the coming fall election, with Clinton expressing his opinion that it was about time women got the vote and he was sure they would all vote for him. Verna smiled to see his confidence and the way Miss Otis nodded her head in agreement to everything that Clinton said. Mr. Derby talked only a little about his work, as neither Clinton or Miss Otis seemed to understand what chemistry even was, much less the importance of the new formulas being tested in Mr. Derby's laboratory.

When making a point about his platform, Clinton rested his right hand on Miss Otis's left hand and she looked into his eyes as if the rest of the world needed to be filtered through his brown irises. After two cups of tea and biscuits overflowing with newly churned strawberry ice cream topped with a sprig of mint, Clinton rose and said they must leave. Verna watched them walk down the sidewalk and enter a hack that had stood waiting outside the Derby's door throughout the lunch.

"Ira, thank you. I don't know if it would have been so pleasant without you." Verna thought, "What a kind man he is, to take the time to be with me through a difficult visit."

"Verna, I know from what you told me his friendship helped you heal. He's a good man. I think he's still a little fond of you. You looked lovely in that green dress." Ira's eyes twinkled as he teased Verna.

"Oh, Ira." Verna laughed. As she shut the front door, she felt another confusing layer of her past life becoming clear like a fast-moving creek that finally reaches the bottom of the hill and becomes still and crystal clear. She knew Clinton would gradually slip into being a friend, an old, dear friend, one never meant to be her lover.

# CHAPTER SIXTY-TWO

## SUMMER BLOOMS

As the azaleas and rhododendrons faded, Verna and Ira sat in stuffed Queen Anne's chairs in the library of his home, taking turns reading aloud to each other. Ellen and Gordon sprawled on the floor, separated by an ivory chessboard. Darcine was upstairs studying. Gordon patiently explained the different moves of each piece, while Ellen furtively watched her mother and Mr. Derby. Verna had found herself growing fond of this quiet man and trusting her inner thoughts to be treated respectfully by him.

"Ira, I think Copperfield's stepfather is a dreadful man. He's heartless. That poor boy."

"Verna, Charles Dickens wrote *David Copperfield* to alarm people about the plight of the poor. Sometimes I think we haven't progressed very far since he wrote this tale." Verna looked into Ira's sympathetic eyes. Deliberating avoiding her gaze, Ira continued, "But I think Dickens is also writing about love. Remember how long it took David to know his heart. Like us, he suffered the loss of his spouse."

Each evening since his wife's death, Ira and his son, Verna, and her daughters gathered in the library taking comfort in each other's presence. The teenagers would play a game, usually cards, but tonight Gordon was teaching Ellen chess. Verna and Ira would read, sitting in the armchairs that flanked the fireplace, cleaned out for the summer.

Occasionally all four played cards together, but usually Verna preferred to read, particularly since Ira started recommending books for her and explaining the author's intent. His intelligence intrigued Verna and his curiosity reminded her of a child's delight in exploring. Respect developed over the months of mutual caregiving, she by looking after his family, he by providing a safe, comfortable home for her and her older daughters to live together.

Looking to see if Ellen and Gordon were listening, Ira leaned forward to ask Verna how she met John.

"Remember, I told you my mother walked out when we were young, less than two years old. John's mother was a cousin of my mother." Verna laughed at his puzzled face. "Don't try to figure it out. We're all related in the hills. According to Granny the Gentrys were one of a few founding families in Madison County, comin' over from Virginia as early as the late seventeen hundreds. And some say they thought they were so special they kept marrying each other." Verna smiled, remembering how her grandmother loved to put that at the end of any bragging about the Gentry family.

Verna went on, seeing Mr. Derby's interest in her story. " When my granny died, John's mother took Grover and myself in. There he was, this handsome eighteen-year-old man. He paid attention to me. I was only thirteen and I fell in love at first sight. Kind of like David Copperfield. We waited to marry until I was fifteen." Verna's eyes never left Ira's as she searched for judgment. Finding none, she leaned back in her chair. Realizing that his opinion of her had become important, she felt the need to deflect attention from herself. "And you, Ira, how did you meet your wife?"

"It was similar. She, too, was the first girl I loved. I met her at a college dance. After that she would come up to Dartmouth and I would travel down to Bryn Mawr. I was determined to marry her and didn't stop asking until she accepted my proposal. I think I wore her down." He laughed self-consciously.

"Dad, what are you laughing at?" Gordon looked up, embarrassed at his father's loud guffaw. Verna, sensitive to the underlying current in the room, decided to divert the teen's attention. "Ellen, tell Mr. Derby your good news."

"Sir, I found out today that I've been accepted as a junior aide at City Hospital. The director of nursing said this will give me a good chance to be accepted into the nursing program the year after I graduate." Ellen's pride showed in her eyes, although she carefully chose words that were not too boastful.

Verna piped in, "She had the highest scores of any applicant." Ira's propensity for seriousness challenged Verna to see if she could get him to smile. "Despite her mother, Miss Foreman welcomed her into the program."

"Ma."

"Tell Mr. Derby about Darcine." Normally cautious to not brag about her children, Verna radiated pride.

"My sister was accepted, too. But we have to wait until July to start." Sometimes Ellen teased her mother that she loved Darcine the most. Verna denied it, but when her mind took its own path, like walking down back-country roads, she found herself thinking of Darcine and how wonderful it was to see her pleasant face in the morning and to kiss her forehead at night.

"Ellen, I'm pleased for you and your sister. I'm sure you deserved the opportunity on your own merits." Verna noticed that Ira's eyes sparkled. She thought, "What a kind man."

After his wife's long illness and painful death, the Derbys welcomed the life-bubbling, unpretentious Collins family. At first Ira didn't understand how this small, smiling woman withstood the tragedy of her losses – husband, children, home. He watched her and saw she took solace in her work and family, as he did. She told him about John's quilt and the support given by her women friends and church in Berea.

As Verna opened up more and told the old stories about her granny, Ira understood the source of her strength. He envisioned Verna's resiliency as a chemical reaction – her grandmother's unconditional love, tenderly conveyed by each brushstroke, changed humiliation into pride. As he watched Verna expect others, particularly men, to find her attractive, he blessed her grandmother for valuing this young girl child so strongly that she did indeed become a beautiful woman. But he kept his thoughts to himself.

He asked Verna to attend St. James Episcopal Church with him on Saturday evenings, so as not to miss the children's Sunday visits. Although apprehensive because Ira's opinion of her had become increasing important, she agreed to go, fearful that the flashbacks of

John's bloody back would return as they had that snowy day when she first came to Louisville or that the minister who comforted her would reveal her craziness, which she kept hidden from Ira. She increasing found she wanted Ira to think well of her. However, the services passed uneventfully, and the minister, while welcoming her back, never referred to her visions. She appreciated that deeply.

One evening, with Ellen, Darcine, and Gordon at the picture show, Ira summoned the courage to inquire. "How did you manage to carry on, Verna, after John's death?"

Looking down at her hands, chapped from antiseptics and bathing patients, she answered quietly. "What choice did I have?"

# CHAPTER SIXTY-THREE

## ANOTHER KIND OF LOVE

The second Saturday in August, Blanche and Hazel came to Louisville for one of their regular monthly visits. In nice weather the friends walked to the park next to the Derby's home. They would sit under a soaring chestnut tree whose gray-rust, peeling bark dropped to the ground like fall leaves.

Blanche tossed her hat on the blanket and peeled the green of a leaf from its veins. "My husband is impossible. He is so mad that women now have the right to vote he tried to forbid me to talk about women's rights at the dinner table. Said it gave him indigestion." Hazel put a hand over her mouth, afraid the uncontrolled laughter would spray her friends.

"Oh, no, Blanche. Really? And of course, you did exactly as he asked."

Hazel tried to look serious but only succeeded in inciting Blanche to stretch the story farther.

"I've taken to helping him hire for his stores in Madison County. He gave me a list of questions to ask the young women. "Where are they from? Have they worked before? How many years of school?" Of course, I checked their references, but I added a question of my own, 'Did you support women's right to vote?'"

"Blanche, you didn't ask them that." Verna knew she should

301

never underestimate her friend's commitment to the cause of women's rights.

"I did, Verna. And the men, too. I'm happy to report that my husband's entire work force, every man and woman, is a dedicated suffragette."

Verna had a story to add. "I'm nursing for an older woman now who fell and broke her leg. Ira referred her to me. She never married and works at the university with him. She's so mad. She told me, 'Verna, I've waited for the right to vote my entire adult life and dreamed of dancing in the streets. Now, look at me!'"

Hazel had remained quiet, before adding in a serious tone, "My principal lost seven family members to the influenza. They aren't thinking of dancing or celebrating anything. I don't understand where some people get the courage to keep going." The words sat on the park lawn like unmovable barriers, allowing only serious conversation to continue. Blanche looked at Verna. They both knew Hazel's principal and cared for the kindly man.

"I wonder also. As I watch Mr. Derby and his family grieve the loss of his wife, I remember John and the children. I wonder how we managed to keep living. There were days I didn't want to get out of bed. Days when breathing seemed too hard. Now I feel hope, like life is again worth the effort. It's comforting to have Ellen and Darcine with me. My heart aches for Son and Nanny Marie – but I know we will be together again.

"Oh, Verna." Blanche touched her friend's arm.

"To love a man again feels too dangerous and yet..." Verna's voice drifted off.

"Verna, you don't have to love a man to enjoy what he has to offer," Blanche shamelessly interrupted.

"Blanche!" Hazel pretended shock and the three friends again began to laugh until Verna held her sides and Hazel admonished, "Stop laughing, you two, or I'll wet my pants."

# CHAPTER SIXTY-FOUR

## STRONG ENOUGH TO WAIT

Time moved by like the Berea to Lexington express train. Verna made the decision to let Nanny Marie and Son stay in Oklahoma for a while longer. She hoped that when Ellen and Darcine were also working the three of them might make enough money to have the young ones return to Kentucky and they would all live together again as family.

Verna awoke in the mornings to the song of migrating birds and watched their flight south. Ira introduced her to the symphony and plays. She taught him to walk for miles without tiring and showed him the beauty of the hills outside Louisville. They went to Lexington to watch the horses run and took the late train home. With Gordon, Ellen, and Darcine, they attended the circus and went to the movies, making Friday nights a ritual night out for all five together.

In late November of 1921, Ira asked to speak privately to Verna. "An Indiana chemical company offered me a position, developing new medicines. I said no. They then included in the offer a new fully equipped and staffed chemistry laboratory – built to my specifications. I had to accept the position. It won't start until July when the laboratory is completed."

"Ma, are you in here?" Ellen entered the library, puzzled by the expressions on her mother's and Mr. Derby's faces.

303

Later at dinner, Ira told Gordon about accepting a position at Eli Lily, in Indianapolis, assuring his son he could finish the school year in Louisville. Gordon protested. Verna attempted to soothe the agitated teen and suggested the father and son talk about it after dinner.

Verna took Ira aside. "Gordon's been interested in learning photography. You might consider buying him a camera."

Ira protested, "He'll think all he has to do to get his way is raise his voice."

Verna answered Ira calmly. "It's hard for a child to move. You could encourage him to take pictures of Louisville, his school and friends, this house – to remember." Tilting her head slightly, she smiled, "It's only a suggestion."

Shortly after their conversation Verna found herself getting cross, more silent with Darcine, snapping at Ellen, even at Ira, who seemed puzzled by the change in her mood.

"Verna, what's wrong? You don't seem yourself." Ira looked at her worriedly, thinking she might be getting sick. She worked so hard.

"There's nothing wrong, I just have so much to do. I have to find a place to live. As you know, I gave up my room at Mrs. Randolph's. Everyone's leaving me again. I miss Nanny Marie and Son terribly. Ellen starts her nursing training in July and will move out. I'll miss her, too. Never thought I'd say that." She smiled a little. "Then Darcine goes the year after. Seems as if just when I was getting set to get everyone together again, they are leaving me."

"Verna, there's no reason for you to move now. I like having you and the girls here. It feels like family. Gordon would miss you. Elizabeth is coming home for Christmas. She's looking forward to getting to know your daughters. Verna, please, for me, don't move, not yet."

Two months later, on a cold February night as Louisville settled into 1921, Ira started a fire in the downstairs library. Ellen and Gordon were off in their rooms writing letters and studying. Verna mended, with a book beside her for when she wearied of sewing. She found the light from the polychrome lamp easy on her eyes. Ira pretended to read a research paper. He looked up, clearing his throat.

"Ira, are you feeling sick? I could fix you a cup of hot tea."

"No. I'm fine." He paused and cleared his throat. "Verna, you've given us the tenderest care we've ever had." There was an uncomfortable silence. Ira began again tentatively. "Gordon asked if you were going with us to Indianapolis."

"I will miss him when you move. Ellen will, too. So close in age. They've gotten to be good friends."

"Verna, you don't have to miss him."

Verna looked up. "Of course, I'll miss him. I'll miss you too. It's been over a year since I came to nurse your wife."

"Verna, I want you to come with us." Ira's voice was soft.

"Ira, I can't do that."

"Verna, we need you. I need the way you bring warmth and laughter into our home."

"Ira, what you're saying isn't proper. I can't keep on living with you like this. I certainly can't move to a strange town with you. I don't know what you must think of me to even suggest it."

"Verna, I'm an awkward man. I don't know how to talk to a woman. I'm used to being by myself in the lab and with my books. Much as I loved my wife we never talked of our feelings. With you I'm different."

"Stop right now. Before I get mad and leave this room."

"Verna, I'm not asking you anything improper. I want you to marry me."

"Ira!"

"Verna, you know I'm not an impulsive man. I've thought about nothing else since Mr. Lily offered me the position. I want you to be my wife and move with us to Indianapolis. Together we will make a home for all the children. Not just mine, but yours. I'll buy a house in Indianapolis big enough for all of us. For my family and for you, Ellen, Darcine, Nanny Marie, and Son. You can continue working, if you want."

Stunned, Verna stared, her mind blank. Then his words started rolling back in. "Be my wife." "A house in Indianapolis big enough for all of us." Son would live with her again, and Nanny Marie, too.

"No, Ira."

"Why?"

"I don't know. I just know I can't. It's not just the work. I would miss my home. Berea, the mountains, the valley. Now at least I have enough money to go home for a few weeks each year."

"Verna, you could still visit Berea each summer. In fact, anytime you wanted." Ira looked into Verna's eyes. "Think about it. I hear

Ellen calling you now. Talk about it with Hazel and Blanche. We have five months until I leave. I won't change my mind. Verna, like David Copperfield I am recognizing a new, different love. I don't expect you to love me now. Just be your loving way with me and my family. That's all we need."

"Ira." Verna wanted to put her arms around him and did. Slowly pulling away, she looked in his eyes, wondering how she had missed the depth of feeling developing between them. Not sensuous and exciting as with John. Trust, respectful conversation, and gentle caring replaced her emptiness and soothed the ache of her loss. She looked forward to seeing his bearded face, hearing his refined voice, and smelling his pipe during their evenings together.

"I feel something for you, too. I don't know yet if it's love. I know that the past few days since you talked about the position in Indianapolis, I've been unhappy, cross. Denying how my feelings for you have grown.

"I can't say yes now. I spent my life waiting for those I loved to return and care for me again – first my mother, my father, my grandmother, then John. Only recently have I learned to trust myself, to know somehow I can take care of myself and my family."

She looked away and then turned back, searching his eyes for understanding. "I've been afraid to love again. Afraid of loss and pain. I'm not ready yet to make a decision. Perhaps you could court me. Yes, I would like that." Verna smiled. "And then we'll see."

Breinigsville, PA USA
26 January 2011
254189BV00001B/2/P